Gilbert Tennent, Son of Thunder

Gilbert Tennent. Attributed to Gustavus Hesselius, American, 1682–1755. Oil on canvas, 36×28½ inches. Reproduced by permission of Princeton University.

GILBERT TENNENT, SON OF THUNDER

A CASE STUDY OF CONTINENTAL
PIETISM'S IMPACT ON THE FIRST
GREAT AWAKENING IN THE
MIDDLE COLONIES

MILTON J COALTER, JR.

A PUBLICATION OF THE PRESBYTERIAN
HISTORICAL SOCIETY

CONTRIBUTIONS TO THE STUDY OF RELIGION, NUMBER 18

GREENWOOD PRESS
NEW YORK ● WESTPORT, CONNECTICUT ● LONDON

Library of Congress Cataloging-in-Publication Data

Coalter, Milton J.
    Gilbert Tennent, son of thunder.

    (Contributions to the study of religion,
ISSN 0196-7053 ; no. 18)
    "A publication of the Presbyterian Historical
Society."
    Bibliography: p.
    Includes index.
    1. Tennent, Gilbert, 1703–1764. 2. Presbyterian
Church—United States—Clergy—Biography. 3. Great
Awakening. 4. Pietism—Influence. 5. Middle Atlantic
States—Religious life and customs. I. Presbyterian
Historical Society. II. Title. III. Series.
BX9225.T397C63   1986   285'.13   [B]   86-9967
ISBN 0-313-35514-8 (lib. bdg. : alk. paper)

Library of Congress Catalog Card Number: 86-9967
ISBN: 0-313-35514-8
ISSN: 0196-7053

First published in 1986

Greenwood Press, Inc.
88 Post Road West, Westport, Connecticut 06881

Printed in the United States of America

The paper used in this book complies with the
Permanent Paper Standard issued by the National
Information Standards Organization (Z39.48-1984).

10 9 8 7 6 5 4 3 2 1

To my patron, muse, and helpmate
Lin

I never before heard such a searching sermon. He [Gilbert Tennent] convinced me more and more that we can preach the Gospel of Christ no further than we have experienced the power of it in our own hearts. Being deeply convicted of sin, by God's Holy Spirit, at his first conversion, he has learned experimentally to dissect the heart of a natural man. Hypocrites must either soon be converted or enraged at his preaching. He is a son of thunder, and does not fear the faces of men.

George Whitefield

CONTENTS

FOREWORD

Since so much of America's religious history centers on evangelism, some observers assert that revivals have been its distinctive characteristic. That would be claiming too much, because in denominations where revivals occurred, evangelists always faced opponents who wished to nurture growth in other directions. Moreover, such a claim would ignore important American communions and theologies in which revivals never received any approbation at all. So revivals are only a portion of American spiritual life. But they are a tremendously influential aspect, considering the impressions made on a great number of churches and the impact made on general culture through an evangelized citizenry. In this important category the first experience of religious awakening merits special attention. It was the first notable popular excitement over religious questions that occurred after the time of colonial planting. It was also the first in a succession of religious upheavals that recurred so often in national experience. Because of its value as precedent and prototype, then, the First Great Awakening has attracted scholarly notice for quite some time.

Gilbert Tennent was recognized in his own day as a leading figure in eighteenth-century revivals, and subsequent investigation has confirmed this verdict. Strange to say, however, no biography worth the name has ever been written about this important person. Professor Coalter of Louisville Presbyterian Theological Seminary has now filled that gap with this careful, judicious study. His admirable work is based on primary research in the archives where Tennent material is scattered.

His patient sifting through original documents is paralleled by a similarly discriminating use of all the rhetoric since expended on Tennent. This biography gets back to basics and affords readers new insight into both the man and the movement.

Knowledge of Tennent's career and contributions is essential to understanding the Awakening. But as Coalter makes clear, once one appreciates religious variegation in the middle colonies, it becomes apparent that there were many awakenings whose emphases do not support the concept of a single effort between Massachusetts and Georgia. Tennent is crucial to understanding the special concerns that emerged in New York, New Jersey, and Pennsylvania. His strategic placement is matched by his controversial role, as evidenced by the subtitle of this book. Coalter's work is also valuable because he traces the influence of German and Dutch Pietism on American revivals, a factor that must be evaluated alongside English patterns for a comprehensive view of what actually transpired during this formative period. Gilbert Tennent serves as a lens through which these larger issues can be investigated in precise detail.

This volume adds to our knowledge in another significant area—namely, in seeing how Presbyterian ecclesiastical machinery grew through stress during its first half century in the New World. If Tennent was a lightning rod that attracted, and occasioned, controversies up to the schism of 1741, his later career instructs us about the uses of diplomacy that led to reunion. As Tennent's personality mellowed, he came to emphasize a religion of the head as well as one of the heart, a lifestyle of stability and cultural influence as well as one of emotions and strenuous reform. Coalter's perceptive interpretation of this changing individual offers valuable insights into the ways in which churches that were gathered under Awakening enthusiasm settled down to assume airs of more ponderous dignity. In sum, this study sheds light on a crucial personality whose biography is long overdue; it speaks additionally to ecclesiastical development, ideas germane to educational expansion, and other factors basic to American culture as it took shape before the outbreak of the Revolution.

—Henry Bowden

ACKNOWLEDGMENTS

This work is the collective product of the good services of many individuals. John M. Mulder and John F. Wilson deserve special credit because they recognized the potential of this study in its infancy. Their advice and encouragement sustained me through the often frustrating exercises of revising and reforming my thoughts into words. I am also appreciative of the patient attention John Murrin, Horton Davies, Paul Ramsey, Henry Bowden, and Richard Cogley gave me during this project. They read about and discussed the life of Gilbert Tennent to an extent far greater than any busy scholars should have been asked to endure.

Tennent's papers were scattered widely throughout the New Jersey–Pennsylvania area. Therefore, the kind aid provided by the staffs of several libraries greatly eased the task of this pilgrim researcher. I am especially grateful for the help of the men and women of Speer Library at Princeton Theological Seminary, Firestone and Mudd Libraries at Princeton University, the Presbyterian Historical Society in Philadelphia, and the Moravian Archives in Bethlehem, Pennsylvania.

Careful analysis of the Tennent corpus was made possible by the unique support offered by Charles Willard, Vernon Nelson, the New Jersey Historical Commission, and the Whiting Foundation. Charles Willard, the director of Speer Library, had Tennent's decaying sermons microfilmed so that they would be preserved for future scholars' investigations and available to this historian for close-order examination. Vernon Nelson of the Moravian Archives taught me to read German

Fraktur and guided me through the rich but intricate maze of Moravian manuscripts when time was at a premium. A grant-in-aid for research in New Jersey history was awarded me by the New Jersey Historical Commission so that I could continue my research on William Tennent, Sr., and Theodorus Frelinghuysen, and a Whiting Fellowship at Princeton University maintained me during the academic year of 1980–1981, when I was composing the initial draft of this work.

Some of the themes found in this work have been highlighted from different angles through publications elsewhere in the literature. Comments on these efforts have been very helpful and have hopefully improved the final product.[1]

I am also grateful to the Presbyterian Historical Society for sponsoring this work for publication and to Louisville Presbyterian Theological Seminary for financial assistance that facilitated its publication.

Finally, the time and emotional commitment required to research, write, and refine a historical treatment of this sort places heavy demands on one's family life. Therefore, I am particularly thankful for my wife, Lin, who typed, edited, and financed this study as well as nurtured its author through both the bright and dismal days of this biography's production.

INTRODUCTION

Gilbert Tennent was recognized by his contemporaries as a major leader of the First Great Awakening in the middle colonies. But his contribution to America's earliest intercolonial revival movement has been eclipsed by the historiographical shadows of George Whitefield and Jonathan Edwards.[1]

Two factors explain why historians have ignored Tennent's career. First, Tennent's corpus of letters and sermons offers ample, but not choice, materials for a biography. Every biographer hopes to expose the private experiences that shaped his subject's public life. Yet in Tennent's case, personal disclosures are rare and anecdotes from friends, family, or foes almost nonexistent. Consequently, Tennent's historical persona has a faceless, impersonal quality that has not attracted scholarly attention.[2]

Equally important in Tennent's historiographical demise has been the limited perspectives from which scholars have viewed the eighteenth-century revivals. Basically, two approaches have been taken. For some the Awakening was the first intercolonial social event and, as such, a significant step in the formation of a uniquely American identity. This perception has led to a search for those aspects of the revival experience that transcended regional boundaries, and this quest has fostered a new appreciation for George Whitefield, since he above all other Awakeners was accepted as the symbolic leader of the Awakening. As Whitefield's stature has grown, however, the relative importance of regional revivalists like Gilbert Tennent has declined.[3]

Another group of historians have taken a different tack in their studies. They have used the New England revivals as a paradigm for understanding the Awakening in other areas of the colonies. This approach has attracted numerous disciples for two reasons. First, the wealth of private and public documents preserved by the Puritans allows scholars to reconstruct colonial New England's experience with precision. The historian requires sources to write an accurate account of the past. Therefore, where the greatest accumulation of materials is located, there too one finds the heaviest concentration of historical research.

The second cause of Awakening historiography's inordinate attention to New England has been American historians' Boston-Jamestown fetish. Until quite recently, students of the British colonies have tended to look to Massachusetts Bay or Virginia rather than Philadelphia, New Jersey, or New York for the key to what America was and would be during the eighteenth century and beyond. Awakening histories in particular have focused on New England because Jonathan Edwards was the most notable representative of the movement in that region. Edwards has long been recognized as the theological genius of the colonial period and perhaps the most original thinker that America has produced. Edwards's brilliance cannot be disputed, but the consequences of his dominance in Awakening research can be questioned, since it has meant that Edwards's contemporaries in the middle colonies and the south have been treated like unattractive stepchildren who were neither so bright nor so interesting as their ''fair-haired'' sibling to the north.[4]

Gilbert Tennent was certainly not the theological equal of Edwards. Where the latter's compositions reflect a perceptive thinker who delighted in deciphering the intricate, interlocking economy of God's plan for humanity, Tennent's works reveal a more practical man whose primary concern was the adjustment of his thought and rhetoric for the most effective promotion of conversion and the practice of piety.

Because Tennent's theology lacks the effervescence of Edwards', scholars have overlooked the fact that one genius did not an Awakening leadership make. The revival message was conveyed to the colonial populace by a multitude of revival ministers who turned to more than Edwards to make sense of the great outpouring of spiritual concern that the Awakening generated. Gilbert Tennent's sphere of influence was extensive. Before the Revolution, Tennent published more than any other clergyman of the middle colonies, and during the revivals of the mid-eighteenth century, he maintained close relations with numerous

New England ministers and practically all of the major middle colony Awakeners.

Tennent's impact on the Awakening was felt most strongly in the mid-Atlantic region, where religious pluralism had reached unprecedented proportions. Unlike Puritan-dominated New England and the Anglican-controlled south, this section of the colonies contained an assortment of northern European churches and sects. By the 1740s an overflow of New England Puritans shared New York with an older immigrant population of Reformed Dutch and French Huguenots. Scottish and Irish Presbyterians lived alongside enclaves of more Dutch in the Raritan valley of New Jersey and coexisted with English Quakers and Anglicans, Swedish and German Lutherans, as well as a variety of German sectarians beside the lower Delaware River and in the city of Philadelphia. Further north, settlements of additional Germans were located on the upper Delaware, while along the western frontiers of Penn's colony, Scottish and Irish Calvinists predominated.

This ecclesiastical and ethnic mix complicated the middle colony Awakening to a degree not experienced elsewhere. In the north and the south, the revivals split religious communities into those for and those against the movement, but in the mid-Atlantic colonies, advocates of new birth were themselves divided by their differing social and theological preconceptions. The result was an intricate pattern of shifting thought and action among Awakeners in this region as revival leaders fought at one moment against critics of the Awakening and, in the next, against fellow revivalists who were believed to be carrying the call for spiritual renewal in directions that were detrimental to the Christian faith.

No one career illustrates the sources and consequences of this conflict on two fronts as well as Gilbert Tennent's. Tennent experienced the conflicting pressures endured by every middle colony Awakener during the period, and his retreat from the revival program in the last years of his life witnesses to the cumulative effect of those tensions on the average revivalist.

The focal point of the many controversies in Tennent's life was the question of experimental piety or, specifically, how a life of Christian piety based on a direct experience of grace in the human heart could best be generated and sustained. Most Awakening historians have overlooked this fact, first, because they have been mesmerized by the struggles over church government that these concerns created in the middle colonies and, second, because they have misread Gilbert Tennent's theological pedigree.

In the introduction to his anthology of Great Awakening documents, Alan Heimert suggested that "the revival impulse [among Presbyterians] expressed itself largely, though not exclusively, as a force battering at the ecclesiastical structure. . . . '' For Heimert, then, "the intellectual history of Presbyterianism in the first years of the 1740s is most striking as an especially vivid illustration of how the Great Awakening 'Americanized' the constitution of a colonial church.''[5] Heimert's view has led to the misinformed perception that the energies of Presbyterian Awakeners were primarily oriented toward the democratization of ecclesiastical government. There is some truth in this, but an equal amount of error. Certainly, Presbyterian revivalists like Gilbert Tennent were involved in far more battles over church polity than their comrades in the north, but the initiative for such conflict should not be credited to them. Controversy over Presbyterian government began before the Awakening and continued through the 1740s as a result of conservative forces within the denomination who were seeking to impose order on the relatively tolerant and unstructured polity of their colonial church. During the Awakening, these same conservatives found their revivalist colleagues unsympathetic to the formation of an authoritative hierarchy of church judicatories. Therefore, they invoked governmental sanctions against the Awakeners. The revivalists reacted by proclaiming the liberation of the laity from their traditional bonds to established parishes, but this move was a reaction rather than an original goal of the Awakening's leaders.

The primary aim of men like Gilbert Tennent was the rejuvenation of a sincere practical piety among the colonial laity. Tennent acquired this goal from the pietistic training that he received from his father, William Tennent, Sr., and his friend, Theodorus Jacobus Frelinghuysen. Because this early instruction of Tennent was misinterpreted in 1949 by the foremost historian of colonial Presbyterianism, the course of Tennent's life and of the middle colony Awakening has been misunderstood. In his classic study of early American Presbyterian politics, Leonard Trinterud admitted that he found it "difficult to understand" why there had been an "ever-recurring attempt [in middle colony historiography] to find the source of Tennent's views in Pietism. . . . '' Trinterud believed that eighteenth-century Pietism was an exclusively German phenomenon. Tennent had traditionally been connected with pietistic views through his early association with Theodorus Frelinghuysen. Yet in his research Trinterud discovered what were to him two telling facts about Frelinghuysen. First, Frelinghuysen's thought was the product of a Dutch Reformed rather than a German Reformed community and, second, Frelinghuysen consistently spurned the title of "pietist" whenever it was applied to his ministry. Trinterud took this evidence to mean that Frelinghuysen was not a pietist and, thus, made no pietist of Gilbert Tennent.[6]

More recently, the error of Trinterud's analysis has been corrected by research on both Pietism and Frelinghuysen. Pietist scholars now claim that Pietism was not a peculiarly German movement. Rather, it evolved from an international ferment of Christian spirituality that found its first expression in the revival of English Christianity known as Puritanism. During the seventeenth and eighteenth centuries, the search for a renewed practice of piety moved far beyond its early Puritan manifestations by crossing the channel through the agency of exiled Englishmen like William Ames. It subsequently was reformulated by Dutch Calvinists, German Lutherans, and continental sectarians and eventually recrossed the channel to alter the theology of its Puritan creators' children.[7]

Despite Frelinghuysen's protestations to the contrary, a recent biographer of Frelinghuysen has also shown that Pietism as formulated by Dutch Reformed theologians had a major impact on the schools where Frelinghuysen studied and the men with whom he associated. In James Tanis's view, Frelinghuysen did not accept the pietist label because of its negative connotations in his day, but he was still a pietist in deed and thought if not in name.[8]

Trinterud's apparent misunderstanding of Frelinghuysen's background and of eighteenth-century Pietism in general suggests the need for a new study that will determine whether pietistic theology and practice were, in fact, important to the middle colony Awakening. The work that follows seeks to fill that need by considering the life of Gilbert Tennent. Because of his close relationship with Theodorus Frelinghuysen and his leadership of revival forces in the mid-Atlantic colonies, Tennent's career offers an excellent test case for such an inquiry.

Tennent's biography shows that Pietism did have a subtle but critical effect on the course of America's first revival. Gilbert Tennent never became a card-carrying pietist, but he was deeply influenced early in his life by his father's emphasis on a sincere life of piety and Frelinghuysen's more definitive pietistic theology and technique. During the first years of his ministry, Tennent fashioned these lessons into a powerful revival program aimed at the regeneration of lay spirituality through an experience of conversion. Tennent's concern for a converting ministry determined his position in the disputes over Presbyterian church government that erupted in the late 1730s and early 1740s. His support of George Whitefield and the First Great Awakening was founded on the belief that both provided the best avenues for promoting pietistic reform, and his retreat from the movement during the last years of his life resulted from his discovery that certain aspects of the revival's pietistic thrust were harmful to the unity of the church and the integrity of the Reformed faith.

Gilbert Tennent, Son of Thunder

1

INSTRUCTION IN THE EXPERIMENTAL MINISTRY: THE CUMULATIVE LEGACY OF TWO EARLY MENTORS

Gilbert Tennent learned the rudiments of his Awakening practice from two men: William Tennent, Sr., his father and tutor, and Theodorus Jacobus Frelinghuysen, his earliest revival colleague. From the former, Gilbert acquired an abiding distrust of Christian rationalists who stressed theological orthodoxy and ritual propriety over heartfelt practical piety. From the latter, he absorbed a uniquely pietistic perspective on the road to salvation, the importance of conversion in that journey, and the methods by which the clergy could best promote both conversion and piety.

WILLIAM TENNENT, SR.

Gilbert's father was a Scotsman who had been educated at Edinburgh University.[1] Following his graduation in July 1695, William Tennent was employed as a domestic chaplain in the Scottish household of Lady Anne, Duchess of Hamilton. Exactly how long he remained in this position is unknown.[2] Indeed, his name does not appear again on the historical record until 1701, when he presented himself to the General Synod of Ulster in Antrim, Northern Ireland. The June minutes of the Synod state that "in this Interloquiter Mr. James Stewart, a Minister, and Mr. William Tennent, a Probationer, who came both to this Kingdom from Scotland, produced their Testimonials, the former one, the latter 3, from Several Places, which were all read: and, after reading, the Brethren met allow the Several Presbyteries within their Bounds to invite and employ them as they shall find Clearness.''[3]

This entry suggests that William Tennent had emigrated to Northern Ireland after being licensed by a Presbyterian judicatory in Scotland and that he was in sufficiently good standing to have received recommendations from three clergymen prior to his departure.

Within a year of his joining the Ulster Synod, William married Katherine Kennedy at Greengraves in County Down. Nine months later their first son, Gilbert, was born at midnight on February 5, 1703, and in the next eight years three more sons and one daughter were added to the Tennent household.[4]

Judging from her family's history, Tennent's new wife was a thoroughgoing Presbyterian dissenter. Her grandfather had served with Cromwell at the battle of Marston Moor, and her father, Gilbert Kennedy, was an ordained Presbyterian minister in Scotland until 1662, when he was ejected for nonconformity. Accounts vary as to how Kennedy made his way to Ireland, but once there he again faced persecution from the Anglican establishment. Kennedy responded to this new test of his convictions by conducting a clandestine ministry in which he preached at night in the open air to secret assemblies of Presbyterians. These underground activities ended in 1670, when Kennedy and his family were allowed to settle at a church in Dundonald.[5]

Despite the staunch dissenting orientation of his spouse and relatives, William Tennent dramatically altered the course of his career only two years after his marriage. In 1704 Tennent received ordination as a deacon in the established Church of Ireland and two years later was made a presbyter by Edward Smith, the Bishop of Down.[6] The young Scotsman left no record of his reasons for deserting the Presbyterian Church, but it appears that the decision involved Irish relations on his side of the family. During 1725 James Logan, William Penn's agent in Pennsylvania and Tennent's distant cousin on his mother's side, wrote James Greenshields of Dublin, a Tennent cousin on his father's side. Logan's letter informed Greenshields that his ''Cousin Tennent came over hither about 6 or 7 years since with his family and after some months spent here found a living in his old and new way viz. the Presbyterian (from which he complains that his Uncle and thee once unhappily misled [him]).''[7]

Anglican-Presbyterian contacts were extremely hostile when William Tennent immigrated into Northern Ireland. From 1702 to 1705 a pam-

phlet war raged between the two churches over the legality of Presbyterian marriages, and in 1704 Irish bishops negotiated the passage of
a Test Act which made attendance at a Church of Ireland communion
service a prerequisite for holding civil and military offices.[8] Tennent's
cousins, the Greenshields, were prominent Anglicans in Northern Ireland society with aspirations for ever higher social and ecclesiastical
preferment. Thus, Tennent's Presbyterian affiliation was a serious embarrassment. In order to rectify this situation, the Greenshields apparently persuaded their Scottish relative that his best career prospects lay
in the established church.

Membership in the Church of Ireland insured a profitable future for
the Greenshields, but the new arrangement was more troublesome for
Tennent.[9] During the fourteen years that he served the church, Tennent
never received a parish of his own, and in 1718 he penned a long list
of personal scruples about the established church's practice and theology. Whether the latter complaints were recent in origin or had been a
long-standing barrier to Tennent's accommodation with the Church of
Ireland is not known. It is clear, however, that by 1718 Tennent considered the offending practices sufficiently odious to cause his immigration to the British North American colonies, where he could return
to the Presbyterian fold.

On September 6, 1718, the Tennent family arrived in Philadelphia.
Eleven days later Tennent requested membership in the Presbyterian
Synod currently meeting in the city. As an explanation for his ecclesiastical about-face, he submitted the following catalogue of complaints
against the Anglican system.

Imprimis. Their government by Bishops, Archbishops, Deans, Archdeacons,
Canons, Chapters, Chancellors, Vicars, wholly antiscriptural.

2. Their Discipline by Surrogates, and Chancellors in their Courts Eccle-
siastic, without a Foundation in the Word of God.

3. Their Abuse of yt Supposed Discipline by Commutation.

4. A Diocesan Bishop cannot be found *Jure divino* upon those Epistles to
Timothy or Titus, nor anywhere else in the Word of God, and so is a mere
human invention.

5. The usurped Power of the Bishops at their yearly Visitations, acting all
of themselves, without consent of the Brethren.

6. Pluralities of Benefices. Lastly, the Churches conniving at the Practice
of Arminian Doctrines inconsistent with the eternal Purpose of God, and an
Encouragement to Vice. Besides I could not be satisfied with their Ceremonial

way of worship. These &c have so affected my Conscience, yt I could no longer abide in a Church where the same are practised.[10]

The Synod admitted Tennent on the basis of this declaration, but not without exhibiting certain doubts about his sincerity. Both in committee and before the Synod, Tennent's case was discussed at considerable length; after his admission, Tennent's written testimony was inserted into the minutes "*ad futuram rei memorium*"; and before providing for Tennent's employment, the Synod instructed its moderator to give the new member "a serious exhortation to continue steadfast in his now holy profession."[11]

Undaunted by this expression of qualified support from the Synod, William Tennent found himself a parish in East Chester, New York, during November 1718. The East Chester congregation had been supplied sporadically before Tennent's arrival by an Anglican missionary of the Society for the Propagation of the Gospel named John Bartow. The members' decision to invite Tennent as their full-time pastor had been occasioned by Bartow's refusal to preach for them on a regular basis, but the call to Tennent created dissension within the membership. This division allowed Bartow to continue visiting the congregation after Tennent's installation and to retain possession of both the church meeting house and £15 of the yearly ministerial salary. In 1719 Tennent tried to halt Bartow's intrusion by asking James Logan to intercede for him with the governor of New York. Unfortunately for Tennent, Governor Robert Hunter, an opponent of the High Church faction in the colony, had just been recalled to England. Hunter's replacement, William Burnet, was the son of Bishop Gilbert Burnet and therefore a strong supporter of the Society for the Propagation of the Gospel. Consequently, Logan was unable to move the new governor, and in 1720 the Tennent family relocated to Bedford, New York.[12]

The ministers and laity of the Bedford area received Tennent's ministry well. Indeed, the new pastor's relations with nearby New York and Connecticut clergymen were so cordial that he was considered a candidate for the Yale College rectorship in 1725.[13] Hopes for this prestigious appointment never materialized, however, and the financial burden of William's large family became increasingly oppressive despite several actions taken in his behalf by Bedford town authorities and the distant Philadelphia Synod.[14]

During August 1726 William Tennent decided his current salary could no longer bear the weight of his expenses, so he sold his New York property and moved to Bucks County, Pennsylvania. Tennent had visited Bensalem in the fall of 1721 to investigate the possibility of settlement, but he waited five years before acting upon the findings of this early exploratory trip.[15]

The Tennents' first autumn in Pennsylvania was not an easy one. Their meager finances forced them to rent a house near Neshaminy Creek along the well-traveled York Road between New York and Philadelphia. There the family's resources were further taxed by travelers who frequently took advantage of their hospitality.[16] At the same time, William began serving two congregations, one composed of Dutch settlers who resided in Bensalem near the mouth of the Neshaminy and another containing Ulster Scots who had settled around the Forks of the Neshaminy. Later this ministry expanded further as Tennent began preaching at Deep Run, a settlement twelve miles to the north.[17]

To save the Tennents from the constant intrusions of York Road travelers, James Logan offered to sell his cousin fifty acres of land at a more secluded location in Northampton Township. There William and his family remained until 1735, when they purchased 100 acres in Warminster Township.[18]

THE LOG COLLEGE THEOLOGY

William Tennent built what became the informal seminary of the middle colony Awakening at his new Warminster home. Housed in a log structure "about Twenty Feet long, and near as many broad," the school was later dubbed by its critics the "Log College." The long-term impact of this so-called college on the First Great Awakening was impressive. Of nineteen young men who studied under William Tennent at The Log College, all but one became Presbyterian revivalists.[19]

The exact composition of the Log College's curriculum is unknown, but the theological content of that training may be deduced from a set of seventeen extant sermons delivered by Tennent between 1706 and 1740.

In the first of these homilies, Tennent dealt with the sin of unbelief. According to the Scotsman, this sin was "notoriously manifested throughout the whole Scriptures; . . . even in those who had a more Iminent and closer demonstration of the mind of God under the Gospel." Tennent recognized that many people in his day considered unbelief to be limited to heathens, Turks, or infidels, but Tennent observed that "too many [unbelievers] are to be found in the very bosom of the church."[20]

To show how this could be so, William delineated two varieties of unbelief. One type, a "negative" unbelief, characterized the heathen to whom the Gospel had never been presented, or the infidel from whom the means of grace had been withheld. "Positive" unbelief, on the other hand, was of two quite different sorts. "Total positive" unbelief involved those who remained infidels even after hearing the Gospel, and "partial positive" unbelief was witnessed in those church members who had "some profession but small practice."[21]

Laypeople guilty of "partial positive" unbelief used several pretenses to claim the status of true believers. Three such excuses that Tennent made a point of condemning were the ideas that birth into a Christian nation, knowledge of Christian doctrines, or mental assent to Jesus as the Christ certified an individual as one of the faithful. None of these were sufficient proof of true belief in Tennent's view, since human beings could absorb the opinions of a "Christian country and not be one bit better than Turks, Jews or infidels"; individuals could "understand their Religion and be able to give a reason of their hope . . . and yet lie under the power of unbelief for all that"; or they could assent to Christ's kingship and yet not believe, since even devils would assent to Jesus' lordship but do not have true faith in him.[22]

The fundamental difference between the believer and the hypocritical professor was practice. As Tennent put it: "Assent is necessary but not sufficient; Laws are not sufficiently owned when they are believed to be the Kings Laws. There is something to be done as well as believed; in primitive times assent was more than it is now, and yet . . . was never allowed to pass for faith."[23]

This distinction between sincere and affected Christianity Tennent considered again in the second of his early sermons. Here, though, the lesson was applied to the Lord's Supper. For Tennent the Supper was no different from any other Christian act, at least in the sense that "the manner of one's religious performance makes it either pleasing or displeasing to God. This turns the scales, and two acts of piety which seem to be the same, many times are not because the manner of the performance makes a vast difference in the values."[24]

Tennent recognized that many men and women participated in communion for the wrong reasons. Some came because they were teased or haunted by their consciences. Therefore, they tried to "bribe [their] conscience with this trifle [of attendance] as we do [bribe] children that cry for a gowd." Others who were ambitious for public office received the Supper in order to satisfy basic legal requirements for their government patronage rather than to fulfill the gracious duties of sainthood. Even ministers, on occasion, celebrated the Lord's sacrifice and yet did not eat the elements as sincere Christians, since "they may do it upon the account of their office and because it is expected of them; but the sense of the end of the Love of God may be wanting which defect makes it a very lame offering."[25] True involvement in the Lord's Supper demanded a spiritual reception in Tennent's view, and the difference between formal and spiritual participation Tennent compared to that "between eating and relishing: betwixt tasting the juice and delicacy of . . . meat, and finding it to be no better than ashes."[26]

In the remainder of Tennent's extant sermons, the theological foundations for his position were outlined. Sin introduced its corrupting influence in the human heart either directly through physical desire and personal habits or indirectly through national and international customs. By definition, sin usurped the Creator's right to absolute obedience and honor from his creatures. Therefore, sinners were essentially rebels, albeit of different varieties. Some rebelled by not knowing God; others by not thinking about him. Some resisted the Divine Sovereign by corrupting the Scriptures, by forsaking God's Word or by refusing to "improve" themselves after experiencing providential afflictions. And still others revolted by relishing every sort of iniquity or by simply offering empty ecclesiastical performances.[27]

The wages of sin and rebellion were temporal and spiritual death, but an antidote for these fatal poisons existed. It was repentance. Repentance for Tennent was not a simple act of the human will. Before individuals could repent, their hearts had to be convinced that they were evil, and before this conviction could take hold, the sinful had to acquire the knowledge "that there is more evil in the sinful nature than ever" they thought; that this evil is fatal to body and soul; and that "liberty from sin is the greatest business in the world."[28]

Such knowledge was not available through reason. The Fall of Adam blinded the human mind so that it no longer understood the constitution of creation, God's present disposition, or even its own workings and nature. Consequently, individuals must look to a source outside themselves for the understanding that prompts conviction and repentance.[29]

This external source was God, and the understanding imparted was "spiritual." In God's plan the individual received spiritual knowledge from without and within. In Tennent's own words, "Instruction External by the preaching of the Gospel is sounded in the Ears of man; and as a concomitant by the good will of God, Internal teaching and Instruction follows. They are inseparable." These two means were inseparable because the latter instruction pierced the heart with an "experience" of that being taught externally. "No knowledge is so distinct as that which the heart circuits to the head." Thus, through divine teaching received directly within the soul, the individual felt and understood as never before the reality of sin, the necessity of repentance, and the comfort of salvation.[30]

By the same process, Tennent believed an individual learned that neither "words without practice nor a profession without reality will do." Christian practice followed naturally from conversion, just as sanctification followed naturally from justification. Although natural, the practice of piety was not automatic. The path to holiness was an arduous journey requiring the service of both laity and clergy as watchmen against the subtle Satan's movements in themselves and others.[31]

Satan's snares were the primary dangers to Christian righteousness, but a secondary danger was "afflictions." Afflictions were part of God's providence sent indiscriminately upon the godly and the ungodly. When visited upon the flagrantly evil, they signaled eternal doom. When visited upon the pious, they represented hopeful warnings for they made the chosen to recognize their sin and turn from it. They humbled God's people and provided exercise for the Christian graces of fear, patience, hope, heavenly mindedness and prayer. Afflictions, then, were God's way of preparing the godly for heaven and protecting them from hell.[32]

This brief synopsis of Tennent's corpus cannot pretend to summarize Tennent's theology or the Log College curriculum. Seventeen sermons out of more than fifty years of pulpit work is hardly a comprehensive sample. Yet the sermons taken together do suggest certain unique emphases in Tennent's definition of true Christianity. Specifically, William Tennent stressed spiritual over external participation in church rites. He distrusted reason as the tool by which the Christian was saved and piety promoted. He believed a conviction of sin was the necessary prerequisite for sincere human repentance, and he was certain that conviction could only result from the supernatural instruction of the human heart. In Tennent's opinion, such tutelage would lead inevitably to the conscientious practice of piety, since profession without practice was the sign of deluded unbelief rather than unmistakable election.

In later years Gilbert Tennent and the students of the Log College included these views in their program for Presbyterian revival. They too assaulted the emptiness of contemporary ritual and mere rational assent to theological tenets. They too proclaimed conviction was the first step to salvation and practical piety the unavoidable culmination of a true experience of divine grace in the human heart. They too emphasized the distinction between the heart and the mind, and, like their mentor, they maintained the heart's condition was the critical difference between those not yet saved and those already saved.

PRELUDE TO GILBERT'S MINISTRY

As the eldest son of William Tennent, Gilbert Tennent became the first student of his father's theology. It is impossible to describe what sort of pupil or son Gilbert was, since his childhood is practically a historical blank. The one exception to this undocumented portion of Gilbert's life is an experience of "law work" that began to torment the young man just a year before his family immigrated to the colonies. According to Gilbert's later accounts of such spiritual trials, "law work" involved a struggle with the biblical moral law wherein an individual recognized with utter seriousness his or her damnable sinfulness before God. Tennent's own law work grew increasingly severe until 1723, when he altered his plans to become a minister and began preparation for a career in medicine. Shortly after this decision, Gilbert experienced conversion, however, and this led him to resume his studies for the ministry.[33]

It was probably no accident that this tumultuous episode in Gilbert's life coincided with the major upheaval of the Tennent family's immigration to America. In 1717, the year Gilbert's law work commenced, William Tennent, Sr., was seriously questioning his past career choices. The Tennent patriarch was disgusted with the Church of Ireland. Yet he must have realized that a return to the communion of the Ulster Synod was impossible because of his earlier defection. His only option, if he wished to sever his association with the Church of Ireland, was immigration. But this move was also fraught with dangers. William Tennent was forty-five years old with a wife and five children in 1717. He had no direct contacts with the clergy of the Presbyterian Synod in

Philadelphia and, thus, had no assurance that that body would accept an Anglican renegade once he and his family had completed the difficult voyage to the New World.

The spiritual turmoil of the Tennents' eldest son reflected the uncertain mindset of his father. Between the ages of fifteen and twenty, Gilbert was faced with the difficult decision of determining his own future career. The onset of law work in this period represented far more than a challenge to Gilbert's ultimate salvation, for it also involved a critical internal battle with himself over the propriety and sagacity of pursuing his childhood dream of entering the ministry. Medicine may have appeared for a time as a much more stable prospect for a young man who understood from firsthand experience the traumatic psychological and physical trials of the clerical vocation. But by 1724 the rigors of the Tennents' ocean voyage had been weathered, and the barriers to establishing William Tennent in a colonial Presbyterian parish had been overcome. Not coincidentally, Gilbert Tennent's personal combat with law work abated at approximately the same time, and gracious conversion overcame his fears of damnation as well as of seeking ordination.

Less than a year after his new birth, Gilbert Tennent visited James Logan in Philadelphia. Logan reported that his young relative was now traveling "on the true call of the Gospellers viz. the best price that they can get for the word." Also he noted that Gilbert had entered the "New Lond[on] College in Connecticut" and seemed "to have got a pretty good stock at his trade for a beginner." Yet Logan wondered whether the younger Tennent did not have "more honesty than that required" for his new vocation.[34]

This mention of Gilbert's enrollment in the "New London College" introduces a new mystery into the Tennent family history. Gilbert Tennent received a master of arts degree from Yale College in September 1725 without having first acquired a bachelor of arts. This would suggest that he was privately educated by his father and then by special arrangement enrolled in the master of arts program at Yale.

Such an arrangement was unusual for a Yale student of the period. The normal course to an advanced degree involved four years of residence for the B.A., three years apprenticeship under a parish minister, and finally examinations for the M.A.[35]

There are three possible factors that could explain an exception being made in Gilbert Tennent's case. First, his father later illustrated his superior abilities as a teacher of classical languages and metaphysics through the alumni of his Log College. Under such tutelage, Gilbert may have acquired a sufficiently impressive intellectual background to convince the Yale authorities to waive the bachelor of arts requirement. Also, the elder Tennent's hopes for the rectorship of Yale in 1725 suggest that he was a respected member of the New England network of ministers involved in the maintenance of Yale College. If this were the case, connections of this sort would undoubtedly have eased the way for his son's admission. But an equally important element may have been the structural instability of the college itself in the year Gilbert received his master of arts. After an unexpected resignation of the school's rector in 1722, Yale's trustees were unable to convince any of their subsequent choices to accept the position until the spring of 1726. During this period of administrative uncertainty, an exception to the rules such as that required for Tennent's son may have easily slipped past the beleaguered officials at Yale.[36]

After receiving his M.A., Gilbert Tennent was licensed for the ministry by the Philadelphia Presbytery and, the following December, admitted to the Presbytery of New Castle as a probationer. At the same meeting of the New Castle Presbytery, Gilbert received a call from a church in New Castle, Delaware, where he had already preached a few Sabbaths "to their good-liking and satisfaction." Tennent gave no answer to the call but instead took it under consideration.[37]

The New Castle invitation was the occasion for the first of many controversies that Gilbert Tennent had with the New Castle Presbytery. Indeed, it may have been the origin of some of the animosity that erupted between the two parties later, during the Great Awakening. In May 1726 George Gillespie was sent to supply the New Castle church in order that he might inquire into Gilbert Tennent's conduct with respect to the call that he had received the previous December. Gillespie reported that he had seen a letter from the young man informing the church at New Castle that he accepted their invitation but that Tennent had subsequently reneged on his commitment. The New Castle Presbytery then ordered Thomas Craighead and Thomas Evans to give a full representation of the matter to the next Synod and to convey the message that the presbytery was "highly dissatisfied with said Irregularity."[38]

On September 23, 1726, the Synod of Philadelphia considered Gilbert Tennent's recent conduct. After some discussion the Synod concluded that Tennent should be reproved and exhorted to "more caution and deliberation in his future proceedings'' since his ''steps were too hasty and unadvised in several particulars.'' Because Gilbert was not present at this meeting, it fell to his father to present his son's explanation for the absence. The Synod approved Gilbert's excuse, but the moderator, Thomas Craighead, publicly reproved the younger Tennent for the New Castle episode at the next meeting of his presbytery.[39]

Why Gilbert backed out of his first call is a mystery. It is clear, however, that some time during this period a group from New Brunswick, New Jersey, asked him to organize a Presbyterian meeting in their village. Gilbert accepted the offer and, during the same autumn that he was reprimanded in synod and presbytery, he was ordained in New Brunswick. This settlement was situated on the south bank of the Raritan River at a point where travelers on the main road between Elizabethtown and Trenton crossed the river by ferry. As yet the town was not officially chartered, but the region around New Brunswick was well populated with English, Dutch, and Scotch-Irish settlers.[40]

Tennent received his call from a group of local residents who were dissatisfied with the nearby Presbyterian minister in Freehold. Both the Presbyterian and Dutch congregations of Freehold had been served by Joseph Morgan since 1709, but in recent years Morgan's ministry had been plagued by controversy. While this dissension was partially responsible for Tennent's call to New Brunswick, it apparently did not create serious animosity between Morgan and Tennent, since Morgan participated in the young man's ordination shortly after his arrival.[41]

THEODORUS JACOBUS FRELINGHUYSEN

Only one other clergyman resided in the immediate area of New Brunswick in 1726. He was the Dutch Reformed dominie Theodorus Jacobus Frelinghuysen. Although by birth a Westphalian German, Frelinghuysen was theologically a thoroughgoing Dutch Reformed pietist. At the age of nineteen Frelinghuysen had been sent to the Cocceian gymnasium at Hamm, and two years later, to the University of Lingen, where he was introduced to the Voetian theology of Johannes a Marck.[42]

Frelinghuysen graduated from Lingen in 1717 and was ordained by the Classis of Emden in East Friesland. He then served a small church in nearby Loegumer Voorwerk until a flood devastated his parish on Christmas Eve. This first pastorate had a significant impact upon Frelinghuysen's later ministry. The dominie's closest friends during this period came from two different circles of confessional pietists in Emden. One group, known to its enemies as the "sanctimonians" or "fijnen" pietists, taught Frelinghuysen to focus his preaching on conversion and to categorize Christians according to their relative progress toward that goal. They also introduced Frelinghuysen to the works of Herman Witsius and Jacobus Koelman. Witsius's covenant theology was well respected throughout the Netherlands, but Koelman had been condemned by various segments of the Dutch Church for his biting criticisms of unconverted clergymen and his unorthodox opinions on church-state relations. From Koelman, Frelinghuysen acquired the idea that ministers were like "watchers on the walls of Zion" whose primary duties included warning the wayward of their spiritual danger and protecting the communion table from the pollution of unrepentant, unconverted sinners.[43]

The other group with which Frelinghuysen was intimate in Emden contained a number of Cocceian pietists. These men offered Frelinghuysen a more moderate brand of Pietism by initiating him to the theology of Johannes d'Outrein. D'Outrein was best known for his support of daily pietistic devotionals and his strong stand in favor of the catechetical instruction of the church's laity. In America, Frelinghuysen would imitate d'Outrein's example by establishing local conventicles of his own.[44]

When Frelinghuysen left Loegumer Voorwerk in February 1719, he planned to accept a teaching position in a Latin school in Enkhuizen. But as he passed through Groningen on his way to his new post, his career was diverted by a call to the "Rarethans." Frelinghuysen then presented himself to the Dutch Reformed Classis of Amsterdam, the ecclesiastical body in charge of all Dutch Reformed activities in the colonies. The Classis accepted Frelinghuysen's credentials in 1719 and in short order reordained him so that by September of the same year he was on his way to America.[45]

When Frelinghuysen arrived in the colonies, seven ministers served the Dutch Reformed churches of New York and New Jersey. In New York City the senior pastor was Gualtherus DuBois. DuBois took a moderate stance in church affairs, but his junior associate, Henricus Boel, was an intense advocate of Dutch orthodoxy and custom. After the English takeover of the New York colony, orthodox dominies like Boel feared the Dutch church might be destroyed either by a swift reversal of the government's tolerant policy or by the assimilation of the Dutch into British society. To forestall the latter threat in particular, Boel attacked all deviations from traditional Dutch practice or theology and encouraged the orthodox Classis of Amsterdam to maintain a strong hold on the colonial church's affairs.[46]

In contrast to Boel, another group of Dutch dominies sought to preserve the integrity of their churches by a different method. Less concerned with doctrinal orthodoxy than the vitality of their laity's spiritual life, these clergymen emphasized the necessity of a sincere practical piety. The eldest representative of this group, Guiliam Bartholf, was the immediate predecessor of Frelinghuysen in the Raritan valley. Bartholf had been a member of Jacobus Koelman's parish while still a young man in the Netherlands and, after immigrating to America, became a fiery supporter of Koelman's pietistic program for reform. In 1683 Bartholf returned to the Netherlands to seek ordination, but he irregularly bypassed the Amsterdam Classis because that body had previously condemned Koelman's theology. This earned Bartholf the wrath of orthodox colonial dominies and, in turn, primed the Raritan valley for the fierce ecclesiastical strife that Frelinghuysen's ministry would later ignite.[47]

Frelinghuysen arrived in New York City early in January 1720. After being welcomed by the city's church leaders, he was asked to officiate in worship. Discussions that followed the service ended in an argument between Frelinghuysen and Boel. The New York minister was offended by Frelinghuysen's emotional "howling prayers" as well as his belief that the Lord's Prayer was unnecessary in the liturgy. These views were direct products of Frelinghuysen's East Frisian Pietism. Following the lead of Koelman, the Emden pietists objected to ritualistic formulas that limited the Holy Spirit's guidance of worship. Therefore, ecstatic impromptu prayer was favored over the traditional Lord's Prayer. These aspects of Frelinghuysen's ministry would have been readily accepted in Emden, but they were singularly unwelcomed by Boel.[48]

Unfortunately for Frelinghuysen, his first conversations with the older DuBois were no better received. Expressing his former colleagues' distaste for ostentatious display, Frelinghuysen boldly chastised the senior pastor for possessing a huge wall mirror in his home.[49]

With both New York City dominies thoroughly offended, Frelinghuysen next traveled to his new parish along the Raritan River, where he preached his first sermon on January 31, 1720. His text was drawn from II Corinthians: "Now then we are ambassadors for Christ, as

though God did beseech you by us: we pray you in Christ's stead, be
ye reconciled to God.''[50]

A group of Frelinghuysen's parishioners soon found their new pastor's
message of reconciliation contradictory to his methods when he began
to examine prospective participants to the Lord's Supper in order to
determine whether their souls were suitably prepared for the sacrament.
Frelinghuysen believed both unprepared communicants and their negligent minister would eat the meal to their damnation if the clergy shirked
this essential duty.[51]

Since these precommunion examinations resulted in the exclusion of
several prominent members from the Supper, vehement opposition to
Frelinghuysen swiftly developed. A complete account of this controversy is beyond the scope of this study, but one document from the
dispute is noteworthy because of the insight it provides into Frelinghuysen's ministry. The dissatisfied laity of the Raritan congregations
discovered in Henricus Boel a willing supporter of anti-Frelinghuysen
sentiment. Indeed, Boel persuaded his lawyer brother in 1725 to prepare
a 150-page *Klagte*, or complaint, against Frelinghuysen's irregular and
unorthodox behavior based on the criticisms of the Raritan dominie's
lay enemies. This document, which was published and sent to the Classis
of Amsterdam for action, criticized Frelinghuysen for a host of sins,
chief among them being his presumptuous judging of individuals' spiritual condition. According to the *Klagte*, Frelinghuysen claimed the
right to decide if a member was suitably converted for the reception of
the Lord's Supper. He ignored authentic certificates of membership from
neighbor Dutch churches, demanded fresh examinations of new applicants' piety, and on two separate occasions, it was alleged, had declared
the Dutch clergy of New York and Amsterdam unregenerate hypocrites.[52]

The *Klagte* objected to the heavy pietistic emphasis upon conviction
in Frelinghuysen's preaching. Frelinghuysen believed a deep conviction
of sin had to precede all conversions. Yet the *Klagte* charged that the
resulting sermonic harangues against his congregations' sins led many
in the Raritan parishes to despair and encouraged the clergyman's supporters to use harsh names and the threat of excommunication to frighten
their enemies. Neither practice actually converted Frelinghuysen's opponents, and the *Klagte* claimed that their real intent was to create
division in the church.[53]

As proof for their charges, the *Klagte* pointed to the current dissension in Frelinghuysen's five congregations as well as the schism that had recently erupted in Joseph Morgan's Freehold churches. Shortly before the publication of the *Klagte*, Joseph Morgan and his son accused Frelinghuysen of luring several Freehold residents into secret conventicles. According to the younger Morgan, Frelinghuysen intended to form his own sect by encouraging conventicle participants to think of themselves as an elite brotherhood of newborn Christians. The elder Morgan supported this claim by denouncing Frelinghuysen for propagating the Dutch separatist ideas of Jean de Labadie.[54]

A time lag in transatlantic communications and the reticence of the Amsterdam Classis to intervene decisively allowed the Raritan controversy to drag on until 1738. But Frelinghuysen's opponents did not wait on the Amsterdam Classis to act against the Raritan clergyman. In the fall of 1725 Dominie Henricus Coens arrived in New York to replace the recently deceased Bartholf and, shortly thereafter, Boel dispatched him to the Raritan valley so that he could conduct services and administer the sacraments to Frelinghuysen's lay adversaries.[55]

LESSONS IN PIETIST THEOLOGY AND RHETORIC

Coens's attempts to organize rival Dutch churches failed, and his actions predisposed Frelinghuysen to distrust Gilbert Tennent when he first arrived in New Brunswick. Frelinghuysen had never met Tennent, but what news he had received about the new clergyman led him to suspect that the young Presbyterian was part of the plot to undermine his ministry. Frelinghuysen had learned that one of his prominent lay critics had contributed to Tennent's salary, and that other disenchanted members of his congregations had been approached for donations. He also knew that Joseph Morgan had played a part in Tennent's ordination. Thus, Frelinghuysen initially avoided Tennent and warned his congregations to do the same.[56]

Tennent's first reaction to Frelinghuysen was more positive. In 1744 he described his first six months in New Brunswick in this way:

When I came *there* [to New Brunswick] which was about *seven Years after* [Frelinghuysen], I had the Pleasure of seeing much of the Fruits of his Ministry: divers of his Hearers with whom I had the Opportunity of conversing, appear'd to be converted Persons, by their Soundness in Principle, Christian Experience, and pious Practice: and these Persons declared that the Ministrations of the aforesaid Gentleman, were the Means thereof. This together with a kind *Letter* which he sent me respecting the Necessity of dividing the Word aright, and giving every Man his Portion in due Season, thro' the divine Blessing, excited me to greater Earnestness in ministerial Labours. I [then] began to be very much distressed about my want of Success; for I knew not for *half a Year* or more after I came to *New Brunswick*, that any one was converted by my Labours, altho' several Persons were at Times affected transiently.[57]

Frelinghuysen's "kind letter" to Tennent may well have been a subtle test of the Presbyterian's theological predilections. Only a few years before, Frelinghuysen had sent a "kind letter" of similar content to Boel, but because of Boel's orthodox background, the letter had been interpreted as an affront and used against Frelinghuysen in the *Klagte* of 1725. Tennent's appreciative response was more likely what Frelinghuysen had hoped for since it calmed some of the dominie's fears about his new Presbyterian neighbor.[58]

Tennent's words show his early esteem for Frelinghuysen, but they also express his unenviable position vis-a-vis the older Dutch dominie. As Tennent's first pastorate, the New Brunswick church was the earliest test of his abilities as a spiritual leader. Yet the first six months of Tennent's ministry manifested no signs of its future fire, while that of his elder associate burned brightly. As a result, Tennent developed serious self-doubts and in the midst of this self-examination, he fell ill. In later years, Tennent recalled:

I was then exceedingly grieved that I had done so little for God, and was very desirous to live one *half Year* more if it was his Will, that I might stand upon the Stage of the World as it were, and plead more faithfully for his Cause, and take more earnest Pains for the *Conversion of Souls*. The secure State of the World appeared to me in a very affecting Light; and one Thing among others pressed me sore; viz. that I had spent much Time in conversing about Trifles, which might have been spent in examining People's States towards God, and persuading them to turn unto him: I therefore prayed to God that he would be pleased to give me one *half Year* more, and I was determined to endeavor to promote his Kingdom with all my Might at all Adventures.[59]

Tennent's illness heightened his awareness of the deficiencies in his ministry, but Frelinghuysen provided the methods by which Tennent would soon fulfill his new pact with God.

Frelinghuysen's early reservations about Tennent disappeared within months of Gilbert's arrival in New Brunswick, and thereafter cooperation between the two men increased dramatically. By 1728 Tennent was preaching in Frelinghuysen's Dutch congregations, and the following year the two pastors led a joint communion service in which Frelinghuysen preached in Dutch and Tennent prayed and administered the covenant seals in English. On later occasions, collections were taken in Frelinghuysen's congregations for the support of Tennent's ministry among English-speaking inhabitants, and members of the Raritan churches were encouraged to attend Tennent's English services when the dominie was either away or too ill to conduct worship.[60]

Tennent's association with Frelinghuysen altered the theology, preaching, and quite likely even the personality of the Presbyterian. Tennent's distant cousin James Logan had remarked in 1725 that Gilbert had "more honesty than that required" for a minister. This quality in the young clergyman would be the source of much conflict in later life, since it led him to ignore the etiquette of ecclesiastical diplomacy in his public declarations. Whether this trait was already embedded in Tennent's character when he met Frelinghuysen it is impossible to say with any certainty. It can be assumed, however, that Frelinghuysen's example did little to moderate this attribute in Tennent and probably exaggerated it.

Frelinghuysen was known and hated for his untempered, almost combative candor both in and out of the pulpit. His detractors were fond of quoting the belligerent poem that the dominie had painted on the rear of his sleigh in order to answer criticisms voiced behind his back.

> No one's tongue, and no one's pen
> Can make me other than I am.
> Speak, evil-speaker, without end;
> In vain you all your slanders spend.[61]

In his pulpit rhetoric Frelinghuysen was no less candid or aggressive, since his pietistic perspective on preaching demanded such an approach.

Frelinghuysen's homiletics was based upon his view of the conversion process, which he pictured in much the same fashion as other Continental pietists of the period. Although this *ordo salutis* was never officially systematized, pietists in German Lutheran, Dutch Calvinist, and English Puritan communions were generally in agreement that full conversion involved three broadly defined steps. The first was law work, or *Busskampf*, as the German Lutherans labeled it; the second, rebirth; and the third, the practice of piety. In confronting the stringent demands of the biblical law, individuals could expect to experience law work during which they were convinced and convicted of their personal sin, brought to despair at their inability to save themselves, and ultimately forced to see in Christ their sole hope for salvation. With the divine gift of grace, the second step of rebirth occurred. This entailed the reception of the Holy Spirit and resulted in the final step of pious acts symptomatic of a new man or woman in Christ. Although joy was a part of conversion, this last step was believed to be an arduous one requiring the full cooperation of heart, body, and mind.[62]

Recognizing that the members of his congregation were at different points in this process, Frelinghuysen carefully directed his sermons to their various conditions. His model for defining the needs of each condition was drawn from the works of the Emden theologian Johan Verschuir. According to Verschuir, four classes of humanity existed. They were

1. "Strong Christian" (*Sterk Christen*), who is converted and is practised in the truths of Christ, as they must be known in contemplation and in particular through experience (*bevindinge*);

2. "Concerned Christian" (*Bekommert Christen*), who is also converted but who still wrestles with much lack of faith and despair;

3. "Literal Man" (*Letterwyse*), who is unconverted, yet instructed and conversant in the truth, without knowing it by experience nor in its power;

4. "Ignorant Man" (*Onkunde*), who is both unconverted and unlearned, but who still seems apt to learn and fit for instruction, and by nature is fairly intelligent.[63]

For each type of individual certain portions of Scripture and styles of rhetoric were considered best suited to promote conversion and the practice of piety. Therefore, Frelinghuysen maintained that "the application [of a sermon] should be discriminating, adapted to the various states of the hearers. . . . In the church are wicked and unconverted persons, moral persons, Christians in appearance and profession; and these," he observed, "constitute the greater number, for many are called, but few chosen. Also are there in the church converted persons; little children, and those more advanced. Each longs and calls," and "each one must be addressed and dealt with according to his state and frame.''[64] For this reason, Frelinghuysen advised Tennent always to ''divide the Word aright'' and, since some would be more receptive to God's Word at one time rather than another, to offer ''to every Man his Portion in due Season.''

Of all the classes of humanity to which a sermon might be directed, the most difficult to reach were the unconverted. Such people did not see the false security of a life without grace. So Frelinghuysen developed several methods by which he could roughly awaken the doomed from their deadly sleep of security. Labeled by Martin E. Lodge the ''preaching of terrors,'' ''holding the mirror to the hearer's soul,'' and the ''searching method,'' the first two of these techniques jarred the listener into conversion either by depicting the frightful future of those not yet converted or by outlining those spiritual attributes in the individual that qualified him or her for damnation. The third method, called ''searching,'' supported the previous two techniques by undercutting any ''conscious or semi-conscious notions which his hearers could use to avoid the awful facts'' that the two previous methods had exposed. This was accomplished by a series of rhetorical questions and answers showing how earlier figures had used the same pretenses to righteousness but found them wanting.[65]

These homiletic techniques were Frelinghuysen's most obvious gift to Tennent's ministry, but the influence of the Dutch dominie did not end there. For Frelinghuysen, all humanity was faced with a choice between two ways of life, which he labeled the ''broad'' and the ''narrow.'' Those who traveled the broad path followed a way ''wherein they are careful, without true Repentance of their Sins, without a narrow Searching of themselves, whereon they seek Self-Honor, Ease and Profit in the World.'' Such individuals ''practice Religion as much as the World can spare, or out of the usual Custom, or for Welfare's sake or for the sake of others to be seen by them, to pass for an honest Man and a good Christian, or to stop the Mouth of their Conscience to keep it from regret, or even to do God Service therewith, and as it were oblige him to save them. . . . '' But, Frelinghuysen concluded, ''their whole Life and Actings is yet Sin, because they only live for themselves and not for God.''[66]

Tennent learned from Frelinghuysen that it was a minister's duty to warn travelers on this broad way that they were doomed. Frelinghuysen's favorite image for the clergy was drawn from Ezekiel 3:17–19:

Son of man, I have made thee a watchman unto the house of Israel: therefore hear the word of my mouth, and give them warning from me.

When I say unto the wicked, Thou shalt surely die; and thou givest him not warning, nor speakest to warn the wicked from his wicked way to save his life, the same wicked man shall die in his iniquity; but his blood will I require at thine hand.

Yet if thou warn the wicked, and he turn not from wickedness nor from his wicked way; he shall die in his iniquity; but thou hast delivered thy soul.[67]

In Frelinghuysen's mind, the clergy was not a "human device, merely contrived for the purpose of keeping the public under restraint . . . [or] to be looked upon as superfluous and unnecessary." Instead, the office of the ministry was "a divine institution . . . [and] a display of the Lord's compassion. We are by nature blind, perverse, and born in the broad way, we wander all as lost sheep, have need of instruction and warning, proceeding from the mouth of God himself."[68]

Ministers were the specially appointed mouthpieces of God. Their role was to warn those on the broad way of their danger and to caution those who veered from the narrow path of their error. Failure to turn either of these groups back to the narrow life did not affect the clerical watchman's future fate, but the watchman was held responsible if he did not sound a clear and penetrating cry of danger.

Frelinghuysen charged that false ministers were a major cause of many a person's damnation. These men did not "faithfully warn the People of . . . [their] dreadful Self-Deceit." They did not show the people "the subtly of Satan, and the Deceitfulness of their Hearts." They were guilty of "not rightly dividing the Word but (Arminian like) throwing out the Promises (in general)," and they too often cried "Peace, Peace," when there was no peace.[69]

True preachers, on the other hand, exposed the false pretension of human self-righteousness before offering gospel forgiveness. If done properly, sinners realized that their family connections, knowledge, wealth, and even participation in the sacraments were insufficient grounds for salvation. If this were left undone, Frelinghuysen was certain that gospel grace was cheapened, and sinful self-deception left untouched.[70]

In a similar vein, Frelinghuysen charged that the common practice of superficial examinations before communion left the laity in a damnable state. Frelinghuysen strictly examined every prospective communicant in his own practice. During such discussions he evaluated the communicant's spiritual condition. If he found it wanting, he warned the sinner to seek conversion. If this warning went unheeded, he banned the unrepentant sinner from the communion table. In this way the ban became the most drastic warning a minister could give to the ungodly.[71]

Frelinghuysen explained false teachers' failure to warn the unrighteous by noting that these men were themselves ignorant of the need for a new birth in Christ. Unconverted clergymen failed to realize that "neither a thorough literary course, nor an ecclesiastical license, nor a lawful call constitute us faithful watchmen." A proper education and official approval might be important for an orderly ministry, but they were the least secure basis for an effective one. Therefore, Frelinghuysen demanded that the clergy severely examine their own souls before they considered the state of others'.[72]

Since proper warning was the truest mark of a Christian minister, Frelinghuysen ignored the ethnic or denominational affiliation of his ministerial associates. With other Reformed pietists in Europe and America, Frelinghuysen practiced a limited "ecumenism." He chose his colleagues according to their "experimental" (i.e., experiential) acquaintance with conversion, their advocacy of a sincere practice of piety, and their adherence to Reformed theology as the proper foundation for evangelical piety. Those who lacked these essential qualifications were considered blind teachers and a dangerous, even devilish, element in the church of Christ whether they were members of his own communion or not. Yet he readily accepted those who shared his pietistic interests whatever their ethnic background or ecclesiastical affiliation. Of course, this limited ecumenism led to severe conflict between Frelinghuysen and orthodox Dutch Reformed clergymen like Boel, but it also produced a close and fruitful collegial relationship with Gilbert Tennent.

From Frelinghuysen's example Tennent learned to choose his allies on the basis of their experimental and Reformed interests. Thus, in later years Tennent aided the Anglican revivalist George Whitefield in the revivals of the Great Awakening and with Frelinghuysen joined the German Reformed clergyman Peter Henry Dorsius in examining and even ordaining a young man in Dorsius's communion.[73]

THE LEGACY OF TENNENT'S TWO MENTORS

Theodorus Frelinghuysen had a pivotal influence on Gilbert Tennent's ministry, but the same can be said of William Tennent. How then do the influences of the two men compare? To answer this question one must first consider their theological backgrounds. Although their ethnic and ecclesiastical pedigrees were quite different, the ministries of William Tennent and Frelinghuysen exhibited several striking similarities. Both men attacked hypocritical participation in the sacraments. Both opposed the idea that one's childhood training, ethnic origin, or theological acumen assured salvation. Both stressed the internal state of the individual over the external observance of liturgical rites, and each emphasized the need for repentance, conversion, and a sincere practice of piety.

These shared beliefs facilitated Gilbert Tennent's acceptance of Frelinghuysen as his second mentor during his first years in New Brunswick. In Frelinghuysen's ministry Gilbert discovered a theology and practice basically in sympathy with the teachings of his father and yet more powerful than the Log College tutor's because Frelinghuysen focused upon conversion as the central experience of the Christian life. William Tennent, Sr., recognized the importance of conversion, but when compared to Frelinghuysen, he gave it a secondary place in his theology. As Martin E. Lodge has noted, "A Tennent sermon of 1729 speaks of this experience [of conversion] as the 'first act of illumination.' . . . It marks the infusion of the grace of God into the sinner, and is but the first step in a growth in obedience, humility, and the understanding of God's teaching. Though such conversion is 'deeply affecting' and 'humbling to the soul,' it is not the shattering experience of Frelinghuysen's evangelism." According to Lodge, then, the elder Tennent emphasized one's " 'growth in grace,' rather than the actual experience of conversion."[74]

Gilbert Tennent never entirely abandoned his father's concern for the Christian's "growth in grace," but he increasingly envisioned this growth in terms of the three-step conversion experience employed by Frelinghuysen. As a result, the style and content of Gilbert's rhetoric began to correspond more closely to that of his Dutch colleague.

This modification of Tennent's ministry had two important long-term effects on Awakening history. In the first place, it transformed an otherwise ineffectual New Jersey pastor into a major revival figure in the middle colonies, and second, it laid the foundation for Tennent's future relations with the Puritan-educated Presbyterian pastors of the New York Presbytery. During his apprenticeship under Frelinghuysen, Tennent's career blossomed. In the late 1720s Tennent sparked his first major revivals among colonial Presbyterians. This brought him both fame and foes.

Because of opposition that developed within the Presbyterian communion against his revival ministry, Tennent would later need the aid of New York Presbyterians to carry his cause. Most of these clergymen had been educated in New England and, consequently, were strong supporters of Puritan theology and practice. Those views held in common by his father and Frelinghuysen were integral parts of the Puritan tradition. On these points Gilbert Tennent and his future Awakening party would eventually forge an alliance with the New York Presbytery's ministers.[75] But this association was delayed for many years because of Gilbert's use of his Dutch friend's rhetorical methods and the concomitant stress upon conversion. Experimental knowledge derived from a converting experience of grace was fully supported by the Puritan tradition. Like Frelinghuysen, early New England Puritans demanded that members of their churches, and especially their clergy, possess a knowlege of God's gracious work in the heart. But the Puritans balanced this call for experiential understanding with a strong insistence on doctrinal enlightenment, respect for the ordained ministry, and the recognition that God alone knew the true state of a human soul.[76]

Doctrine was important to both of the New Brunswick pastors as well. Each man chose his friends and his enemies on the basis of it. But the communication of systematic theology was not the central focus of their revival preaching. Frelinghuysen's homiletics was fashioned to lead individuals to salvation through an experience of conversion. It was not intended to guide parishioners to doctrinal comprehension through an intricate explanation of theological logic.

Frelinghuysen and Tennent also maintained a very high opinion of the ministry. But both men believed clerical authority depended ultimately upon the pastor's firsthand experience with conversion rather than his ecclesiastical certification or formal training.

In a similar fashion, Tennent and Frelinghuysen recognized that God was free to save sinners in any manner he chose. Although no perfect standard existed by which one might judge another's spirit, Tennent believed that educated guesses were possible and necessary for two reasons. First, the Divine Creator was not an arbitrary sovereign. His Spirit's operations on the human heart normally followed a predictable course which could serve as a reasonably accurate measuring stick to evaluate an individual's experience. Second, the converted minister's primary duty was to "divide the Word aright," giving each person his or her portion in due season. But this task could not be accomplished if one did not first ascertain the exact level of progress achieved by individual laypeople in one's congregation.

During the Great Awakening these aspects of Tennent's revival program would create serious doubts in the minds of the New York clergy as to the orthodoxy and long-term benefits of the movement. Troubled by the differences between their own Puritan pietism and the Dutch Reformed Pietism found in Tennent's ministry, the New York Presbytery would, for a time, withhold its support from Gilbert and thereby delay the spread of revivalism within the Presbyterian communion.

2

SOURCES OF PRE-AWAKENING PRESBYTERIAN DIVISIONS: SUBSCRIPTION, ITINERACY, EDUCATION, AND SOVEREIGNTY

During the first years of Gilbert Tennent's ministry in New Brunswick, a conflict erupted in the Synod of Philadelphia that significantly affected Presbyterian politics for the next two decades. On the surface, an "overture" requiring subscription to the Westminster Confession and Catechisms precipitated the crisis. But the call for subscription was itself generated by the discomfort of some Presbyterian leaders with the undefined structure and theology of the colonial Presbyterian system.

The subscriptionist controversy fostered heated debate over the Synod's right to legislate unqualified assent to creeds or practices that were not expressly prescribed by Scripture. Although a supporter of subscription, Gilbert Tennent did not actively participate in these polemical contests in part because he was preoccupied with developing an effective rationale and methodology for revival preaching.

Tennent's efforts in this regard reaped their first fruits in the late 1720s, when several congregations experienced spiritual awakenings under his ministrations. During the following decade, revivalism grew in popularity through the agency of an increasing number of Log College graduates, but Presbyterian subscriptionists soon moved to restrict the new phenomenon, since they viewed their new colleagues' practice as disruptive of church order. This opposition in turn led to a series of ecclesiastical clashes that prefigured the sources and pattern of conflict during the First Great Awakening.

ORGANIZATIONAL AMBIGUITIES IN COLONIAL PRESBYTERIANISM

Middle colony Presbyterians acknowledged their need for an organization to coordinate their common mission by establishing a Philadelphia Presbytery in 1706. This new church body immediately assumed the prerogative to examine and ordain clergy, adjudicate disciplinary cases, and demand attendance at formally called meetings. But it did not formulate a constitution to clarify its ecclesiastical authority vis-a-vis lower church courts, nor did it select a creed as the standard for present and future members' orthodoxy.[1]

These oversights were necessary because of the presbytery's initial composition. Three former New Englanders, three Irishmen, and one Scot attended the first meeting of the Philadelphia organization. The New England clergymen imparted a strong congregational bias to their presbyterianism. Like earlier New England Puritans, they assumed each church society was independent and complete in its ecclesiastical functions because individual congregations of visible saints were the ideal temporal embodiment of Christ's Church. Following logically from this axiom were three corollaries: first, all ecclesiastical power originated in self-sufficient local church societies; second, ministerial authority depended upon a clergyman's formal association with a particular congregation; and third, presbyteries and synods could only advise their autonomous member churches as to proper discipline and orthodoxy.[2]

In the Church of Scotland and the Synod of Ulster quite a different conception of the Church informed presbyterian polity. There the Christian hope for a universal Church determined the ecclesiastical structure. Local congregations were recognized as regional representatives of the worldwide body of Christ, but the will of the highest church judicatories was accepted as the most trustworthy expression of Christ's catholic interests. Ministers in this system were agents of the broader denominational organization regardless of their relationship with individual societies. Power flowed downward through a hierarchy of councils, and higher judicatories possessed the authority to determine the practice and theology of lower courts and member congregations.[3]

These two fundamentally different pictures of presbyterianism prevented a common constitutional agreement in 1706, but they did not stop the establishment of a presbytery for one paramount reason. The central goal of the new association's membership was the spread of

Presbyterian theology throughout the colonial population. This, of course, could not be accomplished if the church's clergy focused on their differences. Therefore, the volatile issue of structural sovereignty was temporarily ignored in the interest of Christian edification and ecclesiastical growth.

For the first two decades of the eighteenth century, the Presbytery (and, after 1716, the Synod) of Philadelphia relied upon immigrant ministers to satisfy its increasing need for leadership. This arrangement proved troublesome, however, since the demand for clergy continued to outstrip the supply and the qualifications of the ministers who did immigrate into the colonies were oftentimes as questionable as their reasons for immigrating. Church authorities tried to monitor the credentials of new ministerial applicants in these early years, but the squeeze of too few workers to service a rapidly expanding population forced a lowering of standards and a decline in discipline. As laxity increased, some Synod members began to question whether the current shortage in staff was not a more serious impediment to church growth than the rising disciplinary lenience.

THE GILLESPIE OVERTURE AND ITS
ANTISUBSCRIPTIONIST REBUTTAL

The first formal protest generated by these misgivings occurred in 1720 after the Synod levied an extremely mild sentence on a clergyman found guilty of fornication. The complaint lodged against this action was ignored, but its formulator, George Gillespie, returned the following year with a motion that allowed members to propose new regulations for church government and discipline wherever a loophole for impropriety existed. The Synod approved this measure, and this precipitated a protest from another segment of its membership.[4]

Six ministers objected to Gillespie's assumption that the Synod possessed the power to prescribe new ecclesiastical rules so long as due process was observed. For a Scotsman like Gillespie, this prerogative was axiomatic, but to the protestors it exhibited gross presumption on the part of a fallible Christian association.

Jonathan Dickinson explained why this was so in a sermon before the Synod during 1722. Dickinson's definition of the problem exposed the fact that the Gillespie rule was being interpreted in the light of contemporary subscription controversies in Northern Ireland. In the early eighteenth century a group of Belfast ministers began meeting for discussions of Scripture and theology. This society included some of the Ulster Synod's most respected clergymen, but it acquired the reputation of promoting heterodox notions about the Divine Trinity. To protect against the infection of such heresy, the Synod passed a rule requiring subscription to the Westminster Confession and Catechisms by all ordained members. The Belfast Society objected to this decision, claiming that human creeds should never replace the Scriptures as tests for orthodoxy. After years of internal debate, the Ulster Synod agreed upon a compromise measure that still demanded subscription but allowed those who conscientiously objected to unqualified subscription to express their faith in their own words. These personal confessions were then reviewed by Synod and, if found consistent with the essentials of the Westminster standards, were accepted in place of subscription.[5]

Known as the Pacific Act, this legislation cooled the conflict in North Ireland until 1721, when a Reverend Haliday refused to subscribe under the prescribed conditions. As he explained his reasons:

My refusal to declare my assent does not proceed from my disbelief of the important truths contained in the Westminster Confession, . . . but my scruples are against the submitting to human tests of divine truth, when imposed as a necessary term of Christian and ministerial communion, especially in a great number of extra-essential truths, without the knowledge or belief of which men may be entitled to the favour of God and the hopes of eternal life, and according to the laws of the gospel, to Christian and ministerial communion.[6]

Dickinson objected to the Gillespie overture in 1722 for essentially the same reasons that Haliday refused subscription in 1721.

Dickinson declared in his sermon that the clergy had no right or need to invent theological statements or ecclesiastical structures to maintain the church's purity. Christ provided in the Scriptures all that was necessary for the "whole work of the ministry." Therefore, human inventions were nothing more than "bold invasions of Christ's Royal Power, and a rude reflection upon his Wisdom and Faithfulness."[7]

Unwarrantable human intervention in the church's affairs took three specific forms, according to Dickinson. The first was "the devising and imposing any part or mode of worship that wants a divine institution." The second involved "the forming or imposing any New Acts or Constitution, in the Government or Discipline of the Church" not clearly

prescribed by Scripture, and the third consisted of a church's pretense
to "any authoritative obligatory Interpretation of the Laws of Christ."[8]
Concerning the last of these, Dickinson acknowledged that "Ministers
of Christ have Commission to Interpret his [Christ's] Laws, and it
concerns them with utmost application to study his Mind and Will, that
they may declare his whole Counsel to his People." But, Dickinson
added, those same ministers have "no claim to Infallibility, [and] can
have no Authority to impose their Interpretations; nor is any Man ab-
solutely obliged to receive Them any further than they appear to him
just and true."[9]

SOURCES OF COLONIAL SUBSCRIPTIONIST AGITATION

Had Dickinson's views prevailed in the Philadelphia Synod, they
would have neutralized the power of future regulations by giving veto
power to every member's conscience. But Dickinson's associates from
Scotland and Ulster were not persuaded by his argument. For these
men, two considerations made formal subscription a necessity. One was
the unprecedented religious pluralism of the middle colonies. While
Dickinson and his supporters ministered to regions in which the population was ethnically diverse but religiously dominated by Reformed
churches, their subscriptionist colleagues served frontier parishes in
Pennsylvania where a common Reformed tradition could not be assumed. The sects and churches vying for the frontier settlers' affections
were even more numerous than the area's unusually varied ethnic
groups. The subscriptionists were all too well aware of the destructive
effects of such pluralism. They knew that the church's corporate identity
and the clergy's local authority were seriously undermined by these
conditions, and in order to combat these tendencies, they advocated a
formally defined structure and theology for their church with subscription as the first step toward that goal.[10]

A further consideration for the subscriptionists was their fear of unorthodox Presbyterian clergymen infiltrating the Synod. It was evident to
all concerned that for an indefinite period of time the church would be
dependent upon immigrant ministers to supply its numerous vacant
pulpits. Yet many of these individuals were infected with the unorthodox
views currently spreading through Europe. If such clergymen were
admitted into the Synod, they could further mislead the already confused

Presbyterian laity. Therefore, a filter was needed to screen out the heterodox before they could corrupt the colonial church with their dangerous notions. Subscription seemed the logical answer since it required an open declaration of new ministers' theology before their entry into the colonial Presbyterian fellowship.[11]

Since most subscriptionists were either Scots or Ulster Irish, they limited their first efforts at enforcing subscription to the presbytery in which their countrymen held a majority. In 1724 the New Castle Presbytery began recording the subscription of all entrants into the ministry. Three years later John Thomson of the New Castle Presbytery proposed a formal overture for Synod-wide subscription. Presbyterian moderates delayed consideration of this measure because they feared it would create a schism, and during the ensuing year, they tried to convince Thomson to withdraw his motion. Their efforts proved futile. In 1728 the subscription overture was again presented to the Synod. This time its passage was recommended by every Scottish or Irish member present, and a vote on the measure was scheduled for the Synod's next meeting.[12]

Before the final vote, Jedidiah Andrews reported to a friend in Boston that the Thomson overture had accentuated the polarization of ethnic groups within the colonial Presbyterian church. Andrews noted that the Scots and the Irish who were in the majority could easily carry the subscription overture. The English, Welsh, and New England members, on the other hand, were "willing to join in a vote to make it [the Westminster Confession] the Confession of our Church, but to agree to make it the Test of Orthodoxy and Term of Ministerial Communion, they say, They will not." These antisubscriptionists were convinced their opponents wished to eject them from Synod because of basic disagreements over discipline and the church's legislative authority. Andrews personally doubted the existence of such a self-conscious scheme, but he did admit his party was "an uneasiness" to the subscriptionists and "tho't to be too much in their way sometimes, so that I think 'twould be no Trouble [to them] to lose some of us."[13]

THE SUBSCRIPTION DEBATE

The sponsor of the offending overture, John Thomson, was well aware that his motion faced stiff opposition, and he feared that the laity would not have an opportunity to consider the issue before a final determination. So he published the measure along with his justification for passage just prior to the 1729 Synod.[14]

Thomson's opponents recognized this ploy to capture their laity's votes. Therefore, Jonathan Dickinson quickly issued a reply to Thomson. Comparing this work with Thomson's, one discovers three fundamental issues that separated the subscriptionists from the Dickinson party. The first related to the nature of a confession, the second concerned freedom of conscience, and the third involved the best means for effecting ecclesiastical union.[15]

Both Thomson and Dickinson accepted the Scriptures as the one infallible rule for the church, but Thomson asked whether it was "the bare Letter [of Scripture], or the Letter together with its true and proper Sense and Meaning, intended by the Holy Ghost, which is the rule." According to Thomson, the earliest Christian communities had no need for creeds because infallible guides living among them directed the church to the text's true meaning. Moreover, when the church finally began to formulate creeds, they excluded them from Holy Writ because they recognized the two forms of writings were significantly different.[16]

The fundamental distinction between creed and Scripture was, in Thomson's view, that the latter was "God's Act and Deed, viz. his Declaration of his Mind to us, and thereby prescribing a Rule for our Faith and Practice; . . . [whereas] Our Confession is the Declaration of God's Thoughts" in our own words. As God's own creation, the Scriptures did not need subscription since their perfection in "form" and "matter" was assured by their source. Creeds and confessions, on the other hand, were formulated by fallible human beings. Their form was necessarily imperfect, but occasionally their matter exactly reproduced the biblical revelation. Confessions that were flawed in form but faultless in matter were the true creeds of Christ's church on earth. The church acknowledged this unblemished matter through subscription and could rightfully impose it upon new members as a test of their orthodoxy and proof of their right to Christian communion.[17]

Although Thomson never stated his underlying philosophy, his argument depended upon the belief that truth could be recognized by a majority of members in any Christian association. On the question of creeds, this meant that a majority could be trusted to distinguish a true confession from imposters and, once that determination had been made, could demand subscription to the truth in that creed. Such a requirement was no more than asking individuals to express their allegiance to the truth. Since declaring for truth was agreeable to the conscience, subscription was compatible with freedom of conscience. For Thomson, tyranny over the conscience only existed where the church forced a person to accept that which was not in Scripture either implicitly or explicitly. Subscription made no such demands. Therefore, subscription was not tyranny.[18]

Dickinson found Thomson's logic faulty. He did not believe creeds were perfect either in form or matter, and he felt Thomson's definition of tyranny was inapplicable even to the paradigm of tyranny, namely, the Catholic Church. Tyranny for Dickinson involved the imposition of anything other than God's explicit word. Subscription to human confessions was such an imposition. Therefore, subscription was a species of ecclesiastical oppression.[19]

As further justification for subscription, Thomson pointed to the fact that the colonial Presbyterian Church was "much like the People of Laish, in a careless defenceless Condition, as a City without Walls" in a time "when Arminianism, Socianism, Deism, Freethinking, etc, do like a deluge overflow even the reformed churches, both established and dissenting."[20]

Dickinson also felt the church lay unprotected, but he denied that subscription was the proper material for building an invincible wall around the Synod's orthodoxy. In his view, subscription prevented the admission of conscientious clergymen who would certainly have scruples about the imperfections found in any creed. Yet it would allow the infiltration of unscrupulous heretics. Equally objectionable was the fact that subscription undermined Synod unity. In the past, heresy and division had erupted wherever subscription was required, so it only stood to reason that a source of schism should not be used as a "Bond of Union."[21]

For antisubscriptionists like Dickinson, church unity could never be codified or imposed. Unity depended upon internalized bonds of sympathy embodied in a flexible church structure. The church had to protect itself from corruption, as Thomson said, but subscription could not accomplish this task. Church vitality depended upon the clergy's unqualified allegiance to God's perfect instruction in Scripture, their experimental knowledge of the Spirit's workings in the soul, and their personal example of the Christian life. For this reason, Dickinson demanded that candidates be more carefully examined during their ordination trials and that errant ministers be severely disciplined.[22]

Thomson, in contrast, viewed church union in a mechanical fashion. As Howard Miller has described his perspective, "Union did not evolve naturally and unaided from the shared interest of a society. Rather, it followed the vigorous codification and public adoption of those interests. Thus, a union was viable only when its true members—and enemies— were identified and its physical and intellectual boundaries demarked and defended."[23]

THE ADOPTING ACT OF 1729

When the Philadelphia Synod finally met in September 1729, a vote on subscription could no longer be delayed. During its first session the Synod appointed a committee which included representatives from both sides of the issue in the hopes that together they might formulate a balanced agreement acceptable to all parties. On September 19 this group presented a proposal to the Synod that was, as one historian has described it, a "judicious compromise based on the Irish Pacific Articles with a preamble in Dickinson's spirit."[24]

The preamble specifically required that ministers and future candidates "declare their agreement in, and approbation" of, the Westminster Confession and Catechisms and adopt said documents "as the confession of our faith." But those who harbored doubts about certain portions of the Westminster standards could express them to either their presbytery or the Synod, and those bodies would decide if the confessed scruples affected essential elements of the standards. If not, the minister in question would be admitted without further examination.[25]

During the afternoon session of September 19, the full Synod membership subscribed to the Westminster standards with two qualifications. The twentieth and twenty-third chapters of the Westminster Confession were renounced by the entire Synod. These chapters concerned a civil magistrate's power over the Synod's clergy, the magistrate's right to prosecute individuals for religious reasons, and the English crown's relationship to the church.[26]

The Synod hoped this Adopting Act would end the subscription controversy, but it did not. Like most compromises, the new rule left all parties dissatisfied. The subscriptionists had achieved a Synod-wide subscription, but their outnumbered opponents had seriously qualified the new requirement through the preamble. The preamble implied that certain doctrines in the Westminster standards were not essential for membership, but it left unspecified which tenets were optional. Moreover, the preamble allowed the presbytery or the Synod to decide cases of conscience, but it avoided designating one of these bodies the final arbiter where the two might disagree.

Four days after the Synod passed the Adopting Act, the fourth part of the Westminster standards, known as the Westminster Directory, was considered. This document dealt specifically with worship, discipline, and the respective powers of judicatories within the church's governmental structure, but it had not been included in the Synod's subscription. After discussing the Directory, the Synod recognized it "to be agreeable in substance to the word of God, and founded thereupon." But the Synod simply "recommended the same to all their members, to be by them observed as near as circumstances will allow, and Christian prudence direct." This equivocating stance on the Directory left unresolved the relative powers of the Synod and its presbyteries, and in cases of conscience where the Synod and a particular presbytery disagreed, ultimate authority remained open to question.[27]

THE DETERIORATION OF THE ADOPTING ACT COMPROMISE

Due to these loopholes in the Adopting Act, presbyteries dominated by subscriptionists chose to ignore its preamble. In 1730 and 1732 the New Castle and Donegal Presbyteries imposed unqualified subscription to the Westminster standards. At the same time, a novel interpretation of the Synod's action began to circulate. According to this new reading, the preamble had been only a "preliminary act" and, thus, had not been intended as part of the approved subscription process. This of course neutralized the preamble's conditions.[28]

The Synod formally accepted this reinterpretation of subscription in 1736 because of the heresy trial of a young Irish clergyman named Samuel Hemphill. Hemphill had requested admission to the Synod of Philadelphia in September 1734. On the basis of written testimony from Ireland, the petition was granted and the new member was made an assistant to Jedidiah Andrews in the Philadelphia Presbyterian Church.[29]

Hemphill's preaching was well received by a certain portion of the Philadelphia population which included the printer Benjamin Franklin. But it was not appreciated by his superior in the Philadelphia church. Convinced that Hemphill was a Deist and a Socinian, Andrews presented a formal complaint against his youthful associate to the Synod's commission in April 1735. After nine days of deliberations, the commission found Hemphill guilty of propagating several heterodox beliefs.[30]

The Hemphill trial generated considerable adverse publicity for the colonial Presbyterian Church. Using his press to defend Hemphill, Benjamin Franklin attacked the Westminster Confession and the Presbyterian Synod's authority to dictate theology for its membership.[31] This unflattering assault prompted even Jonathan Dickinson to champion the cause of subscription. In a publication entitled *Remarks Upon a Pamphlet, Entitled, A Letter to a Friend in the Country*, Dickinson reiterated his antipathy for creedal subscription, but he also admitted that contemporary trends required such an extreme measure. In Dickinson's opinion, the current age was far too liberal in its notions. Variations in theological views were beneficial to the church in some instances since they encouraged charity and mutual forbearance. But the recent proliferation of differing doctrinal perspectives was not such a case, for it had sown unorthodox beliefs so widely that infidelity rather than charity had resulted. To curb the current growth of heresy, Dickinson conceded that subscription was necessary.[32]

This pamphlet by Dickinson illustrates how the Hemphill case temporarily united the Synod over the subscription issue by aggravating Presbyterian fears of theological corruption from incoming immigrant clergy. After the Hemphill affair, no member of the Synod wished to repeat the embarrassing mistake of admitting an unorthodox European minister. Therefore, at the suggestion of the subscriptionist party the 1736 Synod approved a more stringent reading of the 1729 Adopting Act. This overture, which was accepted without objection, declared the Adopting Act minus its preamble was the ''true Intent'' of the Synod's 1729 action.[33]

This radical redefinition of the original subscription act was a peculiar reaction to the Hemphill trial. Instead of proving the value of unqualified subscription as a defense against the infiltration of heterodox clergymen, the Hemphill case showed just the opposite. Once in Ireland and again in Philadelphia, Hemphill had subscribed without qualification to the Westminster standards, and yet his views were still heretical. Nevertheless, because Synod subscriptionists continued to blame the Adopting Act's preamble for Hemphill's admission into the colonial Presbyterian ministry, they campaigned for and won a negation of its stipulations.[34]

The Dickinson party cooperated with this move by passively avoiding a decision. The entire membership of Dickinson's East Jersey Presbytery chose not to attend the Synod's 1736 meeting, thereby leaving a clear subscriptionist majority to decide the issue.[35]

Gilbert Tennent was one of the absent East Jersey Presbytery members, but his reasons for not being present were not likely the same as Dickinson's. Tennent had not been actively involved in either the controversies over subscription or the formulation of the 1729 compromise. His exact views are unknown. But he did subscribe to the Adopting Act in 1729, and his father and three brothers subscribed without qualification to the standards at one time or another between 1729 and 1737. All this suggests that the Tennent family accepted subscription as a valid means of insuring the clergy's orthodoxy.[36]

The Tennents, however, were not subscriptionists in the fullest sense of the word. The subscriptionist program included far more than a simple allegiance to the Westminster standards. Men like John Thomson viewed subscription as only the first step in a larger effort to define the Synod's power over the church. The subscriptionists' ultimate goal was a system of judicatories with ascending authority that would determine with one voice the beliefs and practices of middle colony Presbyterians. This, they felt, would best insure the church's vitality. Gilbert Tennent did not support subscription for this purpose. Throughout his life the Westminster standards were a major reference point for his theology and piety. Therefore, their preservation as a norm for orthodoxy was important to Tennent. But Tennent also believed that the church's survival depended first and foremost upon its members' piety, and such piety required the spread of experimental knowledge. One source of this belief was the instruction that Tennent had received at the hands of William Tennent, Sr., and Theodorus Frelinghuysen. A second source was the New Jersey minister's pastoral experience in his home region during the period that the subscription controversy raged in the Synod.

PRIVATE AND PUBLIC RESPONSES TO TENNENT'S CONVERTING MINISTRY

In 1728 John Tennent and William Tennent, Jr., joined their brother's household in New Brunswick. It was customary during the eighteenth century for ministerial candidates to live with a pastor for a period after completing their formal education. Normally they spent this time preparing for ordination examinations and assisting the local pastor in his parish duties. But the tenure of Gilbert's brothers in New Brunswick was anything but normal.

John and William Jr. fell ill shortly after their arrival in New Brunswick. Although William was more seriously ill than John, John's deep fear of death precipitated severe internal struggles over the state of his soul. Gilbert realized John's sins were minor, but remaining true to the example of his Dutch friend, Frelinghuysen, he explored the errors of John's past life in order to bring him to a sincere conviction of his unrighteousness.[37]

Like "a man going to be put upon a rack, or gibbet," John wrestled four days and nights with his sins until his eldest brother became alarmed at the intensity of the combat and altered his method. Instead of exposing his brother's guilt before God, Gilbert began to offer him "encouraging supports . . . from every promissory part of the sacred scriptures." This did not immediately calm John. Wearied and depressed by his spiritual exertions, the young man asked to be left alone so he could pray in private. Shortly thereafter, gracious relief arrived. When Gilbert entered his brother's room the next morning, he found to his amazement "a great alteration in his [brother's] countenance." John explained that he had begged with the dogs for a crumb of mercy from the Lord's table, and Christ had answered his request generously.[38]

While John Tennent received gracious table scraps from his Master's table, William's illness precipitated a spiritual journey of an entirely different sort. William did not remain conscious during his sickness. Instead he fell into a coma that led the entire Tennent household to assume he was dead. Preparations for his interment were interrupted, however, when an attending physician discovered the faintest hint of warmth under his arm. The doctor insisted that the funeral be rescheduled. Gilbert complied with this request but found to his dismay that the physician wanted another postponement when the agreed upon date for his brother's last rites arrived. Convinced that his brother was no longer of this world and that further delay was both irrational and indecent, Gilbert entered William's room to insist the funeral commence. There he found the doctor attempting to moisten his patient's tongue with oil. Tennent was incensed by this apparent effort to force-feed a corpse, and he began to tell the offender as much when suddenly William opened his eyes, "gave a dreadful groan and sank again into apparent death."[39]

The unexpected resurrection of William Tennent confirmed the doctor's analysis of his malady, and thereafter Gilbert and his sister, Ellenor, nursed their ailing relative back to health. William suffered total amnesia for a time, but when his memory returned, he recounted the strange voyage he had completed during his stupor. He recalled that a "superior being" had guided him to a place where "an innumerable host of happy beings surrounding the inexpressible glory" engaged "in acts of adoration and joyous worship." William wanted to remain among this splendid assembly, but his companion informed him that he must return to earth. In that instant he opened his eyes to behold his eldest brother standing above him arguing with his doctor.[40]

Oddly enough, Gilbert Tennent never commented publicly on the experience of William Jr. Perhaps out of guilt for his impatient demands for a burial or simply from an uncertainty about the meaning of the event, Gilbert avoided mention of the occurrence.

John's soulful struggles were a different matter, however, for Gilbert used them in one of his earliest publications as an instructional model of Christian conversion. John's experience paralleled what Frelinghuysen had taught his Presbyterian colleague to expect. Thus, for Gilbert this intimate family event left no doubt that Frelinghuysen's insights were valid and his methods sound.

Not coincidentally, Gilbert's preaching ministry sparked its first genuine revival shortly after his Dutch mentor's instructions were confirmed by the spectacular spiritual adventures of John Tennent. During the late 1720s Tennent frequently supplied pulpits on Staten Island in addition to pursuing his regular duties in New Brunswick. In the midst of one such supply visit in 1728, Tennent discovered that the people in the congregation "were generally affected about the State of their Souls; and some to that Degree, that they fell upon their Knees in the Time of the Sermon, in order to pray to God for pardoning Mercy: Many went Home from that Sermon; and then the general Inquiry was, what shall I do to be saved?"[41]

Similar spiritual awakenings in other parts of New Jersey followed this revival and, together with his brother's recent "new birth," convinced Gilbert that the pietistic ministry that he had adopted from Frelinghuysen was the best antidote for spiritual apathy in his own communion. Consequently, in the early 1730s Tennent began to propose specific measures to the Synod that would make such an approach the norm rather than the exception among the Presbyterian clergy.

TWO OVERTURES FOR A CONVERTING MINISTRY

Gilbert Tennent introduced two overtures to bolster the Synod's current legislation against "the declining power of godliness" in its congregations during 1734. The first of these measures exhorted all Synod ministers to take "due care" in searching for evidences of the grace of God in those whom they admitted to the Lord's table and to "make it their awful, constant, and diligent care, to approve themselves to God, to their own consciences, and to their hearers, [as] serious faithful stewards of the mysteries of God, and of holy exemplary conversions." All presbyteries were also asked to inquire "into the conversations, conduct, and behavior" of their ministerial candidates and "diligently examine . . . their experiences of a work of sanctifying grace."[42]

In Tennent's second overture presbyteries were instructed to oversee the propriety and diligence of their ministers' practice. The preaching of every minister was to be reviewed to see

whether he insist in his ministry upon the great articles of Christianity, and in the course of his preaching recommend a crucified Savior to his hearers as the only foundation of hope, and the absolute necessity of the omnipotent influences of the Divine grace to enable them to accept of this Savior; whether he do in the most solemn and affecting manner he can, endeavor to convince his hearers of their lost and miserable state whilst unconverted, and put them upon the diligent use of those means necessary in order to obtain the sanctifying influences of the Spirit of God; whether he do, and how he doth, discharge his duty towards the young people and children of his congregation, in the way of catechizing and familiar instruction; [and] whether he do, and in what manner he doth, visit his flock and instruct them from house to house.[43]

After unanimously approving these proposals, the Synod ordered that its presbyteries insert a copy of the new acts into their minutes so that they could be read at every presbytery meeting. If any clergyman failed to satisfy any of the rulings' particulars, his presbytery was to censure him, and if the presbytery's censure was not taken to heart, the minister was to be brought before Synod.[44]

These measures were the first ever proposed by Tennent, but they already contained the seed of his future Awakening program. For Tennent the church's revival demanded action on all three levels of the church's membership. Among the laity the young should be nurtured in the faith through catechetical instruction and family training. Adult members should be regularly visited for close examinations of their behavior and, during private precommunion conferences, tested in their experimental knowledge of grace. With regard to ministerial candidates the church should insure that these potential shepherds of the faithful led exemplary lives themselves and were intimately acquainted with the normal workings of the Holy Spirit in the sinful soul. Familiarity with the Spirit's movements was especially important to Tennent since these young men would never know how to examine or preach to their sin-sick congregations without it. Finally, with the ordained clergy, Tennent felt the church should be particularly cautious. The clergy were crucial to the maintenance of a vibrant lay piety because it was their responsibility to warn the sinful and guide the faithful. To be sure their warnings were timely and their guidance true, ministers gathered together in presbyteries should examine one another periodically. During these examinations, presbyteries should be especially conscientious in monitoring preaching. Like most Calvinists, Tennent was convinced that the sermon was the clergy's most important duty. Preaching, according to Tennent, involved two essential tasks. The first was the communication of what he called a "historical faith," i.e., the laity's understanding of and assent to Christianity's essential doctrines. Coordinate with this chore and perhaps even more important was a second duty, namely, aiding the Holy Spirit in providing an "experimental Knowledge" of that divine grace that transformed the mental historical faith of the believer into the heartfelt experiential faith found only in converted Christians. This inevitably led to a vibrant piety throughout the church.

The Synod's unanimous approval of Gilbert Tennent's suggestions shows that, at least in theory, the entire membership recognized the need for church-wide revitalization. But already Gilbert Tennent and the subscriptionists were promoting different remedies for the church's flagging piety. Most subscriptionists believed the church's current problems could best be solved by imposing uniformity on the disparate elements of the Presbyterian constituency. For the Tennents, on the other hand, the solution depended upon the preaching ministry.

GILBERT TENNENT'S HOMILETIC SYSTEM FOR REVIVING SINNERS

In a preface to one of John Tennent's sermons published by Gilbert Tennent after his brother's untimely death in 1732, Gilbert described the ideal preaching ministry by recalling his brother's methods. John was "awakening and terrible (to unbelievers) in denouncing and describing, with the utmost vehement *pathos* and awful solemnity, the terrors of an offended *deity*, the *threats* of a broken *Law*, the miseries of a sinful *state*: . . . this subject, . . . he insisted upon, because he found it by experience, . . . the most effectual and successful *means* to alarm the secure sinners." At the same time, Gilbert noted, John was "as tender and compassionate . . . to gracious souls, as he was awful and awakening to others; he knew as well how to open and apply the gospel balsam to sick souls, as to brandish and apply the law's lance to the secure; and he was willing to do the one, as the other." John was, however, "very cautious of misapplying the different portions of the word to his hearers, or of setting before them a common mess, (as the manner of some is) and leaving it to them to divide it among themselves, as their fancy and humour directed them: for he knew well that that was the bane of preaching."[45]

Here one has Gilbert Tennent's earliest description of what should be included in a sermon and how that content should be ordered. The harsh reality of sin's consequences had to alarm the sinner before the soothing balsam of gospel promises could properly be applied to calm the convicted and to strengthen the converted. If a minister mixed these two messages or reversed them, he created a "common mess" that only perpetuated the sinful self deception of human self-righteousness and obstructed the much needed renewal of piety.

The practice of "denouncing and describing . . . the terrors of an offended deity, the threats of a broken Law [and] the miseries of a sinful state" was known to Tennent and his contemporaries as the "preaching of the terrors." It was the first part of a two-step homiletic process by which a minister led his congregation to conversion. Preaching terrors was based on the rhetorical methods that Frelinghuysen had taught Tennent during his early ministry, and, as with Frelinghuysen, its use generated strong opposition.

In order to answer the critics of this method as well as to satisfy the increasing demand from his admirers for copies of his sermons, Tennent prepared his first publication in 1735. Entitled *A Solemn Warning To The Secure World, From The God of Terrible Majesty, Or, the Presumptuous Sinner Detected, his Pleas Consider'd, and his Doom Display'd*, this sermon was Tennent's first extended defense of "terrors."[46]

Tennent illustrated in the homily how sinful humanity's pretenses to righteousness were far greater obstacles to human salvation than sin itself. Obstructing the sinner's view of his or her vices, arrogant affectation of spiritual propriety made the sinful person comfortable and secure in a quagmire of unrighteousness. The clergy were to awaken sinners from this deadly security, but to do so they had to preach terrors. Preaching the terrors involved the annihilation of self-righteousness, first, by exposing its sources and, second, by comparing the sinner's supposed "works" with the humanly impossible perfection demanded in the biblical law.

Although the sources of self-righteousness were legion, Tennent singled out thirteen common causes of the deadly malady. Eight of these were inherent aspects of the sinful personality such as ignorance, negligence, self-love, inconsideration, pride, pretensions to perfection, palliatives for imperfections, and false conceits to all the Christian graces, affections, privileges, and performances. Five others were tempting external circumstances or agents like prosperity, the Devil, the bad advice of wicked folk, the false preaching of unconverted ministers, and the wicked example of neighbors.[47]

Each of these factors kept the sinner ignorant of his or her sin by discouraging careful self-examination and by urging the unrighteous to judge their spiritual condition by surface appearances. According to Tennent, the sinful believed a pious education, a good reputation, and formal church membership or orthodox beliefs were sufficient evidences of a right relationship with God. But Tennent warned that "all presumptuous Persons are not guilty of Prophaneness or Immorality, no no; some of them make a fair shew in the Flesh, are regular in their external Conduct, and have the strict *Form* of Godliness, though they are destitute of the Power of it." Therefore, self-satisfaction rather than overt impropriety was the truest mark of the sinner.[48]

The major external agent perpetuating the sinner's deadly self-righteousness was the Devil, but his most capable human allies were the unconverted clergymen. Ministers of this sort were to Tennent a dangerous fifth column in the church. Maintaining a "loose Carriage" and a "frothy, chatty, jocose Discourse," they neglected their duty to examine sinners' souls. They allowed a "lax and promiscuous admission of unworthy Guests" to the communion table, and they propounded "those erroneous, nature soothing, but soul damning Doctrines of Free Will, universal Grace, and universal Redemption" in their preaching. Seeking personal honor and gain rather than the salvation of sinners, these men catered to graceless people's wish "to hear of nothing but

Love, Peace, Promises [and] Comforts.'' They avoided offense by classing "their Audience into one common mass" so that no one recognized his or her own graceless state, and they applied the terrors of the biblical law and the comforts of the Gospel out of sequence so that conviction seemed unnecessary for conversion.[49]

To this smooth and soothing practice Tennent addressed two questions: "Are not Ministers called the Salt of the Earth? [And] has not Salt a biting, painful Quality?" To Tennent the answer was obvious. The ministry was both biting and painful to sinners because the clergy were ordained to roughly awaken fallen humanity from its deep sleep of false security. The manifold causes of human self-deception made this task difficult and necessitated a far more violent method than that practiced by unconverted clergymen.[50]

As for the evidence of the need for terrors, Tennent compared the preacher to an individual whose neighbor was "sleeping securely and dreaming pleasantly" while his house was afire. In such a situation, Tennent observed:

You would not surely go to whisper in . . . [your neighbor's] Ear some soft round about Discourse, that his House was you feared not in the best Condition possible, it might perhaps take Damage if suitable Care were not taken to prevent it. I say would you go thus about the Bush with a poor Man in a Time of such Danger? No, I believe Not: I fancy you would take a rougher method, without Ceremony or Grimace.

By the same logic, Tennent declared that preaching terrors was the proper method of a saving ministry. Although jarring, preaching terrors was more merciful than the lax homiletics of unconverted ministers since it alone rescued sinners from the horrible pain of eternal damnation.[51]

The comforts of gospel promises so commonly found in the pulpit rhetoric of the unconverted had their place in Tennent's sermons, but they were not so indiscriminately applied. Tennent reserved the Gospel for the already convicted, and he preceded all such comforting discourse with the threat of terrors to the not yet saved. In *A Solemn Warning*, Tennent justified this homiletic pattern in three ways. First, he claimed the sequence of "terrors first, comforts second" coincided with God's own treatment of the soul. The Holy Spirit converted the human heart by convicting it of its sins before supplying the gospel balsam to sin's deep wound. It was appropriate, then, that the clergy should synchronize their public proclamations to the Spirit's internal actions. The presentation of terrors before comforts was justified by "natural reason" as well. Tennent noted that wise builders did not build their houses before digging deep foundations, nor did experienced farmers sow their fields before plowing up the hard ground. So too, Tennent claimed, good ministers should not build faith before digging a deep foundation of conviction in the soul, nor should they cultivate faith before applying the plow of terrors to the sin-hardened heart. As a final rationale for his preaching style, Tennent pointed to the psychological handicaps of fallen humanity. "Unconverted People have a clearer Notion of Pain, both bodily and mental, than of the Pleasures and Comforts of a pious life, for They have had the Experience of the one, but not of the other. . . . Unconverted people are [also] governed . . . by Hatred against the good God. . . . How then can it be reasonably expected that such Persons will be much moved by Love Arguments when they are without that noble generous *Passion* in any Degree of *Luminence* towards God." According to Tennent, sinners could not be expected to respond to that which they did not understand or apprehend. Therefore, they must be awakened in the only way their crippled natures would allow, i.e., through the threatened pain of terrible damnation.[52]

Tennent's *Solemn Warning* was a harbinger of future conflict in the Presbyterian communion. Because of the homiletic system Tennent outlined in this sermon, the middle colonies' population would experience a rude spiritual awakening before the end of the decade. Since this large-scale revival would disrupt Presbyterian order and de-emphasize doctrine in the interest of promoting conversion, schism between Presbyterian subscriptionists and their Awakening associates would result.

In 1735 no one, including Gilbert Tennent, expected such a struggle because most Presbyterians shared at least a passing concern for those aspects of the Christian witness that Tennent and the subscriptionists championed. But by the late 1730s this situation would change dramatically. Between 1737 and 1739 the church witnessed a series of inadvertent clashes between the advocates of order and doctrine and the disciples of terrors and conversion. These skirmishes led to the formation of self-conscious parties and encouraged an escalation in the claims of each group for their particular program of church renewal.

SKIRMISHES OVER ITINERACY

The first concrete indication of differences between Tennent and the subscriptionists occurred in 1737. On his way to the Synod, Gilbert Tennent preached a sermon on the last judgment to a Presbyterian congregation in Maidenhead, New Jersey. The church lay within the jurisdiction of the Philadelphia Presbytery, but Tennent did not seek presbytery approval for his visit. As yet the Synod had no regulations concerning ministers preaching beyond the boundaries of their presbytery, and since the Maidenhead church had no settled pastor, Tennent quite likely viewed his visit as an innocent attempt to provide spiritual sustenance to a church in need of temporary pulpit supplies.[53]

Synod subscriptionists, however, did not interpret Tennent's actions so favorably. They believed that Tennent had slighted the authority of the Philadelphia Presbytery both by not seeking permission for his visit and by ignoring the fact that David Cowell and Eleazar Wales had already been assigned to supply the church. As a result, the aggrieved party presented an overture to the Synod's committee in 1737. This measure stipulated that a probationer should not preach in a vacant congregation without the approval of both his own presbytery and the vacant church's presbytery, and that a minister or probationer should not be invited to preach in a vacant pulpit of another presbytery without the approval of the presbytery in which the preaching would occur. This motion was referred to the Synod's executive committee for consideration.[54]

Tennent could hardly have missed the message of the Philadelphia Presbytery's action, that being that a politic minister should avoid further unauthorized excursions beyond his presbytery's boundaries. Tennent was anything but diplomatic when it came to preaching and revivals, however, so he returned to Maidenhead in October to lead a communion service. Again Tennent's ministrations were well received by the local laity, but not much appreciated by the presbytery. Technically, Tennent had not violated any Synod law but he had shown a blatant disregard for his subscriptionist colleagues' sense of order and propriety.[55]

To prevent further visits like Tennent's at Maidenhead, unidentified members of the Synod proposed that a formal rule be adopted in 1738 that would ''prevent irregularities . . . by some ministers and probationers preaching to vacant congregations without the bounds of their respective Presbyteries.'' This suggestion met serious opposition until a complicated compromise was formulated by the Synod. In this agreement, a minister called to preach in a vacant pulpit of another presbytery could comply if the church's presbytery or the Synod previously authorized the supply work. Lacking such official permission, the itinerant had to avoid the call if any clergyman in the shepherdless congregation's presbytery warned that the invited minister's preaching would ''likely . . . procure divisions and disorders.'' A minister whose itinerations were vetoed in this way could override the warning by applying to the congregation's presbytery or the Synod, but in the interim he was not to preach in the vacant church.[56]

For men like Gilbert Tennent who regarded itinerancy as the solution to the church's desperate need for clergy, this compromise was a negative blessing. The 1738 itineracy act was an improvement over the overture submitted the previous year since it did not require that itinerants in every case waste their time attending the meetings of neighboring presbyteries in order to acquire permission for their traveling ministries. But the new regulation had one significant drawback, that being that a single pastor could unilaterally stop a roving minister from serving a vacant church. Over this point, serious controversy would later develop.

DISCORD OVER CANDIDATES

The morning after the Synod accepted this compromise, it approved a request for the creation of a New Brunswick Presbytery in New Jersey. With boundaries stretching from the Raritan River in the north to just above Maidenhead in the south, the new body encompassed the parishes of five Presbyterian clergymen, three of whom were Log College graduates. For the first time in Presbyterian history, then, a group of William Tennent's students formed the majority in a colonial presbytery.[57]

Gilbert Tennent admitted to George Whitefield in later years that the application for a New Brunswick Presbytery had been a self-conscious maneuver by his party to acquire control over the mechanism by which godly young men could be introduced into the Synod's ministry.[58] This strategy was successful, but not because of a lack of opposition. At the same Synod meeting, an overture presented by the subscriptionist-dominated Lewes Presbytery threatened for the first time the previously unchallenged sovereignty of presbyteries over the ordination of ministers. The measure suggested the appointment of a Synod examining committee that would test the proficiency of privately educated candidates for the ministry in the areas of philosophy, divinity, and the biblical languages. If the committee found a candidate sufficiently qualified, it would notify his presbytery in writing, and this certification would be accepted in lieu of an official college diploma. The Synod recognized that this act should not be imposed immediately since many candidates could not be informed of the new regulations in time. Therefore, for one year it established two examining committees, one for the north and one for the south. Gilbert Tennent was one of seven clergymen assigned to the northern committee.[59]

Subscriptionist ministers had several reasons for supporting this legislation. First, the examining act was a logical extension of their general preference for uniformity and order dictated by an all-powerful Synod. Also, the act permitted stricter regulation of educational standards for the church's future clergy. Clerical education was especially important to the subscriptionists since they believed it had a direct bearing on the process of salvation. The subscriptionists did not accept Tennent's contention that a minister's spiritual state affected his effectiveness as an instrument of the Lord. Moreover, they considered determinations of a clergyman's converted status tentative at best. Consequently, the subscriptionist party did not stress the examination of candidates' experimental knowledge.

Doctrinal and biblical competence was another matter. Such expertise could be tested with exactitude and, indeed, had to be verified because the communication of the ''right'' Word of God through preaching was assumed to be the means by which the Holy Spirit saved souls. That a proper education was essential for ministerial candidates followed logically from this belief. Appropriate training in philosophy, theology, and literature provided young men with the knowledge of what God's ''true'' word was and how it should be conveyed to the laity. An inadequate education, on the other hand, inevitably led to the promulgation of errors in doctrine and/or practice as well as a short-circuiting of the salvation process.[60]

The subscriptionists realized that formal theological training was difficult to acquire in the middle colonies.[61] There was no local college, and the cost of attending a school in Europe or New England was prohibitive for most young colonials. Therefore, many candidates sought an education privately from a local pastor or at an informal institution like William Tennent's Log College. These private options were unacceptable to Synod subscriptionists because of the variations in approach and standards that resulted from a plurality of tutors. For example, students at the Log College received particularly good preparation in the biblical languages, but many subscriptionists questioned the Tennent patriarch's competence in philosophy and theology. For this reason they demanded the formation of a Synod committee to maintain certain basic standards.

Besides these theoretical and practical considerations, ecclesiastical politics also demanded that the subscriptionists support the examining act. As the majority in the Synod, the subscriptionist party could control the composition of that body's examining committee and thereby determine the future leadership of the church by screening out certain "undesirable" applicants before local presbyteries even considered their candidacy.

Synod subscriptionists needed such preemptive powers because of the current character of the New York and New Brunswick Presbyteries. Clergymen of Jonathan Dickinson's persuasion dominated the New York Presbytery. Therefore, they could not be expected to produce candidates who vigorously supported the subscriptionist program. The New Brunswick Presbytery, on the other hand, was an unknown quantity, but several factors suggested that it too was a threat. Two subscriptionist presbyteries had recently expressed serious reservations about the preparation of Log College graduates for the ministry. In 1736 the Philadelphia Presbytery sustained the trials of Charles Tennent for ordination "with Remarks," and later the New Castle Presbytery refused to license John Rowland because he was in their opinion "remarkably deficient in many parts of the useful Learning required in our Directory."[62] Equally troubling to subscription advocates was the New Brunswick group's lackadaisical attitude toward ecclesiastical order, as exemplified by Gilbert Tennent's visits to Maidenhead.

The examining act passed by a "great majority" in 1738. How Gilbert Tennent voted is unknown, but it is unlikely he supported the act since he and his associates protested its passage in 1739. Why Tennent did not immediately object can only be surmised from subsequent events. Less than three months after the Synod adjourned, the newly created New Brunswick Presbytery met for the first time. On this occasion, John Rowland requested that the presbytery begin his trials for ordination. Rowland had been privately educated at the Log College, so the presbytery recognized that the examining act must be addressed. After discussion on the matter, the presbytery unanimously agreed that "they were not in point of Conscience restrained by said Act from using the Liberty and Power which Presbytery have all along hitherto enjoyed." The members then examined Rowland on the usual parts of learning as well as "his experience of a Work of converting Grace in the soul," and on September 7, 1738, they licensed the young man to preach.[63]

The New Brunswick Presbytery neglected to explain why it was not bound by conscience to observe the new examining act, but events shortly conspired to force a public declaration. The Philadelphia Presbytery had been unable to find a permanent pastor for the Maidenhead church. Therefore, it suggested that the congregation seek a replacement outside the judicatory's boundaries.[64] The church issued a call to John Rowland, but before Rowland could fill his new pulpit, David Cowell warned him away on the basis of the 1738 itineracy act. Rowland ignored the admonition, so the Philadelphia Presbytery acted against him at its September meeting. Invoking both the itineracy act and the examining act, the presbytery declared Rowland's licensing invalid and ruled him guilty of intrusion.[65]

"THE APOLOGY OF THE PRESBYTERY OF NEW BRUNSWICK"

This hostile action startled the New Brunswick Presbytery. At the next Synod meeting, in May 1739, the revivalists carefully examined the previous year's minutes in order to determine the legality of the Philadelphia clergymen's ruling. To their dismay they discovered that the judgment was faithful to the letter of the 1738 regulations. This led Tennent and his associates to present a "paper of objections" questioning the validity of the year-old acts and the authority of the Synod to make such laws.[66]

This document proposed scriptural, pastoral, and practical objections to the itineracy act. The New Brunswick Presbytery claimed the measure was contrary to Scripture in at least two ways. First, it prevented ministers from fulfilling their duty to preach constantly "in and out of season," and second, it contradicted the Apostle Paul's "generous Temper" which made him happy that the Gospel was preached anywhere. The Tennent party also labeled the legislation improper on pastoral grounds since it barred the laity from their positive duty to hear approved ministers. The act compounded the already serious problem of a scarcity of ministers by hindering laypeople from hearing those ministers who were available. And it encouraged suspicion and distrust between Synod clergy when supposedly they accepted each other as qualified ministers of the Word. In sheerly practical terms, the New Brunswick clergy asserted that the new rule unfairly allowed a single uncharitable minister to "lord it over" his colleagues. It contradicted the laws of nature, nations, and God by condemning ministers before an actual offense had been committed, and it ignored the fact that division resulting from a minister's itinerations was the work of the Devil rather than the intent of the itinerant. If the Synod so feared the preaching of false doctrine because a particular minister might be fallible, Tennent and his associates suggested that the Synod's clergy should cease preaching altogether, since no minister was infallible.[67]

Concerning the examining act of 1738, the New Brunswick Presbytery noted three scriptural principles that required its revocation. First, there was a parity of power among gospel ministers. Second, Christ had delegated to presbyteries exclusively the power to ordain, and third, this presbyterial prerogative assumed a prior right to control the examination of candidates. In order to bolster these fundamental objections to the examining act, the revivalists also noted how the measure was unnecessary and contrary to traditional presbyterial practice. Since 1706 colonial presbyteries had ruled supreme over candidates. Therefore, the New Brunswick party asked, why change now? After all, the presbyteries' primary purpose was the supervision and ordination of candidates. This new act destroyed that purpose, and worse yet, the proposed investigating committee encouraged a new form of prelacy in which a few clergymen could negate the power of their far more numerous colleagues in presbyteries.[68]

The New Brunswick clergy were convinced that the Synod's recent rulings represented the imposition of new human additions to the church's divinely appointed presbyterian structure. Consequently, the presbytery's most fundamental argument against the contested statutes recalled those expressed earlier by Jonathan Dickinson against subscription. Like Dickinson, the Tennent party called it a "false hypothesis"

that a Majority of Synod or other Church-Judicatories have a Power committed to them from Christ to make new Rules, Acts, or Canons about Religious

Matters on this Ground or Foundation, viz. that they judge them either to be against or agreeable to the general Directions of the Word of God, and serviceable to Religion; which shall be Binding upon those that conscientiously dissent therefrom, under certain Penalties which are to be inflicted even upon those who judge the Acts they enforce to be contrary to the Mind of Christ, and prejudiced to the Interests of his Kingdom.[69]

Such legislative power was never delegated by Christ, was utterly inconsistent with the perfection of Holy Scripture, and was an invasion of Christ's kindly office. Hence, laws such as those just passed by the Synod represented an encroachment upon the rights of individual conscience and private judgment and, even worse, made the discipline of Christ subject "to the Lusts, Fancies and Traditions of Men."[70]

By so opposing the Synod's legislative authority, the New Brunswick group radically reduced the judicatory's powers. The Synod retained the right to review errors of discipline or improper conduct. But the New Brunswick party maintained that Synod judgments in such matters were only "advice" except where God had given "particular obvious Direction in his Word . . . and even then" the Synod does "no more than show from Scriptures what is the Mind and Direction of God in such Cases, and declare their own Resolution to act according thereto."[71]

These complaints against new religious laws were vintage Dickinson, but the goals of their argument were radically different. Where in 1722 Dickinson had employed the same logic to combat the imposition of man-made creeds, the New Brunswick party now used it to protect an experimental ministry. The New Brunswick clergy openly declared in their petition their fear that the Synod's committee would be prejudiced against a candidate because of some metaphysical nicety. What they left unsaid was their common apprehension that an excessive concern for such niceties might lead to the rejection of young men with superb insight into the workings of the Holy Spirit on the human heart.[72]

To be fair to Gilbert Tennent and his associates, one cannot simply dismiss their defense of presbytery authority as an expedient smoke screen designed to protect their party's interests. The subscriptionists' guidebook for church government was the Westminster Directory, which did not specify the locus of the power to ordain. Ordination was delegated to "presbyters" in the Directory, but which group of presbyters (the presbytery or the Synod) was not defined. Thus, the New

Brunswick Presbytery's claims for presbytery autonomy were as faithful to the Directory's principles as the subscriptionists' counterclaims for Synod sovereignty.[73]

The opinions expressed in the New Brunswick petition did not prevail. When the Synod reviewed its 1738 actions, it refused to alter the examining act, and it strengthened the itineracy act.[74] Interestingly enough, Tennent and his associates only protested against the Synod's review of the examining legislation. The revised itineracy rule was passed *nomine contradicente*. The selectivity of the revival party's complaint indicates that before George Whitefield's arrival in October 1739, experimental Presbyterian ministers of Tennent's persuasion were more interested in protecting presbytery sovereignty over the licensing and ordination of future clergy than they were in securing a place for itineracy in the church's polity.[75]

The New Brunswick clergymen's failure to safeguard their presbytery's powers left John Rowland's licensure equally insecure. The irregularities in the young man's licensing came to light when his presbytery's minutes were inspected. The Synod revoked Rowland's membership and admonished his presbytery for acting improperly.[76]

These transactions of the 1739 Synod altered the politics of colonial Presbyterianism irrevocably. No longer were the church's clergy under any illusions as to the contradictory policies of the revival and subscriptionist parties. The latter group now understood that their New Jersey colleagues shared neither their view of Presbyterian government nor their standards for ministerial certification, and the men led by Gilbert Tennent recognized the subscriptionists' plan to control the polity and personnel of the denomination through their majority in Synod. From such insights a schism in 1741 was born.

3

THE GREAT AWAKENING: CATALYST FOR SCHISM

The 1739 Synod brought the conflicting purposes of its membership out into the open, but no party as yet preferred open schism to the current troubled union. This would soon change for two reasons. First, Presbyterian revivalists would continue to defy the Synod's instructions, and second, the unexpected appearance of the charismatic English evangelist George Whitefield would turn the laity's affections to the New Brunswick party's favor.

Whitefield's first tour through the middle colonies ignited widespread enthusiasm for the experimental cause, and this in turn inflamed Gilbert Tennent's rhetoric. Experimental piety became *the* test by which Tennent judged his lay and clerical associates, and his assaults on the unconverted ministers who questioned the validity of such examinations acquired a vigor and venom never before witnessed in his ministry. The New Brunswick revivalist would later regret the severe judgmental tone of his sermons in this period. But while under the spell of a peaking Awakening fervor, he was unable to recognize the potential dangers of his intemperate polemics.

In the spring of 1740 Tennent's escalating militance and that of his fellow Awakeners occasioned the first overt subscriptionist attacks on revivalism. Rather than producing the desired cooling of revival excitement, though, these countermoves only exacerbated the already explosive tensions in the colonial Presbyterian community.

MORE TROUBLE OVER JOHN ROWLAND

The Tennent family continued to promote John Rowland's ministry even after the Synod had clearly counseled against such action. In September William Tennent, Sr., invited his former student to preach to his church at Neshaminy. This move was doubly hazardous for the elder Tennent because of the Synod's admonition and because Tennent's relations with this congregation were brittle at best.[1]

The Tennent patriarch's difficulties with the Neshaminy church stretched back to the summer of 1736, when a group of his parishioners charged that he was not their pastor since he had never been officially installed. In July Tennent requested a clarification of his status from the Philadelphia Presbytery. The presbytery decided in Tennent's favor, but the judgment was appealed to the 1736 Synod. Tennent was vindicated once again and his lay opponents chastised both for their complaint and for their appeal.[2] But two years later Tennent's lay critics expressed their continued discontent with a new petition to the Philadelphia Presbytery. This time a clerical assistant was requested. After initially resisting the suggestion, Tennent withdrew his protest in order to avoid further animosity. The presbytery chose a young licentiate and subscriptionist sympathizer, Francis McHenry, to aid Tennent at Neshaminy.[3]

Tennent and McHenry had been sharing the Neshaminy pulpit on various schedules for about a year when William offered an invitation to Rowland. This clear violation of the Synod's recent ruling permitted Tennent's critics to complain another time to presbytery. The Philadelphia presbytery had already planned to meet at the Neshaminy church on September 19 for the ordination of Tennent's new colleague. So after the McHenry ceremony, the complaint was considered. When asked to explain his actions, Tennent declared the presbytery had no authority to intervene in such matters and "contemptuously withdrew." The presbytery's response was to condemn Tennent both for his invitation to Rowland and for his "indecent" withdrawal.[4]

As one might have expected, the New Brunswick Presbytery immediately came to William Tennent's aid by asking the Log College tutor to join its membership as a correspondent. Offers of this kind were common among colonial presbyteries, but the use to which the elder Tennent put the invitation was atypical. Between 1739 and his death in 1746, William Tennent never again attended the Philadelphia Presbytery, preferring to meet instead with the New Brunswick Presbytery, where his sons and former pupils ruled.[5]

In addition to assisting William Tennent, the New Brunswick revivalists also defied the Philadelphia Presbytery and Synod by ordaining John Rowland at their October meeting. Presbyterians customarily ordained their candidates to service in a particular congregation, but in Rowland's case, no call had been extended. Therefore, the young man was given the unusual title of evangelist to the church at large. This new office exposed the Tennent party's growing concern for the many pulpits left vacant by the current shortage of ministers as well as their willingness to alter the church's polity wherever need so dictated.[6]

The New Brunswick clergymen recognized that their church's staffing problems could not be solved by simply ordaining young candidates to roam the middle colonies supplying pulpits. True church renewal required experimental ministers who preached the proper complement of terrors and gospel to enliven the local laity's souls. Candidates of any theological persuasion were scarce at the time, but revival-oriented applicants were even fewer in number and would be rarer in the future if one took account of the elder Tennent's advanced age. William Tennent, Sr., was sixty-six years old in 1739. Thus, the long-term survival of the Log College was at risk. This school had been the revival party's primary source of new experimental clergy, so some alternative had to be secured to insure a continuous flow of suitable young men into the Presbyterian Church's leadership. In order to fill the expected gap left by the Log College's demise, the presbytery authorized a letter to Jonathan Edwards. Edwards had recently emerged as the leader of experimental interests in New England, so the New Brunswick party asked him to recruit pious New Englanders for the New Jersey ministry.[7]

This request represented a significant miscalculation of Edwards's powers and their Neshaminy mentor's vitality. In April 1740 Edwards informed his New Jersey correspondents that experimental candidates were as scarce in New England as they were in the middle colonies. Therefore, he would be unable to assist them. William Tennent, on the other hand, far surpassed his colleagues' expectations by producing eleven more graduates of the Log College between 1739 and 1746 and by persuading George Whitefield to cast his lot with the Presbyterian revivalists.[8]

GEORGE WHITEFIELD

Although the Awakening seed had been sown and cultivated in the colonies for many years before George Whitefield entered the middle colonies, the spiritual harvest known as the Great Awakening began when Whitefield stepped ashore at Lewistown, Delaware, on October 30, 1739. Whitefield had already sparked major revivals in Great Britain. Yet rather than remain in England to organize his followers, he had decided to visit the North American colonies in order to procure funds for an orphanage that he had established in Georgia.[9]

Whitefield's ministry generated furious controversies in the colonies which, paradoxically, made him a phenomenal success. His appeal depended in large part on the long-standing conflict between his own Church of England and the English dissenting community. For the religious opponents of the established church, Whitefield became a "Dissenter Priest." By frequently attacking the integrity of fellow Anglican clergymen, he confirmed the widely held belief that they had abandoned their communion's original Reformed foundations in favor of a corrupting Arminian rationalism. Since the seventeenth century, dissenters had been leveling such charges at the Church of England, but Whitefield was particularly convincing because he spoke as an insider against this trend in Anglican theology.[10]

With few exceptions, colonial dissenters supported Whitefield's assaults on the Church of England's clergy, but many did not accept Whitefield as their leader because of a second element in his colonial persona. Whitefield promoted what might be called a "new-birth ecumenism." In his view conversion alone distinguished the true believer from the atheist or the mere professor of Christianity. Therefore, all other prerequisites for fellowship were unnecessary barriers to Christian unity.[11] Most colonial dissenters accepted the need for a new birth in Christ, but many believed that Whitefield overemphasized conversion at the expense of their denominational doctrines, government, and liturgy. For these men and women the practice and theology of their particular church were based upon Scripture. Thus, Whitefield's cavalier attitude toward such matters was considered suspicious at best and perhaps even blasphemous. Some colonials also felt that Whitefield encouraged hazardous emotional excesses. They believed his appeals for a sudden new birth focused too much on the passions and thereby tended to arouse unseemly religious enthusiasm in reborn Christians.

CAUSES OF THE TENNENT-WHITEFIELD ALLIANCE

The Tennent family did not support religious enthusiasm, but they did find Whitefield's special brand of ecumenism compatible with their own program to revive the church. The first member of the Tennent family to make contact with Whitefield was the father of the clan, William Tennent, Sr. Less than two weeks after Whitefield's arrival at Lewistown, Tennent visited the young celebrity in his rented quarters in Philadelphia. William explained to Whitefield the history of his academy in Neshaminy, the work of his sons in New Jersey, and the interference of the Philadelphia Synod in the family's experimental ministry. Much impressed with this "old grey-headed Disciple," Whitefield immediately associated the "persecution" of the Tennents with contemporary attacks upon his allies in Scotland and England. As he described his thought in his journal,

As far as I can find, both he [William Tennent, Sr.] and his Sons are secretly despised by the Generality of the Synod, as Mr. Erskine and his Brethren are hated by the Judicatories of Edinburgh, and as the Methodist Preachers are by their Brethren in England. Though we are but few, and stand as it were alone like Elijah, and though they, like the priests of Baal, are many in Number, yet I doubt not but the Lord will appear for us, as he did for that Prophet, and make us more than Conquerors.[12]

How God would make them "more than Conquerors" was not immediately evident, but the way was shown within a few days when Whitefield received a call from Thomas Noble to visit New York City.[13]

Setting out on November 12, Whitefield made New Brunswick his second stop. Gilbert Tennent was ten years Whitefield's senior, but the two men quickly discovered that their theological and pastoral interests were hardly distinguishable. Like his Anglican visitor, Tennent preached the necessity of a new birth in Christ and promoted the same sort of new-birth ecumenism that Whitefield practiced. In the years to come Whitefield would discover Tennent's ecumenism was more limited than his own, since Gilbert balked at cooperation with non-Calvinists. But this difference was not immediately evident at their first meeting. Therefore, Whitefield eagerly accepted Tennent's offer to accompany him on his tour to New York.

Whitefield was unfamiliar with the middle colonies, so he needed a local revivalist like Tennent to introduce him to sympathetic clergymen and guide him to the ripest fields for spiritual harvest. In this respect Tennent served Whitefield well. During the few days they traveled together, Gilbert led his new friend to practically every congregation in New York and New Jersey that had exhibited a receptive ear to the call for new birth.

The potential benefit for Tennent of an alliance with Whitefield must have been apparent to the New Brunswick pastor as soon as he learned that his itinerary could include stops in northern New Jersey and New York City. This territory was dominated by members of the old antisubscriptionist party. During the recent period of tensions between the New Brunswick Presbytery and Synod subscriptionists, the antisubscriptionists had sided against Tennent and his associates because of what they considered the divisive effects of the revival mania.

The most extreme instance of revival-inspired division had erupted just prior to Whitefield's arrival. In the early fall of 1739, several members of the Woodbridge, New Jersey, congregation began to criticize their pastor, John Pierson, for his lack of enthusiasm for the experimental cause. The Tennents themselves never attacked Pierson, but the fact that their supporters had done so caused Pierson and his friends in the New York Presbytery to question the ecclesiastical benefits of revivalism.

In a sermon to the Woodbridge church given at the October meeting of the New York Presbytery, Jonathan Dickinson summarized the antisubscriptionists' objections to the current revivals. Entitled *The Danger of Schisms and Contentions With Respect to The Ministry and Ordinances of The Gospel*, the homily attacked four arguments that were being used by revival supporters to rationalize separation from a settled pastor who did not support their cause. The first involved the claim that another minister with "superior gifts, graces or ministerial qualifications" would probably be more beneficial to the soul. Dickinson had no objection to a "bare preference" for a more gifted minister, since reason and observation proved that God gave some clergymen more gifts than others. But he did condemn laypeople who intentionally avoided their pastor because of his lesser gifts. Such action was unchristian in Dickinson's mind because it overlooked the fact that the church was one body, with each part serving an essential function. Furthermore, Dickinson believed this type of thinking inappropriately honored the instrument rather than the agent of spiritual edification. God, not ministers, saved souls. A minister's ordination was a sign that God planned to edify his people through him. Thus, Dickinson claimed that "if we do not find spiritual Edification under a faithful Minister of Christ, whether of the most eminent Capacities or not, it is our own Fault."[14]

A second defense for separation related to the minister's style. Some revival supporters maintained that their pastor's gifts were ample, but that his methods were not suited to their particular sentiments. Although he did not deny the existence of differences in taste among the laity or style among the clergy, Dickinson emphasized how the Scriptures specifically instructed the laity to support their settled pastor. According to Dickinson, this requirement was one of the more obvious duties enjoined by Scripture and was reinforced by the customary covenant between laity and clergy that was sealed at the time of a minister's call.[15]

A third explanation for separation concerned the clergy's personal experience with conversion. Many revival advocates believed their pastor had "not experienced those Convictions and Humiliations as are necessary Preparations for a saving conversion to God, or such Joy and Peace in believing, as those that are the true Children of God have experienced,—Besides," they complained, these ministers "find Fault with those [of us] that have had these Experiences."[16]

Dickinson opposed the first part of this complaint because he doubted human beings' ability to judge the spiritual condition of their fellows' hearts. Verbal testimony was unreliable since the most sincere Christian was too humble to boast about gracious attainments, and measurements of others' experience on the basis of one's own was questionable because the "holy one of Israel" was not limited to any one method of conversion.[17]

Dickinson did, however, sympathize with those laypeople who had been criticized for witnessing to their rebirth. He accepted new birth as an authentic and necessary event in the Christian life. Therefore, he condemned those clergy who slighted their converted parishioners.[18]

As a final justification for separation, many revival advocates suggested that division was required whenever a clergyman refused to preach terrors. Dickinson assumed that the terrors of the biblical law played an essential part in the salvation of sinners. As he said, "if we [ministers] were so cruel to the Souls of our Hearers, as to leave 'em in their Stupidity and sinful Pursuits, without warning them of their

Guilt and approaching Misery: or were *prophesying smooth Things and Deceit* to 'em; There would then be just cause for Complaint.'' But Dickinson was not yet convinced, as the Tennents were, that the clergy of his church neglected the terrors in their sermons. Although some did not preach their warnings ''with the same Elevations of Voice, as some others are capable,'' that did not mean they avoided warning their parishioners entirely.[19]

This statement was a clear declaration to all interested parties that the New York Presbytery was still unpersuaded that the subscriptionists were as negligent or the current revivals as edifying as the New Brunswick group maintained. Indeed, Dickinson expressed the commonly shared belief of his colleagues that the censorious character of the revivals was like ''a dead Fly in the Apothecaries Ointment'' and that it seriously compromised their potential contribution to the Presbyterian church.[20]

Gilbert Tennent realized that these misgivings had to be eliminated if the revival cause was ever to succeed in Synod. In 1739 the revival party was woefully outnumbered, and for that reason recent Synod decisions had consistently undercut Tennent's program for church renewal. To reverse this trend, Tennent and his associates needed more votes. Bringing more revival candidates into the presbytery was not the answer because the Rowland affair had shown that Presbyterian subscriptionists would block such efforts. It was unlikely in the near future that the subscriptionists would have a sudden change of heart. Therefore, the only viable alternative was to force a wedge between the current alliance of former pro- and antisubscriptionists. Certain concerns of the latter group offered material for the formation of such a wedge. Specifically, their long-standing support of an experimental ministry and their opposition to the centralization of ecclesiastical power made New York clergymen uncomfortable with the subscriptionist program. If Tennent could accentuate these differences and, at the same time, persuade his associates to the north that revivals were beneficial to the Presbyterian community, his own plans for experimental reformation would win out not only in Synod but in the church at large.

Tennent recognized in Whitefield's proposed tour the means for accomplishing this twofold strategy. The dynamic young minister could only increase the popular appeal of the revival cause and might at the same time sway antisubscriptionists to accept Tennent's views.

Exactly how much Tennent determined the course and message of

Whitefield during their journey to New York is uncertain, but on certain occasions the New Brunswick pastor's guiding hand seems evident. Upon their arrival in New York City on November 14, Whitefield sought permission to use the local Anglican church, but when his interview with Commissary Vesey degenerated into an exchange of mutual recriminations, Vesey banned Whitefield from his pulpit. Whitefield initially responded by holding an interdenominational open-air service, but Tennent swiftly used his contacts with New York's Presbyterian pastor, Ebenezer Pemberton, to acquire a pulpit for Whitefield. During the next three days, Whitefield preached at least twice a day to considerable crowds in Pemberton's meetinghouse and, in the process, moved the church's pastor to the Awakening side.[21]

Leaving New York late on November 18, Whitefield and Tennent proceeded to Elizabethtown, New Jersey. There again Whitefield had words with the local Anglican priest before Jonathan Dickinson invited him to dinner and offered him the use of his pulpit. Tennent no doubt told Whitefield that Dickinson was not yet a convinced supporter of the revivals because Whitefield used this occasion to speak "against both ministers and People among the Dissenters, who held the truth in unrighteousness, contenting themselves with a bare, speculative knowledge of the doctrines of grace, but never experiencing the power of them in their hearts."[22]

Whitefield's phenomenal success during his first tour through the middle colonies forced other antisubscriptionist leaders like Dickinson and Pemberton to reconsider the possibility that the Tennents' revivals had been a foretaste of a true work of God in the making. Whitefield's attacks on ministers who were "well versed in the doctrines of grace, having learned them at university, but notwithstanding are heart hypocrites, and enemies to the power of godliness" laid seeds of doubt about the motives of subscriptionist opposition to the revivals, and as these seeds took root, the antisubscriptionist party moved ever closer to an alliance with the Tennents.[23]

Whitefield aided his new friend's interests in a number of other important ways as well. The Anglican clergyman spread the message of new birth far beyond the confines of either the New Brunswick Presbytery or the Presbyterian Church. As a member of the Church of England, Whitefield was not bound by the Synod's itineracy act, and his ecumenical approach attracted laypeople of all theological persuasions. Whitefield's popularity and skillful oratory in turn focused the attention of the public press on local awakenings, and his personal endorsements of the Tennent family heightened the prestige of the New Brunswick party.

THE DANGER OF AN UNCONVERTED MINISTRY

All these factors pushed Gilbert Tennent to new heights of rhetorical polemics. Shortly after Whitefield's departure from the middle colonies, Tennent confessed in a letter to Whitefield that the recent trip to New York had greatly increased his wrath against "carnal Ministers." On March 8, 1740, Tennent expressed this anger publicly by delivering a sermon entitled *The Danger of An Unconverted Ministry* during a visit to the Presbyterian congregation in Nottingham, Pennsylvania.[24]

The death of Rev. John Paul had left the Nottingham pulpit vacant in September 1739. As a temporary measure, the Donegal Presbytery assigned five ministers to supply the church. Two of these men, Alexander Craighead and David Alexander, were staunch revivalists, while the other three were uncompromising subscriptionists. Through the late autumn and early winter of 1739–1740, the Nottingham congregation was courted by both parties. The two revivalists managed to spark a revival at Nottingham with the help of Samuel Blair, but when opposition mounted against their efforts, Tennent was called in to convince the congregation that a revival minister should be chosen to fill the Nottingham position.[25]

Tennent treated the Nottingham congregation to his most scathing attack on unconverted ministers. As in previous sermons, Tennent declared the ministry of natural men "uncomfortable" to the Christian soul because their sermons were generally too short, always out of season, necessarily lacking in authority, and inappropriately divided.[26] But for the first time in his career, Tennent made the further charge that such a ministry was "unprofitable" and "dangerous" to the laity's souls.

The Ministry of natural Men is dangerous, both in respect of the Doctrines and Practice of Piety. The Doctrines of *Original Sin, Justification by Faith alone* and the other Points of *Calvinism* are very cross to the Grain of unrenew'd Nature. And tho' Men, by the Influence of a good Education, and Hopes of Preferment, may have the Edge of their natural *Enmity* against them blunted; yet it's far from being broken or removed: It's only the saving Grace of GOD, that can give us a true Relish for those Nature-humbling Doctrines.

And alas! What poor Guides are natural Ministers to those, who are under spiritual Trouble? They either slight such Distress altogether, and call it *Melancholy* or *Madness*, or daub those that are under it, with untemper'd Mortar.[27]

Because of the danger such a ministry presented to a parishioner's salvation, Tennent went on to suggest that it was both "lawful and expedient" to leave one's settled but unconverted minister in order to hear more "Godly Persons."[28]

Tennent's reasons for making such a radical proposal were both numerous and varied. In the first place, Tennent was more concerned with saving souls than maintaining ecclesiastical order. He agreed with Dickinson that ministers were but instruments of salvation in God's gracious hands, but he also believed those clergymen who had experienced conversion in their own lives were better tools for the work to which they were ordained. Consequently, transfer of one's membership to a church with such a minister was both proper and prudent.[29]

To those who claimed that God alone could judge men's souls, Tennent noted the Apostle Paul's commendation of the church at Ephesus for carefully examining those who said they were Apostles. On the basis of this passage, Tennent asked: "Does not the spiritual Man judge all Things? Tho' he cannot know the States of subtil Hypocrites infallibly; yet may he not give a near Guess, who are the sons of Scova, by their Manner of Praying, Preaching, and Living?"[30]

Opposition to laypeople's choosing which pastor they would follow was based in Tennent's opinion on two false presuppositions. The first assumed that choosing between pastors had been condemned by Paul when he chastised the Corinthians for favoring Paul over Apollos or Apollos over Paul. Quoting the Dutch Reformed pietist Voetius, Tennent denied that this passage eliminated choice. As Tennent put it, because the Apostle

reproves an excessive Love to, or Admiration for particular Ministers, accompanied with a sinful Contention, Slighting and Disdaining of others, who are truly godly and with Sectmaking: To say that from hence it necessarily follows, That we must make no Difference in our Choices or in the Degrees of our Esteem of different Ministers, according to their Different Gifts and Graces . . . is an argument of as great Force, as to say, Because Gluttony & Drunkenness are forbidden, therefore we must neither eat nor drink, or make any Choice in Drinks or Victuals, let our Constitution be what it will.[31]

Tennent also believed Presbyterian opponents of revivals suffered under the delusion that ruptures in the temporal body of Christ could and should be avoided at all cost. So long as the church remained a mixture of saints and sinners, he claimed that divisions were inevitable because the promotion of true religion invariably stirred up opposition from Satan's servants within the church. Christ's faithful advocates should not be faulted for the resulting schisms, since they were only the "innocent occasion" for such disruption. Tennent warned, however, that disciples of Satan would try to make it appear otherwise. "Very often natural men, who are the proper Causes of the Divisions, aforesaid, are wont to deal with God's servants, as Potipher's wife did Joseph: they lay all the Blame of their own Wickedness at . . . [the godly's] Doors, and make a loud Cry!"[32]

This statement is a key to the middle colony Awakeners' understanding of the divisions that the Great Awakening precipitated in local congregations. For men like Tennent such events were the unwelcomed results, but not the fault, of revivals. They were unwelcomed because schism in the body of Christ was always regrettable. They were the consequences of the revivals because a resurgence of true piety was invariably opposed by Satan's agents. Yet they were not the fault of the Awakening because spiritual ferment only provided the "occasion" for heart hypocrites to foment dissension.

Tennent's sermon at Nottingham created a stir within the Presbyterian communion because it contradicted certain axioms of the subscriptionist and antisubscriptionist programs. Against the former group, Tennent opposed the idea that unconverted ministers were as effective as their converted colleagues and further charged that their ministry was dangerous to their congregations. Against the latter party, Tennent suggested that piety, not unity, should be expected when promoting a resurgence of piety.

In *The Danger of An Unconverted Ministry*, Tennent also loosened the bonds of the church covenant between the laity and their clergy. Although Tennent advised his revival supporters to follow normal procedures for dismissal from their congregation, he nevertheless urged these laypeople to take the initiative and choose their future pastors on the basis of their experimental knowledge. Implicitly this message was a challenge to the local laity to decide the current conflict in the Synod. Freed from the traditional restraints of geographical parishes and church covenants, middle colony Presbyterians were now asked to determine by their transfer of membership which party would grow and prosper.[33]

No doubt one factor that emboldened Tennent to rest his fate in the hands of the laity was the knowledge that George Whitefield would soon return to the middle colonies for his second revival tour. Since Whitefield's earlier travels had electrified the local population, Tennent could anticipate a second visit would further magnify the revival party's popularity.[34]

WHITEFIELD'S SECOND TOUR

Tennent's expectations were only partially fulfilled by his English friend's performance in the spring of 1740. Arriving in New Castle on April 13, Whitefield proceeded to Philadelphia, where he enjoyed larger crowds than before. On April 23 Whitefield began a journey through Neshaminy, Skippack, Amwell, New Brunswick, Woodbridge, Elizabethtown, New York City, Amboy, Freehold, Allentown, and Burlington. When he returned to Philadelphia, Whitefield's adoring public offered to build a church where he and his associates could preach. Whitefield refused the offer, but his supporters built the so-called New Building anyway. On May 12 Whitefield left Philadelphia to travel to Derby, Wilmington, White Clay Creek, Nottingham, and Faggs Manor before departing by ship from Lewistown.[35]

Although Whitefield's second tour was the most successful of all his efforts among the middle colony populace, it generated the first open opposition to his ministry from Presbyterian clergymen. During a major revival at Faggs Manor on May 15, Francis Alison challenged Whitefield to a public debate. Whitefield initially refused because he felt the circumstances were inappropriate for such a contest, but when Alison persisted, Whitefield yielded. The debate between Whitefield and Alison was short-lived because the crowd grew ugly when it realized Alison opposed Whitefield. Nevertheless, Alison was able to question Whitefield on his doctrine of assurance. Alison objected to Whitefield's claim that those who lacked an assurance of their salvation were in a "damnable condition." Whitefield denied that he had ever stated his position in such bold terms, but he did maintain that assurance was an attainable goal for any converted Christian.[36]

After Whitefield's visit in 1740, Jonathan Dickinson also expressed qualms about the evangelist's message in a letter to a friend in Boston. Dickinson admitted that Whitefield had impressed him during his first stay in Elizabethtown because "his Discourse was excellent, [and] the Method of his Address the most affecting that I had ever known." Whitefield's more recent appearance, on the other hand, had troubled Dickinson and the ten other ministers who had been present. According to Dickinson, "Many were stumbled at, [and] few or none affected with . . . [Whitefield's latest] Discourse." Of his personal reaction, Dickinson remarked: "I cannot stand surety for all his Sentiments in Religion, particularly his making Assurance to be essentially necessary to a justifying Faith; And his openly declaring for a Spirit of Discerning in experienced Christians, whereby they can know who are true converts; and who are close Hypocrites."[37]

These doctrines prevented the New York Presbytery from joining forces with Presbyterian Awakeners until 1745. Dickinson's party believed assurance was only enjoyed by a small number of the elect. Furthermore, they considered accurate discerning to be an illusion. Since God's sovereignty allowed him to save sinners in any way that he chose, New York Presbyterians felt that there was no trustworthy measuring stick by which the saint could be distinguished from the hypocrite.

Whitefield and Tennent, on the other hand, considered assurance the inevitable fruit of a sincere conversion. Like the practice of piety, it flowed naturally from the experience of being born again in Christ. The revivalists also believed that the Spirit normally converted sinners in a predictable fashion, and that an experienced Christian who knew the Spirit's usual practice could recognize the marks of conversion in another.

PAPERS OF COMPLAINT AGAINST THE SYNOD'S MINISTRY

As Dickinson and his associates took a step back from the Awakening, Presbyterian Awakeners pushed the advantage that Whitefield's second round of travels had given them with the laity. The Tennent party used the occasion of a Synod meeting in May 1740 to continue the revival that Whitefield had sparked in Philadelphia. Before his departure from Philadelphia on May 12, Whitefield had publicly recommended the Tennents to his local disciples. Because of this personal commendation, the Tennent brothers and their allies, Samuel Blair, John Rowland, and

James Davenport, were permitted the use of the platform that had been built for Whitefield on Society Hill. During the six days that the Synod met, these five men preached fourteen different times at Society Hill and, on several occasions, led worship in the local Presbyterian and Baptist meetinghouses. The fact that no other member of the Synod was given similar privileges shows that the local laity accepted the Tennent party as surrogate leaders in Whitefield's absence.[38]

The Tennents simultaneously promoted the Awakening cause in the Synod by reopening the question of the 1738 itineracy and examining acts. Shortly after the Synod opened, an alternative to the examining act was offered. The measure was debated for two days, until the Synod decided not to alter the act unless "some other expedient could be found that will answer the design of that government." This decision precipitated a protest from the same men that had complained against the act in 1739, only this time they were joined by four more ministers and eleven more elders. The increased number of protestors plus the fact that a majority of these individuals were laymen indicated Gilbert Tennent's recent call for lay support was producing significant results.[39]

Three different alternatives were considered to placate the Tennent party's objections, but each in its turn was found unacceptable. Therefore, the Synod finally decided to defer further discussions of the act for several days.[40]

On the last day of Synod before the issue of examinations could be reopened, Samuel Blair rose to read a list of complaints against the "many Defects" in the Presbyterian ministry. Blair asked that his paper be heard in closed session, but the membership refused. So Blair publicly declared that too many of his colleagues ignored the most important doctrine of new birth in their sermons, preferring instead to emphasize works righteousness. He charged that the faithful were unable to gauge their spiritual development since the marks of a true disciple were never clearly delineated from the pulpit, and he bewailed the consistent neglect of parishioner and candidate examinations.[41]

Gilbert Tennent had prepared a similar catalogue of objections to current clerical practice independently of Blair. So when his friend had finished, the New Brunswick pastor rose to offer his thoughts on the matter. Tennent chided his fellow ministers for "crying up Duties, Duties, and urging natural Men to them almost constantly as if outward Things were the whole of Religion." Such a message only flattered sinners into a deadly security that left their hearts corrupt with hidden presumptions. He also chastened the Synod's clergy for their "Great Stiffness in Opinion, generally in smaller Matters where good Men may differ," and he expressed his resentment over the recent attacks upon revivals and the scrutiny of laypeoples' and candidates' spiritual condition. Acknowledging that infallible knowledge of a person's rebirth was impossible, he continued to maintain that "satisfactory knowledge" of the same was not only attainable but required. For this reason he chastised those who made light of candidates' examinations by noting that such neglect was symptomatic of the Synod's greater "zeal for outward Order than for the main Points of practical Religion."[42]

As a warning that his critique should be taken seriously, Tennent concluded with this statement: "Rules that are serviceable in ordinary Cases, when the Church is stocked with a faithful Ministry, are notoriously prejudicial when the church is oppressed with a carnal Ministry."[43] This idea Tennent would develop into a full-blown rationale for ignoring Synod laws that interfered with his promotiom of the Awakening. Four months after the 1740 Synod adjourned, Tennent would openly defy the 1738 itineracy act by visiting the congregation in Nottingham, Pennsylvania, again. There he would declare: "Certainly, it must be acknowledged that Church Rules do not bind when they hinder the Edification of the Body, for which they are suppos'd to be made. And is it not reasonable to conclude that Rules which may be proper in ordinary Cases, may be hurtful in extraordinary [ones]?" If so, Tennent asked:

May there not be a Suspension of some Rules for a Time when the Church is in an extraordinary Situation, without the overthrow of Discipline. Do not general Rules admit of Exceptions; and do not the Formers of Church Rules acknowledge them to be alterable according to various Circumstances? To be more zealous about the Observation of some Rules, than for the spreading Power of Godliness, does it not look like the Pharisees tything Mint and Annis and Cummin, while in the mean Time they neglected the weightier Matters of the Law?[44]

If Tennent wished to remain a Presbyterian minister in good standing and also continue his revival work, he needed such an argument since the Synod's current rules made the two efforts incompatible. But expediency was not the only factor leading Gilbert to favor this position. Tennent firmly believed that his opponents were making church law the master rather than the servant of the Christian community. Regulations in and of themselves were not offensive to Tennent; they had a very specific function in that they aided the orderly promotion of God's work. Yet Tennent recognized that in certain unusual circumstances ecclesiastical polity could impede rather than promote the edification of the church. In such instances, Tennent considered it the Christian's duty to ignore temporarily the offending regulations for the greater glory of God. Tennent was persuaded that the Awakening was such an exceptional occasion and that certain Synod laws had to be circumvented in the interest of God's reviving spirit.

Unfortunately for Tennent, his logic was lost on Synod subscriptionists. In their view, Tennent and Blair had publicly insulted not only their party but the entire Synod by charging malfeasance without specifically naming the guilty ministers. Samuel Blair later stated that he and Tennent had intentionally omitted names because they hoped to procure a Synod pronouncement that would remedy the situation without requiring the potentially acrimonious process of individual trials. Their opponents, on the other hand, interpreted the omission as an underhanded attempt to slur reputations without offering proof of the charges or an opportunity for a proper defense.[45]

The papers presented by Tennent and Blair killed the already slim chances of a compromise on the 1738 acts. The Synod adjourned without voting on any of the compromise proposals that had been submitted and without dealing with the ill will generated by the charges of the two revivalists. The neglect of the latter in particular primed the already volatile relations in Synod for a schism one year later.[46]

GRIEF, TRAVEL, AND FURTHER OPPOSITION

Before that schism erupted, Gilbert Tennent experienced a year of great personal sorrow and public success. Tennent's grief resulted from the death of his first wife, about whom precious little is known. Her name, the date of her marriage, and the exact time of her death is lost to history, but George Whitefield recorded in his published journals that Tennent delivered a funeral sermon for his wife shortly before beginning a revival tour through southern New Jersey, Delaware, and upper Maryland in the late summer of 1740.[47]

Most likely a call from several churches in southern New Jersey provided Tennent with a much needed diversion from his recent loss.

Southern New Jersey contained only two settled pastors, both of whom opposed the Awakening. Therefore, the invitation offered the added attraction of carrying the experimental message into enemy territory. Tennent's exact itinerary is uncertain, but it appears that he also used the occasion to visit the friendly congregations of Christiana Bridge and White Clay Creek, Delaware, as well as Bohemia Manor, Maryland.[48]

While Tennent traveled the lower middle colonies, the subscriptionist party began to take action against his associates. During a Donegal Presbytery meeting on September 7, Francis Alison and John Thomson formally charged Alexander Craighead, David Alexander, and Samuel Blair with intruding into their parishes. Three days later, several members of the New Castle Presbytery presented a list of objections to George Whitefield's theology. A challenge to either answer the criticisms or allow the document's publication was included with this catalogue of Whitefield's errors. Since Samuel Blair and Gilbert Tennent were present at this meeting, Blair attempted to defend Whitefield by noting that several of the English evangelist's statements had been lifted from their original context by the authors of the petition. But the presbytery rejected Blair's apologetics and authorized the printing of the petition. Early the next year this document appeared under the title *The Querists*.[49]

At the same meeting of the New Castle Presbytery, Blair and Tennent were asked to substantiate the charges they had made against the Presbyterian ministry at the 1740 Synod. If any of their members were guilty of the offenses described by the two revivalists, the presbytery demanded that they declare the names of the guilty parties at once. Caught off guard and unprepared, Tennent and Blair refused to answer the New Castle Presbytery's challenge.[50]

Tennent returned to his congregation in November 1740 only to leave again within a few short weeks. In a conference with Whitefield at his New Brunswick home, Tennent was asked to make a revival tour through New England. Whitefield had just completed a month and a half of travels in the north where his preaching had been extremely well received. Now he wanted Tennent to stoke the Awakening fires that he had ignited by retracing his steps.[51]

Whitefield's choice of Tennent was not accidental. During their trip to New York, Whitefield had been so deeply impressed with Tennent's preaching that he wrote in his journal:

I never before heard such a searching sermon. He convinced me more and more that we can preach the Gospel of Christ no further than we have experienced the power of it in our own hearts. Being deeply convicted of sin, by God's Holy Spirit, at his first conversion, he has learned experimentally to dissect the heart of a natural man. Hypocrites must either soon be converted or enraged at his preaching. He is a son of thunder, and does not fear the faces of men.[52]

According to several accounts, Whitefield's contact with Tennent had an immediate effect on the Anglican's homiletics. The *Boston Weekly News-Letter* reported in 1740 that when Whitefield visited New York "a roughness was noticed by his hearers which was said to have been lately acquired." Quite likely the noted "roughness" was the consequence of Whitefield adopting Tennent's method of preaching terrors.[53]

Whether this was so or not, it is clear that Tennent's searching pulpit style struck such a sympathetic chord in Whitefield that he chose Tennent to follow up his efforts in New England. Whitefield recalled in his journal that his colonial colleague "was at first unwilling [to make the trip], urging his inability for so great a work; but afterwards, being convinced it was the Divine Will, he said, 'the will of the Lord be done.' "[54]

To insure a good reception for Tennent, Whitefield penned a letter of recommendation to the prorevival governor of Massachusetts, Jonathan Belcher, and sent a young tutor from Harvard to accompany Tennent to Boston.[55]

The winter that Tennent chose to visit New England was the worst the region had experienced in thirty years. Ice covered the entire Boston harbor, and roads into the city became so clogged with snow that mail carriers were forced to abandon their horses and move about on snowshoes.[56]

Despite these difficulties, Tennent stopped in almost as many towns as Whitefield had the previous fall. From New Brunswick Tennent made his way to Long Island, where he caught the ferry to Westerly, Rhode Island. There he took to horseback on the overland route to Boston. Arriving on December 13, he preached at several churches within the city and in the nearby towns of Charlestown, Newton, Roxbury, and Cambridge. Then he proceeded to York, Maine, stopping along the way to offer his Awakening message to congregations at Hampton, Malden, Chelsea, Marblehead, Hamlet, Ipswich, Greenland, and Portsmouth. After returning to Boston, Tennent paused only briefly before starting the trek homeward. As he moved southward, he made a loop through southeastern Massachusetts and concluded his tour by leading a number of revivals in the major coastal towns of Rhode Island and Connecticut.

Unlike the success of Whitefield, what success Tennent enjoyed cannot be attributed to the publicity surrounding his visitations. Where Whitefield's planned itinerary had been advertised in local newspapers, Tennent's movements received little or no attention from the press. Tennent also admitted in later years that he never warned a minister that he would visit his parish. Instead, he waited until his arrival in a community to announce his presence and then requested permission to use a local pulpit.[57]

Reactions to Tennent's preaching were mixed. On the negative side, Timothy Cutler, an Anglican missionary in Boston, recalled that the New Brunswick minister was an impudent and noisy "monster" who told all that came to hear him that "they were damn'd! damn'd! damn'd! This charmed them! and in the most dreadful winter that I ever saw, people wallowed in the snow night and day for the benefit of his beastly brayings." Charles Chauncy had a similar impression of Tennent. Tennent was in his view

a Man of no great Parts or Learning; his preaching was in the extemporaneous Way, with much Noise and little Connection. If he had taken suitable Care to prepare his Sermons, and followed Nature in the Delivery of them, he might have acquitted himself as a middling Preacher; but as he preached, he was an awkward Imitator of Mr. Whitefield, and too often turned off his Hearers with mere Stuff, which he uttered with a Spirit more bitter and uncharitable than you can easily imagine.[58]

Much of the rest of New England found Whitefield's successor a very attractive figure. The Reverend Thomas Prince, Sr., of Boston noted that Tennent "did not . . . at first come up to my Expectations; but afterwards exceeded it. In private Converse with him, I found him to be a Man of Considerable Parts and Learning; free, gentle, [and] condescending: . . . He seem'd to have as deep an Acquaintance with the experimental Part of Religion as any I have convers'd with; and his Preaching was as *searching* and moving as ever I heard."[59]

A young Samuel Hopkins was equally complimentary. When Tennent came to New Haven in March 1741, Hopkins claimed that the revivalist created a major awakening of spiritual concern among the Yale students. As for his personal response, Hopkins admitted: "When I heard Mr. Tennent, I thought he was the greatest and best man, and the best preacher, that I had ever seen or heard. His words were to me, 'like apples of gold in pictures of silver.' And I thought that, when I should leave the College, as I was then in my last year, I would go and live with him, wherever I should find him."[60]

Similar plaudits were recorded by ministers in most of the towns on Tennent's itinerary. In those places where Whitefield had preceded Tennent, the New Jersey pastor was credited with bringing home the Awakening message with a force greater than that witnessed during Whitefield's stay, and in regions untouched by the Anglican evangelist's ministry, Tennent was recognized as the source of a resurging religious piety.[61]

Tennent's own evaluation of his work contained a mixture of pride and humility. In a letter to Whitefield on April 25, 1741, he thanked his colleague for insisting he make the journey. He further admitted that he had met with success "much exceeding" his expectations.[62] But Tennent did not assume that his eloquence was the primary cause for his warm reception. When asked by one of his female admirers "what there was in the matter or manner of his addresses . . . that produced such a wonderful and irresistible effect," Tennent replied, "Madam, I had very little to do with it. I did not preach better than common and perhaps not so well: for I was often much fatigued with travelling, and had little time to collect or arrange my thoughts. But I went into the pulpit and spoke as well as I could, and God taught the people."[63]

Judging from his only published sermon during this period, Tennent was perhaps too modest about the "matter" of his addresses. In this homily, entitled *The Righteousness of the Scribes and Pharisees considered*, the middle colony clergyman exhibited shrewd insight into the religious pretensions of his New England audience, for in it he attacked the two pillars of their spiritual pride, those being their scrupulous observance of the biblical law and their family ties to the great Puritan "saints" of the seventeenth century.

Tennent used the Jewish Pharisees as an example of religious folk who were meticulously careful in their external religion. But he observed that such superficial conformity had always been empty of righteousness as well as an ineffective means of salvation without an internal transformation of the heart by the gracious experience of new birth. Also he warned that modern-day Pharisees could not fall back on their parent's virtue when their own conduct failed to justify them before God. "What will your good Parentage avail you, unless you walk in the steps of their Simplicity, Faith and Holiness, but to aggravate your everlasting Pains? . . . What our Parents and our Grandparents have done, are not our's."[64]

Tennent's effort in New England was clearly his finest hour. Traveling alone and without pay, he traversed the snowbound roads of the northern colonies in order to crush the pretensions of the self-righteous with his terror-filled attacks on pharisaic piety. Reports of his successes reached all the way to Great Britain and prompted Whitefield to ask his colonial associate to follow him to Scotland.[65]

Because the severe winter had wreaked havoc on his "constitution," Tennent declined with the following explanation: "I am since inwardly weak and have in a great measure lost my usual Voice so that I believe I can hardly speak so as to be heard by a large Audience. I have also been much troubled with an inward Fever and am unable to endure much fatigue without occasioning a Relapse."[66] In the same letter Tennent disclosed that he had recently remarried. His new wife was Cornelia Bancker de Pyster Clarkson, a woman ten years his senior. Cornelia brought several children to the marriage, since she had been wedded before to a Captain Matthew Clarkson, Jr., a merchant of some wealth in New York City.[67]

PUBLIC TUSSLES IN THE PRESS

Tennent's damaged health and a necessary adjustment to his new domestic routine demanded that he keep close to his New Brunswick home for almost a year, but an equally important factor in his decision was the rising opposition to the Awakening that began to appear first in the regional press and later in Presbyterian judicatories.[68] Middle colony newspapers were generally sympathetic to the revival movement before the autumn of 1740. Only one-fifth of the articles on Whitefield that were printed in Philadelphia's *Pennsylvania Gazette* and the *American Weekly Mercury* included criticisms of his work, and only one in four items concerning Tennent's Society Hill revivals carried unflattering comments.[69]

This trend ended, though, with the publication of *The Querists*. Unofficially credited to David Fvans of the New Castle Presbytery, this pamphlet castigated George Whitefield for a number of unguarded statements in his printed journals and sermons. Evans shared his fellow subscriptionists' suspicion of the Anglican minister's pietistic rhetoric. He questioned Whitefield's description of conversion as a process whereby Christ was formed within the sinner's soul. Such language was in Evans' opinion a dangerous imitation of the Quakers' "Christ within" and a proof of Whitefield's shallow understanding of Calvinism. *The Querists* also accused the popular revivalist of promulgating a host of superstitious, unrefined notions that corrupted the clergy and transformed the laity into a disorderly rabble. One idea that received special attention was Whitefield's promotion of evangelical cooperation. While laudable in the abstract, Evans charged that Protestant ecumenism would eventually lead to a fatal rapprochement with the Papists.[70]

The first Awakener to respond to *The Querists* was Gilbert Tennent's youngest brother, Charles. His defense of Whitefield was almost identical to that expressed by Samuel Blair when the publication of the work had been discussed in the New Castle Presbytery.[71]

George Whitefield first encountered *The Querists* in New York City after his triumphal itinerary through New England. Recognizing the gravity of the challenge, he immediately formulated a letter that addressed only two of *The Querists'* complaints. Whitefield confessed that he had not received sufficient training in the Calvinist system at Oxford, and he asked that his critics pray for his knowledge to be increased by the Lord's instruction. As for his ecumenism, Whitefield declared his plan had always been to avoid the two extremes of ecclesiastical disorder and religious bigotry. To prevent the latter, he insisted that open fellowship with all newborn Christians, whatever their denomination, must be maintained.[72]

As one might have expected, Whitefield's critics were not satisfied with his response. Therefore, they published a rebuttal, which occasioned a further apology for Whitefield by Samuel Blair. Thereafter no further *Querists* dealing specifically with Whitefield appeared, but public opposition to the Awakening continued.[73]

Early in 1741 David Evans produced a second anonymous work for public consumption. This time his target was the revival experience as a whole. Evans entitled his satirical creation "A true and genuine Account of a wonderful Wandering Spirit, raised of late (as is believ'd) by some Religious Conjurer; but whether in the Conclave of Rome, or else where, is not so certain.'' While this work correctly associated the colonial Awakening with contemporary pietistic revivals in England, Scotland, and Germany, its major thrust was to connect Whitefield and his cohorts with the blind dogmatism of Rome and the quixotic irrationality of religious enthusiasts. The "Wandering Spirit" of the new movement was, as the author phrased it,

Don Quixot turned Saint-Errant, and like him, can see Wonders by Hearsay. It abhors Reason, and is always for putting out her Eyes; but loves to reign Tyrant over the Passions, which it manages by Sounds and Nonsense. It is so blind itself that it walks by feeling; and yet sets itself up for an unerring Guide to all others. Old *Infallibility* learnt it the Lesson to Wrest the Bibles out of Men's Hands, which it performs effectually, by persuading all its Votaries, that nothing but its suggestions are God's Mind in the Scriptures; and all that will not give away Scripture and Reason tamely, for its inward Feelings and Experiences, are proclaimed carnal Men, who cannot understand, but pervert the sacred Oracle.[74]

Samuel Blair answered this slander with an equally caustic article in April 1741. Blair observed that it was easy ''for a wanton prophane Wit, to represent anything, the most sacred and venerable, in a false and ridiculous Dress.'' Then, to prove Evans guilty of such a performance, he presented a brief composition supposedly written by an old Pharisee. The Pharisee repeated selected passages from the ''wonderful Wandering Spirit,'' but he footnoted each quote with a biblical reference justifying the Awakening practice that had been censured in the earlier publication.[75]

As Whitefield drew fire from one segment of the Awakening's opposition, Gilbert Tennent soon received his share of criticism from another sector. On January 12, 1741, the *Boston Weekly Post-Boy* printed an anonymous letter critical of Tennent's New England tour. The author of the epistle suggested that only one of two reasons could have moved Tennent to make his disruptive journey. Tennent either believed that the northern clergy were unfit spiritual shepherds or he considered himself superior to them all. Whichever of these misconceptions had motivated the New Brunswick pastor, his unidentified critic declared Tennent guilty of irresponsibly abandoning his New Jersey congregation in order to act out his pretensions to grandeur in New England.[76]

Stung by this attempt to discredit him, Tennent paused briefly in the midst of his travels to compose a reply. Tennent denied that he harbored contempt for the Puritan clergy or an overblown opinion of himself. He recalled his initial reticence to attempt the tour because of his "mean Qualifications of Mind, and cold Constitution of Body," and he insisted he had only agreed to accept the task after listening to the reports of "a lamentable Decay of . . . Godliness" from Whitefield and various New England divines who demanded he "come over to their *Macedonia* and help them." Tennent also noted that he had arranged for ample supplies to his shepherdless congregation in New Jersey and that, to date, he did not "repent" his decision to leave his home church since "in diverse Places . . . that GOD (who will not seal a Blank) has graciously, visibly, and uncommonly bless'd my poor Labours, to the spiritual Good of many Souls."[77]

Later the same year, Tennent was again attacked in the press, but this time by the now infamous Querists. Entitling their work *Querists, Part III*, the authors did not concern themselves with Tennent's exploits in the northern colonies. Instead, they focused on his Nottingham sermon against hypocritical "Pharisee-Teachers." According to the Querists, Tennent was the real Pharisee since he had spawned "a Sect of precise, vain glorious Separatists" who judged the state of other's hearts at every opportunity. The Querists believed a *probable* judgment of another's state on the basis of observable fruits of grace was perfectly in keeping with the Gospel, but *infallible* judgments or even "near guesses" were no more than blind surmises and impositions on the divine prerogative.[78]

Querists, Part III chastised Tennent as well for laying too heavy a burden on the laity by "uncivilly denouncing" and "devilizing" them in his terror-filled sermons. By proclaiming his "rough terrifying Error instead of Truth," it suggested Tennent was like "an unmerciful and unnatural Father that gives a child crying for Bread, a Stone to break his Teeth." The errors taught by the New Brunswick revivalist were declared legion, but those singled out as most heinous were three. The Querists rejected the notion that all the saints shared a certain assurance of their salvation. Only some of God's elect were blessed with such a conviction. Therefore, Tennent's demand that every saint experience assurance led to unnecessary despair among the godly.[79]

Tennent's belief that converted clergymen alone were profitable to a sinner's salvation was labeled an equally mischievous fiction. If such a claim were true, the Querists reasoned, success in reforming the laity's lives was the surest criterion for judging a minister's heart. Yet this contradicted both common sense and Holy Scripture, "for how often shall we find that decoyed Villainy has been successful, when real Virtue strove against the Tide to no Purpose . . . [and that] God told his chosen Servants that they would not be successful in their ministry."[80]

The Querists also opposed the laity's right to leave less gifted ministers in order to place themselves under a more converting pastorate. A minister and his laity were bound together in a marriage. Therefore, they asked, should a husband "despise his own virtuous Wife, because some fine Lady in the Town is more beautiful than she? . . . is not Truth, in her sober homely Garb, more edifying than gaudy Error, spruced up with all the Fineries of the Scene or Stage, or bug-beared with all the Horns that can stick upon its hydratic Heads?"[81] The answer was a resounding "No!" The clergy had the right to demand the constant attendance and support of their parishioners. The bond between the two parties could not be severed unilaterally for any reason and certainly should not be broken for the "secret reason or surmises in a Man's own breast" about his spiritual leader's salvation.[82]

THE TRIAL OF TWO AWAKENERS

During the winter of 1740–1742, opposition to the Awakening did not limit itself to the printed word. The subscriptionists of Donegal Presbytery attempted to discipline two young revivalists in December. David Alexander and Alexander Craighead were perhaps the two most vulnerable members in the Tennent party since they belonged to a presbytery dominated by revival critics and because they were clearly guilty of intruding into the parishes of John Thomson and Francis Alison.[83]

Their trial infuriated fellow Presbyterian Awakeners, but it had an even more inflammatory effect on their enemies in the Donegal Presbytery. The presbytery was repeatedly interrupted during its deliberations by the two defendants and a crowd of sympathetic laypeople that had assembled to offer moral support. Indeed, hostility between the presbytery and onlookers became so intense at one point that a change of venue was necessary.[84]

When the presbytery asked Craighead to answer its indictment, the young minister turned the tables on his accusers by accusing them of whoredom, drunkenness, Sabbath breaking, and lying. The assembly insisted on two separate occasions that Craighead hand over a written list of the charges he had made so that the ministers named therein could offer an open defense. Craighead refused and informed the presbytery that it had no authority to try him since it was acting both as judge and prosecutor. This impudent reply earned Craighead a suspension.[85]

The disciplining of Alexander Craighead hurt the revival party, but it did not slow local agitation against Awakening antagonists. When the Donegal Presbytery met again in April, it received a petition for the severance of John Thomson's pastoral relationship with his congregation in Chestnut Level, Pennsylvania. The presbytery rejected the request after several persons whose names appeared on the document denied ever having seen it. But this action precipitated a great outcry from the prorevival laypeople attending the meeting.[86]

Once order was again restored, John Thomson rose to offer a new overture. His proposal represented a significant escalation in the subscriptionist agitation against the Awakening. Thomson suggested that the Presbyterian laity should be required to subscribe to the Westminster standards just as the clergy had done and that penalties for participation in revivals be imposed. As he put it in his measure, all lay participants in the Lord's Supper must "personally . . . acknowledge and receive the Westminster Confession and Catechisms as the Confession of their Faith, . . . promise to submit to the Government of the presbyterian churches as laid down in the Westminster Directory," and pledge never to "countenance or encourage" itinerant preaching by attending a revival service. If these conditions were neglected or broken, the offending layperson could be barred from the communion table. The overture also stipulated that the presbytery must censure any of its members, whether clergy or lay elder, who went to hear a traveling evangelist in another church or allowed such a minister to preach in a pulpit for which they were responsible.[87] This essentially was a declaration of war on the Awakening, but it was passed by a great majority because the subscriptionists in the presbytery, like their colleagues throughout Pennsylvania, had reached the limits of their tolerance. The papers presented by Blair and Tennent in 1740 and the disorders encountered at the Craighead-Alexander trials had bruised their reputation and offended their sense of due process. They now believed the revivals were a cancer on the body of Christ and had to be excised at all cost, for their personal good and the good of the church.

SCHISM ERUPTS

The Synod of Philadelphia convened on May 27, 1741, at Jedidiah Andrew's meetinghouse in the City of Brotherly Love. Caught between the raging conflict of Awakeners and subscriptionists, the New York Presbytery chose to avoid the meeting in the hopes that their absence would prevent further acrimonious debate over the examining act. The plan worked only in part. The examining act was not discussed, but rancor continued.[88]

Contention first arose over Alexander Craighead. Despite his recent suspension, the controversial young man attended the Synod. Several members interpreted his presence as an affront to the Donegal Presbytery's authority and, therefore, insisted that Craighead be barred from participation. The revival party responded by fiercely disputing the proposal for two whole days.[89]

By June 1 Presbyterian subscriptionists were infuriated by their inability to overcome their opponents' protection of Craighead. Aware that Samuel Blair was ready to present a protest against David Evans for his malicious "wonderful Wandering Spirit," they feared that Blair might divert the Synod's attention to their own contentious behavior. So they decided to take drastic action. As one historian has described their next move, the "champions of order" agreed to commit an "act of supreme disorder."[90]

After attracting the attention of the moderator, Robert Cross of the Philadelphia Presbytery presented a written protestation to the Synod. Signed by twelve antirevival pastors and ten elders, the document included five demands. First, it declared it was the Synod's "indispensable duty . . . to maintain and stand by the principles of doctrine, worship, and government . . . summed up in the [Westminster] Confession of Faith, Catechisms, and Directory." Second, it asserted that "no person, minister or elder, should be allowed to sit and vote in this Synod" if he did not subscribe to those standards or was found guilty of violating them. Third, it insisted that those individuals who had objected to the Synod's legislation in 1740 should not be permitted to remain members in good standing. Fourth, it proposed that anything "done, voted, or transacted" by the Synod while those men were still participants would be of "no force or obligation" to those who now protested; and fifth, it proclaimed that the undersigned petitioners would consider themselves the "true Presbyterian church in this province" and look upon the former protestors "as guilty of schism" if the latter group remained members of the Synod.[91]

Eyewitness accounts agree that the Philadelphia Synod fell deathly silent during the reading of this ultimatum, but they do not concur on much else. Cross sympathizers later claimed that the protestation had been created without malice or forethought. It was signed in a calm and orderly fashion, but Samuel Blair quickly destroyed the decorum of the moment by rising to demand that the complainants withdraw since they were a minority. When Cross and his associates declared themselves the majority, Blair requested a roll call vote. This prompted lay observers who accepted the Awakener's views to shout from the gallery for the ejection of all revival critics, but this clamor halted when the vote proved Cross's party was indeed in the majority. Shocked, embarrassed, and angered by their defeat, the revival contingent along with its rebellious gallery of admirers vacated the house in a great confusion before the meeting ended in prayer.[92]

Gilbert Tennent's recollections of the same moments in time were quite different. Tennent believed that Cross had conspired with his fellow petitioners prior to the 1741 Synod in order to expel their main competitors, the Awakeners. Cross had shrewdly worded his complaint so that it implied that he spoke for the entire Synod, but when a vote was taken to determine who truly represented the majority, the tally was evenly split between Cross's sympathizers and revival proponents. This result was ignored, however, because the complaining party created such confusion with their loud speech and their mad rush to sign the Cross document. Tennent also recalled that he and his compatriots did not leave the Synod until the moderator had concluded the session with prayer.[93]

Although the contradictions in these reports and the vested interests of the witnesses make a perfect reconstruction of the event impossible, certain facts can be assumed. Robert Cross did have the support of a majority of those present and voting. With the New York Presbytery absent from the deliberations, the Tennent party had no chance of outvoting the protestors. The revivalists, on the other hand, had ample grounds for complaint. The authors of the protestation had improperly assumed that they were the "voice of Synod" before a confirming vote proving that fact could be taken. Their voting strength depended upon the absence of the New York Presbytery, and they made no attempt to follow the normal judicial procedure of presenting a formal list of charges that could later be answered during disciplinary trials.[94]

Frustrated by the Awakeners' past disregard for due process, Cross and company offered their own crude ultimatum to the asembled presbyters. They could either accept the proposed document and eject the revivalists from their fellowship or they would be rejected as a bogus synod.

Those who were neither listed with Cross as signatories of the protest nor known Tennent supporters were later divided as to the propriety of the 1741 purge. Jedidiah Andrews, the Synod's moderator, had for some years been a pacifier of tensions within the communion, but on this occasion he sided with Cross. As he told a member of the New York Presbytery in a letter almost a month later, ''If it [the Protestation] had not been done now, . . . it must in my mind have been done within a little time, unless we would be contented to be a Babel, both as to Principles and Practice.''[95]

Another member, George Gillespie, took the contrary position. Gillespie was a staunch supporter of the Scotch-Irish presbyterian tradition, but he also applauded the Tennents' efforts to reawaken lay piety by scrutinizing the experimental knowledge of church members and ministerial candidates. The morning before the schism erupted, Gillespie had confronted Gilbert Tennent with the accusation that ''he was for a Separation in our Synod.'' But Tennent had convinced Gillespie that he had no such desire, and in fact, wanted only that ''our Synod would fall upon some Methods to keep our church pure.''[96]

Gillespie was appalled to hear Cross's protestation read in Synod. He later remarked that the event opened his eyes to the fact that the Awakening's opponents rather than the revivalists ''were hottest for division,'' and this discovery prompted Gillespie to join the ejected members as well as to defend the Tennent party's actions in a published letter to the New York Presbytery.[97]

The day after his expulsion from Synod membership, Gilbert Tennent met with fellow presbyters who had chosen to maintain their allegiance to the experimental cause. Their first act was to establish two ''conjunct'' presbyteries that would serve henceforth as a Synod for those churches affected by the purge. The old New Brunswick Presbytery was kept intact but was enlarged to include the congregations of Richard Treat and William Tennent, Sr. Its counterpart was given the name the

Londonderry Presbytery and was formed by combining the communions served by Samuel Blair, Alexander Craighead, David Alexander, Charles Tennent, and George Gillespie.[98]

In order to combat the recent charges leveled against them by the Cross protestation, the new body declared that its allegiances to the Westminster standards had always been as "close and firm . . . as even the Synod of Philadelphia in any of their Publick Acts and Agreements about them." Then it appointed Gilbert Tennent to prepare an answer to the allegations found in the Cross complaint, and Samuel Blair to the task of composing an official account "of the Differences in our Synod for some years past."[99]

CONTRASTING PERSPECTIVES ON THE CAUSES OF THE SCHISM

While Tennent and Blair went to work on their apologies, their opponents took the offensive by publishing two pamphlets—one by Robert Cross and the other by John Thomson. Cross offered in his publication a complete copy of the 1741 *Protestation* along with a prefatory statement to explain why it had been necessary. Many churchpeople blamed his party for precipitating the Presbyterian schism, but Cross suggested that his protest had done nothing more than expose the obvious, i.e., that the Awakeners had for some years past been united to the Synod in name only.[100]

John Thomson took a different tack in his critique of his now separated brethren. Concentrating on their *Apology* of 1740, Thomson charged that Tennent and his associates were guilty of promoting an "unorthodox" theory of presbyterian government. Tennent had claimed in the *Apology* that Christ delegated the power of ordination to individual presbyteries, but Thomson maintained that the term "presbytery" was "equally applicable to any ecclesiastical Judicatory, from a Session to an ecumenical Council." Furthermore, he noted that in "orthodox" Presbyterian circles the prerogatives of lesser judicatories were assumed to be included within those of superior councils. Therefore, the Philadelphia Synod had an even greater claim to the power of ordination than the presbyteries under its jurisdiction.[101]

The *Apology* had proposed that a minority had the right to ignore the decisions of a majority for conscience' sake. Thomson agreed that a minority should not submit to a majority decision so long as their conscience told them that the decision contradicted God's written word. Yet he rejected the notion that a majority must tolerate that same minority's conscientious objection. Minorities could always appeal an ecclesiastical act that contradicted their convictions, but when their appeal failed, the majority was duty-bound to demand their colleagues either obey or separate.[102]

As a final objection to Tennent's *Apology*, Thomson questioned the revival leader's definition of a new religious law. Tennent had suggested that all church rules must be based upon the clear example or the express instructions of the Scriptures. Thomson maintained that "the Lord Jesus Christ had invested his church with Authority to make Orders, Acts, or didactic Rules, for the regulating of Circumstances of ecclesiastical Matters, which are not, nor possibly could be all condescended upon in Scripture." Such "explications and applications" of the "general rules" found in Scripture were not new religious laws. They were instead a necessary use of "common sense and the light of nature" by Christ's authorized officers.[103]

From the perspective of most Scottish and Irish Presbyterians, Thomson's account of ecclesiastical government was biblical. But Samuel Blair viewed things quite differently. Blair took almost three years to complete the assignment given him by the Conjunct Presbyteries, but the time was well spent. When Blair's *Vindication of the Brethren* was published in 1744, it offered a masterful summary of revivalist views on church government. Where Thomson had pictured the Awakeners as radical extremists who willfully fostered anarchy and chaos, Blair insisted that "there is a proper Medium between Tyranny and Anarchy; between unjust Opposition and lawless Confusion: And . . . we have only rejected the one, without inferring the other of these Extremes." According to Blair, Thomson had overlooked this important distinction because he assumed there was no difference between civil and ecclesiastical societies. The survival of both associations, in Thomson's view, depended upon the majority's ability to rule authoritatively. Blair, on the other hand, believed that there was

a great Difference between the church of Christ and merely civil secular Societies; . . . Civil Societies . . . are only concerned about their temporal Interests and Advantages; . . . so [they] may make whatsoever Constitutions and Agreements for themselves they please in those Matters. . . . They may make all these Agreements Terms of Union and Membership; for there is no superior Law to the contrary; and their Orders and Agreements do not affect the Consciences of their Members; nor is it [a] Matter of Conscience with them Whether to continue [as] Members or not; . . . But the judicatories of the Church are solely Religious Societies. Their Concern and Business is only about the spiritual Interests of Men, all their Affairs relate to Matters of Religion and Conscience; and the Renting and Breaking of the Union of the Church is in itself a weighty Matter of Conscience . . . and of very sad Consequences to the highest Interest in all the World.[104]

For all these reasons, Blair charged that church councils were justified in imposing the majority's will in only two instances. First, where the specific duty enjoined was "itself particularly declared, appointed, or forbidden by God in holy Scriptures," and second, "when the Majority of a Judicature judge a particular Thing or Rule, to be a good prudential Expedient, in present Circumstances, to answer the Design of some general Direction or Injunction of God's Word" *and* the minority could submit in good conscience even though they did not judge the legislation prudent or expedient. Where the minority was convinced that the proposed ruling was contrary to the express Word of God, Blair suggested that the judicatory had to tolerate their conscientious disobedience. Otherwise, the minority would be asked to make a choice between two equally sinful options, i.e., either remain a part of the church and sin by submitting to the rule, or leave the church and sin by destroying the unity of Christ's body.[105]

Gilbert Tennent published his reply to Cross's remonstrance under the title *Remarks Upon A Protestation*. In this work Tennent denied the charge that his party had been in a state of schism before the 1741 Synod. He acknowledged that the Awakeners may have "differed with our Brethren in respect to some acts and canons they had made, yet we designed no separation. We thought mutual forbearance would be the best Expedient . . . so we were far from a desire of imposing our Judgment upon our Brethren, or imagining that there was a Necessity of Separation upon the Account of the aforesaid Diversity of Sentiment."[106]

While Tennent's enemies may have found this hard to believe, it is likely Tennent was faithfully reflecting the opinions of his colleagues prior to the schism. The revivalists did not need to impose their views through the Synod. Their fortunes were on the rise, and so long as they were tolerated by the rest of the Synod, they could expect their increasing popularity among the laity to bolster their numbers and power in that body. Presbyterian critics of the Awakening, on the other hand, had neither the inclination nor the luxury of pursuing such a policy. They assumed that the membership must conform to the majority's will, and their following among the populace was deteriorating so rapidly that their long-standing control of the Synod was in jeopardy.

The fifth demand of Cross's *Protestation* illustrates the extremes to which the antirevivalists' predicament had pushed them. It declared that no one should be allowed to remain a member who did not act in accordance with any rule either ordered by Synod or found in the Westminster Directory. This Tennent considered unreasonably severe and even contradictory to his opponents' own practice. After all, in 1736 the Synod had adopted the Directory with the important proviso that all should conform to it "as far as was suitable to the Circumstances of the Church in this Country." Presbyterian subscriptionists had used this clause on several occasions to rationalize their own variations from the Directory's rules. Yet Tennent noted that they were not willing to allow similar liberties to their rivals.[107]

A group led by Francis Alison responded to Tennent's criticism of the *Protestation* by publishing a point-by-point rebuttal. The authors confessed that they were mystified by their rivals' logic, especially as it related to the Synod's unity.

What Sort of Conscience, on the one Hand, represent[s] their Brethren as carnal, wicked wretches and prophane Opposers of God's Work . . . and yet, on the other, design[s] no Separation from such? And when Disagreement was concerning the very Fundamentals of social Union, or Terms of ministerial Communion: How was mutual Forbearance practicable, without either an Agreement on the Head, or either Sides Condescending, for Peace Sake, to give up their Rights of Conscience?[108]

Alison and company insisted that the "rights of conscience" were a two-way street, and as proof, they offered a comparison between the present controversy and a fictitious argument between a thief and his judge. According to this analogy, the Tennent party was like a thief who "pleaded for Liberty of Conscience to steal because he judged all Things should be common; and as he was pleading for Life, he said, he hoped the Judge was too good to deny him Liberty of Conscience." Yet the judge (or the antirevivalists) replied, "If you must have Liberty of Conscience to steal . . . I must have Liberty of Conscience to hang Thieves, when catched in my Bounds; because they transgress the Law. . . . ''[109]

Portraying Presbyterian Awakeners as thieves was unfair, but the comparison held a precious kernel of truth. Both parties in the 1741 schism considered themselves conscience-bound to pursue their present program for the greater good of the church. But the revivalists believed their conscience dictated infractions of the law in the present case, while their opponents assumed that only a complete adherence to the letter of the law could bring about the intended good.

4

TROUBLES WITHIN THE REVIVAL CAMP: SEEDS OF SELF-DOUBT

The 1741 schism of the Presbyterian Church did not shake Gilbert Tennent's confidence in the justice of his cause. Indeed, if anything, the split only strengthened his faith in the Awakening since it confirmed his expectations that fierce opposition from the Devil's minions was the price to be paid for a concentrated effort at experimental revival.

Tennent did not anticipate trouble arising from within the Awakening camp, however, and in the weeks and months that followed the acrimonious division, he learned the cruel lesson that one's supposed friends can on occasion be a greater test to one's convictions than one's enemies.

EMBARRASSMENT, SUCCESSION, AND ENTHUSIASM AMONG FRIENDS

Little more than a fortnight after their expulsion from the Synod, the revival party experienced its first serious scandal. On June 15, 1741, John Rowland was tried for stealing a horse. A man impersonating Rowland had committed the theft, but the thief, Tom Bell, was such an accomplished confidence man that his imposture had not been detected.

When Rowland appeared before the Court of Oyer and Terminer in Trenton, New Jersey, his defense consisted of alibis from William Tennent, Jr., Benjamin Stevens, and Joshua Anderson. Each man testified that he had attended a worship service in Pennsylvania led by

Rowland at the same time that the alleged crime had been committed. On the basis of this testimony, Rowland was acquitted.[1]

The scandal surrounding this trial might have quickly dissipated had not Joshua Anderson been indicted for perjuring himself. Anderson was tried and convicted, and this led naturally to indictments against Rowland's other two witnesses. When William Tennent, Jr., was brought to trial in March 1742, he pleaded innocent to the charge of perjury, but the jury was unable to decide whether he was telling the truth. A second trial was scheduled for June. When no witnesses surfaced to corroborate William's earlier testimony, his lawyers suggested that he take advantage of a loophole in the law to escape punishment. The penalty for perjury included a public humiliation on the steps of the local courthouse and a heavy fine. Yet William steadfastly refused to use a legal technicality to circumvent a possible conviction. Fortunately for him, his principled obstinacy paid off, for just as he and his brother Gilbert were walking to the courthouse for the commencement of the trial, two witnesses arrived to testify in William's behalf. On their testimony he was acquitted of all charges.[2]

Although William Tennent, Jr., and John Rowland were exonerated, their court battles caused serious embarrassment for the Awakening party. The revivalists had for some time attacked their foes as unprincipled opportunists in search of personal profit. Now they found the names of two of their most prominent associates dragged through the legal system in connection with the low crimes of horse thievery and perjury.

As the Rowland-Tennent affair progressed through the courts, the integrity of middle colony Awakeners was further compromised by the experimental excesses of other colleagues. Enemies of the Awakening nicknamed the revivalist party the ''New Lights'' shortly after the schism. The term was a derogatory one borrowed from the Irish subscription controversies of the 1720s. In Ireland it had been applied to the antisubscriptionist party in order to suggest their views were an unorthodox departure from traditional Presbyterian theology. Since several members of the Irish antisubscriptionist party did become Arians in later years, the label had acquired a particularly odious association with heresy and disorder by the 1740s.[3]

Colonial New Lights like Gilbert Tennent were neither heretics nor anarchists. They sought a balance between the demands of individual conscience and ecclesiastical structure, between ecumenical cooperation and denominational integrity, and between heartfelt piety and doctrinal probity. The New Lights soon discovered, though, that balances of these sorts were not easily sustained in periods of spiritual awakening and ecclesiastical schism.

At the first formal meeting of the Conjunct Presbyteries in June 1741, the dangers of loosening ecclesiastical bonds were painfully evident. After the presbyteries declared their allegiance to the Westminster Confession, Alexander Craighead proposed the adoption of the Solemn League and Covenant. This covenant had been formulated in 1643 by the General Assembly of the Church of Scotland. Its adherents had sworn to protect the Reformed religion and promote the reformation of the English church, presumably on the Scottish pattern. Had the Craighead overture been approved, the Conjunct Presbyteries would have set themselves on a course of imposing Reformed theology and presbyterian polity on the entire colonial community.[4]

Gilbert Tennent opposed Craighead's plan, as did the rest of the presbyteries' membership, because this type of "league" was "a national work, belonging to the three Kingdoms [of Great Britain], and not to two presbyteries." But Tennent had more than one reason for rejecting the proposal. Tennent strongly objected to mixing religion with civil politics, and he found the "Covenanting scheme . . . too narrow a Foundation to build any great Superstructure upon."[5] The superstructure to which Tennent referred was the ecumenical alliance of newborn Christians that he and Whitefield had been encouraging through the Awakening. The Craighead proposal did not allow for that tolerance of nonessentials among churchpeople that was essential to interdenominational cooperation.

Unfortunately, the fiery Craighead did not understand this point. Therefore, when the Conjunct Presbyteries rejected his motion, he separated from the presbyteries and formed an independent Covenanters movement. To justify his action, Craighead soon began spreading the word that the Westminster standards were never truly adopted by either the Philadelphia Synod or the Conjunct Presbyteries and that all true Presbyterians should rally around him.[6]

Since Craighead took with him a number of the revival party's lay supporters, his departure was a setback, but an even greater blow was inflicted on the movement by two contemporary developments in New England. Following Gilbert Tennent's tour in 1740–1741, a number of New England laymen began to travel through Connecticut and Rhode

Island preaching the message of new birth and experimental piety. Many of these men had heard Tennent's attacks on unconverted ministers and interpreted his words as a call to the converted to spread the spiritual awakening.[7]

After learning that he personally was being blamed for this increase in unauthorized lay preaching, Tennent collected his thoughts into a letter which he sent to several prominent New England ministers in the fall of 1741. Tennent carefully distanced himself from the lay preachers in the northern colonies. If this practice "be encouraged and continued," Tennent warned, "it will be of dreadful consequence to the church's peace and soundness in the faith. I will not gainsay but that private persons may be of service to the Church of God by private, humble, fraternal reproof, and exhortations; and no doubt it is their duty to be faithful in these things. . . . But for ignorant young converts to take upon them authoritatively to instruct and exhort publicly tends to introduce the greatest errors and the grossest anarchy and confusion. . . . It is base presumption," Tennent claimed, "for any persons to take this honour to themselves, unless they be called of God as Aaron." Therefore, he suggested that all who "fear God should rise up and crush the enthusiastic creature in the egg."[8]

The lay itinerants of New England had woefully misread Tennent when they assumed his assaults on empty pharisaic piety were appeals for the laity to preach without proper ecclesiastical authorization. Tennent was no supporter of a ministry based on charisma alone. Experimental knowledge may have been an essential qualification for ordination, but proper trials and procedures were in Tennent's opinion equally necessary for God's ministers.

Tennent's letters on lay preachers calmed the fears of New England ministers somewhat, but they did not remove doubts about the Awakening, since one of Tennent's ordained colleagues was currently promoting even greater disorders. James Davenport was a Presbyterian pastor from Southhold, Long Island. He had shared the Philadelphia stage with Gilbert Tennent during the Society Hill revivals of 1740, and while Tennent toured New England, he served briefly as a supply to Tennent's New Brunswick pulpit.[9]

In July 1741 Davenport traveled to Connecticut and Rhode Island to promote the experimental cause. During this tour of several months' duration, Davenport converted many souls, but he also prompted numerous excesses. On several occasions Davenport encouraged congregations to parade through the streets singing praises to the Lord. At other times, he allowed laypeople to speak or pray publicly in worship, welcomed emotional paroxysms during his sermons, and attacked local ministers by name from the pulpit.[10]

Tennent liked Davenport personally, but he strongly disapproved of his methods. Emotional outbursts during revivals did not surprise Tennent, since he believed the Holy Spirit's influence often overpowered the frail human frame. But in his own ministry Tennent did not encourage expressions of religious passion and, indeed, cautioned his followers not to take such experiences as proof of their conversion. Davenport's congregational parades and his use of lay assistants were also condemned by Tennent. The New Brunswick revivalist saw nothing wrong with formal licentiates aiding an itinerant, but he considered the practice of laypeople preaching to the faithful a major step toward wild and fruitless enthusiasm.[11]

Tennent had a reputation for slandering clergymen, but he condemned Davenport's attacks on ministers from the pulpit. Davenport customarily asked pastors in the churches that he visited to give him an account of their rebirth. If they refused, Davenport assumed they were unregenerate sinners and declared as much in his next sermon. Tennent, on the other hand, never made such demands of ordained clergymen, and he never exposed the names of unconverted ministers from the pulpit. To his way of thinking, such charges were best reserved for formal ecclesiastical proceedings.[12]

Many of Tennent's contemporaries may have seen little difference between his practice and that of Davenport. Others may have viewed Davenport as the more honest of the two men, since he openly declared which men he opposed while Tennent's general attacks on unconverted ministers besmirched the reputation of the entire clergy. Nevertheless, Tennent was personally convinced that Davenport's methods were quite different from his own and that Davenport had moved far beyond the bounds of ecclesiastical propriety.

Tennent had good cause to be concerned about his colleague's activities. The Southhold pastor's disorderly behavior in New England soon affected Tennent's own reputation. In newspapers throughout the colonies Davenport's antics were reported and associated with the ministries of both Tennent and Whitefield. One example of this linkage is a poem that appeared in the *New York Weekly Journal*. Rather than openly name the subject of his work, the poet chose to identify his three protagonists by their home bases in the colonies.

> Three preachers in three distant places born,
> Georgia, New Brunswick, and Southhold did adorn,
> The first to strike the passions did excell,
> The next was famed for sending souls to Hell,
> The last had nothing of his own to show,
> And therefore wisely joined the former two.[13]

THE UNITAS FRATRUM

On the heels of the Craighead separation and Davenport's escapades, Tennent encountered what would become an even greater threat to his Awakening leadership. In the early winter of 1741, Tennent was introduced to the German nobleman Count Nicholas Ludwig von Zinzendorf. Zinzendorf was the founder and patron of a religious group known formally as the Unitas Fratrum and familiarly as the Moravians. The Count had sent a representative of his church to America in 1736 to investigate the possibilities of settlement and missions. His recommendation had been to establish a community in Georgia, but when a select group of Moravians settled in that colony, they decided within only a few years that Pennsylvania was more fertile ground for their mission.[14]

George Whitefield played an important part in the Unitas Fratrum's migration to Penn's colony. In order to smooth the way for their departure from Georgia, Whitefield offered to buy whatever possessions they left behind, to provide free passage to Philadelphia on his ship, the *Savannah*, and to employ the Moravians in the construction of a school he had planned at Nazareth, Pennsylvania.[15]

Despite Whitefield's kindness to the Moravians, their leader, Peter Bohler, assumed a rather condescending attitude toward his people's benefactor. Bohler reported to Zinzendorf that the Englishman wanted to gather a few well-grounded brethren around him. This, Bohler believed, was fortunate since Whitefield's associates lacked a satisfactory foundation in experimental Christianity. Concerning Whitefield's relation to future Moravian missions, Bohler remarked that Whitefield loved Zinzendorf's followers "very much and would do everything which we tell him."[16]

This confidence that Whitefield could be easily manipulated was quickly discovered to be unfounded. In November 1740 Bohler and Whitefield met to discuss the Moravians' progress in building the Nazareth school. On Bohler's side, there was very little to report since recent rains had seriously delayed the work. This soured the atmosphere of the meeting, but an even greater source of contention was the two men's theological differences. During their conversation Bohler argued with Whitefield over the doctrine of predestination. Like most Moravians, Bohler believed in the eventual salvation of all humanity. Whitefield, on the other hand, had been persuaded by his Calvinist friends that predestination and a limited election were God's true plan. Over these differing opinions a heated discussion developed that prompted Whitefield to order the Moravians off his property at Nazareth.[17]

Whitefield received word shortly after his break with Bohler that Moravian missionaries in England and Georgia were attracting many of his disciples into the Unitas Fratrum by preaching doctrines that differed radically with his own views.[18]

Whitefield's replies to these letters are particularly helpful in understanding the extremely negative reaction that colonial Calvinists later had to the Moravians' presence in the middle colonies. In addition to the doctrine of universal salvation, the Moravians preached perfectionism and "stillness." "Stillness" was a Moravian tenet based in part on a verse in Psalm 46— "Be still, and know that I am the Lord." Moravian ministers employed this text to prove the error of the Calvinist doctrine of "striving." Reformed revivalists in Great Britain and America considered conversion an exclusive work of the Holy Spirit which came only to those who had been elected before creation through God's predestination of the saints. Somewhat paradoxically though, these Calvinists also maintained that sinners could and should "strive" for their salvation by employing the divinely appointed means to salvation stipulated in Scripture and embodied in the church's rites and practices.[19]

This apparent contradiction in their message resulted in a harsh double bind for those who were not yet converted. Calvinist congregations learned that they must work with all their might for salvation, yet they might not be saved since election was limited and predetermined. In stark contrast, Moravian preachers insisted that Psalm 46 warned sinners not to strive, "for the Lord is the Lord and he will save you by Himself for he saves all men."[20]

Moravian missionaries also claimed that human perfection was possible for Christians in this life. Although they customarily qualified such a statement by noting that perfection was only infrequently accomplished, Calvinist revivalists regarded their concession as no concession at all. Reformed theology taught that original sin had so infected human nature that complete obedience to God was an unreachable ideal. The saints should certainly improve their behavior over time, but perfection remained illusive until the next life.[21]

Because of their close cooperation during the latter part of 1741, it is safe to assume that Whitefield informed Tennent of his conversations with Bohler and of the troubling correspondence he was receiving from his followers in Great Britain and Georgia. This warning was reinforced by reports from Tennent's New Brunswick colleague, Theodorus Frelinghuysen. When the Amsterdam Classis of the Dutch Reformed Church discovered that a group of Moravians planned to immigrate to America, it prepared a letter cautioning its colonial clergy against contact with the Unitas Fratrum. This letter was sent to Theodorus Frelinghuysen in August 1739 and was followed the next year by a book describing the "dangerous errors of Zinzendorf and his Moravians.[22]

These unfavorable communications about Zinzendorf's disciples predisposed Tennent to expect the worst from their leader. Zinzendorf, on the other hand, probably knew very little about Tennent. From his perspective, there was no apparent need to know Tennent. Tennent's reputation, after all, had barely spread beyond the colonies. Local Moravians regarded him as little more than one of Whitefield's lieutenants, and he had no direct connection with the threefold mission that Zinzendorf had set for himself.

Zinzendorf came to America to convert the American Indian, to supervise the establishment of a Moravian settlement at Bethlehem, Pennsylvania, and to organize an ecumenical "Congregation of God in the Spirit." The last of these goals would generate the greatest opposition to his ministry. Zinzendorf had developed the model for his Congregation of God in the Spirit out of the contemporary pietist idea of reforming the church through "*ecclesiolae in ecclesia.*" The founder of German Lutheran Pietism, Jacob Spener, had envisioned these *ecclesiolae* as the means by which practical piety would be promoted systematically, first among dedicated groups of Christians and later throughout the ecclesiastical community. Meeting together for regular Bible study and discussion, pietist conventicles were to encourage spiritual renewal from within the church while at the same time maintaining a close watch against sectarian pride among their fellows.[23]

The particular *ecclesiola* that Zinzendorf employed for this uplifting work was the Moravians. After John Hus's execution in 1415, his followers in Bohemia and Moravia organized the Unitas Fratrum. The brotherhood spread into Poland, East Prussia, and Hungary during the sixteenth century, but it was almost destroyed in the next century by the Thirty Years War and survived only in small enclaves throughout Moravia. The church's future looked bleak until a group of its members migrated to Zinzendorf's estate in Bethelsdorf during 1722. From that time forward, Zinzendorf placed his considerable resources behind the Moravians, and in the process, the Unitas Fratrum was transformed by his unique brand of pietistic Christianity.[24]

Unlike other German pietists whose *ecclesiolae* remained almost exclusively Lutheran, Zinzendorf sent missionary parties into all parts of the Western world. Their instructions were to seek converts to Christ and to avoid conflict with local Christian denominations. Converts came quickly but so did conflict because of Zinzendorf's unusual vision of Christianity. Zinzendorf regarded the current ecclesiastical divisions in the body of Christ as both positive and negative. On the plus side, each communion emphasized different elements of the Gospel, which in turn attracted a unique segment of the world's population. But this multifaceted witness also had its drawbacks since the varying pictures of Christ's good news provided by different church systems obstructed the laity's vision of the Church's fundamental unity by particularizing the biblical revelation.[25]

Zinzendorf planned to provide a concrete example of Christian brotherhood in the Church Universal through his Unitas Fratrum. To accomplish this task, he advised his followers to avoid becoming another church among many and, instead, to provide a meeting place for the worship and communion of Christians from all communions. Joining the Moravians, then, did not involve renouncing one's Reformed or Lutheran theology or even rejecting one's membership in the Reformed or Lutheran churches. In Germany, the Netherlands, and Great Britain, enclaves of Moravians were established that identified themselves as both Moravians and Lutherans, or Moravians and Reformed.[26]

Traditional church leaders recognized very quickly their laity's attraction to the Moravian ecumenical witness, but they suspected the brotherhood's open admission was a shrewd ploy to lure gullible lay-people into a new church. This suspicion was justified in part. Moravian leaders did on occasion teach doctrines that contradicted the theology of their followers' former communions, and in their efforts to build a united fellowship, they sometimes ignored or disparaged denominational differences in worship, polity, and theology.[27]

By the 1740s, outside opposition to the Moravians was forcing the brotherhood in Europe to seek government recognition. Zinzendorf hoped this trend could be avoided in the middle colonies because of the region's unusual religious pluralism. Indeed, Zinzendorf planned to establish a Congregation of God in the Spirit which would be "a league of members of every sect who would be bound together by spiritual ties instead of by an externally formulated association. In this league the denominational doctrines were not to be stressed, but rather the Spirit that gave rise to those convictions." As such, the new organization would serve as an ecclesiastical umbrella under which members from every colonial denomination could gather, and in which their differences would be relativized by their common universal perspective.[28]

Zinzendorf's evaluation of the differences between the religious situation in America and the situation in Europe was both sagacious and simplistic. Popular participation in the Awakening proved that the colonies were ready for some form of interdenominational cooperation, and many of the pietistic notions preached by the Moravians had already been introduced with great success through the revivals. But, as John B. Frantz has pointed out, pietists in the mid-Atlantic region came in several different varieties, and the distinctions between them presented significant barriers to their union. Pietists everywhere shared a concern for practical piety and new birth, but they disagreed radically on the degree to which they should adhere to the rites and doctrines of the established churches of Europe. Sectarian pietists like the Dunkers or the Seventh-Day Baptists at Ephrata were separatists who sought in their separation the creation of "pure religious communities." They spurned the traditions of established European churches while maintaining a strong allegiance to the rituals and beliefs that they had developed within their own sects. The confessionalists were, like Gilbert Tennent, strong advocates of both the rites and dogmas of their traditional communions. They recognized the emptiness of such ecclesiastical symbols when unaccompanied by the practical piety of the laity, but they believed such symbols could contribute to the creation of vibrant discipleship.

Ecumenists like the Moravians, on the other hand, strove for a union of all Christians and were willing, if not eager, to achieve that end by ignoring differences of creed or form.[29]

After some time in the colonies, Zinzendorf would discover that these varying pietist perspectives were as great an obstacle to his Congregation of God in the Spirit as the Europeans' penchant for established state churches. But this revelation was still far in the future when Zinzendorf encountered Gilbert Tennent in the early winter of 1741–1742.

TENNENT MEETS ZINZENDORF

Zinzendorf arrived in New York City for his first and only visit to the colonies during the last days of November. Zinzendorf had planned to travel straight to Philadelphia, but his journey was briefly interrupted in New Brunswick by two short interviews with Gilbert Tennent and Henri Visscher, Theodorus Frelinghuysen's lay assistant. Of his purpose in meeting with Zinzendorf, Tennent later remarked that he and Visscher "thought it their Duty, diligently and impartially, to acquaint themselves with their [the Moravians'] Principles, [so] that they [Tennent and Visscher] might not, on the one hand, neglect any Appearance of God, and the Operations of his Spirit, in these declining Times; nor, on the other, receive such as his Messengers, who might be engaged in the Introduction of Error and Confusion among us."[30]

The circumstances for the interviews were rather curious, according to Tennent's account. Zinzendorf would not allow Tennent and Visscher to converse with him at the same time so long as their discussion dealt with religious matters. Tennent later interpreted this rule as a devious maneuver to prevent two witnesses from testifying against Zinzendorf's unorthodox views.[31]

The conversation was conducted in Latin. Peter Bohler had cautioned Zinzendorf to learn English before his trip to the colonies, but there is no indication that Zinzendorf spoke English sufficiently well for an extended theological discussion at this point in his visit. In the aftermath of his meeting with Tennent, it is probable that Zinzendorf deeply regretted this oversight.[32]

Tennent probably understood Latin, since his parent-tutor, William Tennent, Sr., was a noted linguist and his communication with the Dutch-speaking Frelinghuysen had been limited to that tongue. Zinzendorf was also well trained in languages, but James Logan remarked Zinzendorf's Latin was difficult to understand. As Logan put it, Zinzendorf's French was difficult to follow, but his Latin was "still more odd than his French—in some parts carrying a show of elegance, but in others mere nonsense; in other places plain enough, in others perfectly unintelligible."[33]

The capacity of Tennent and Zinzendorf to communicate in Latin is only important because of a Moravian sympathizer's later report of their conversation. According to this anonymous individual, Zinzendorf denied ever holding a conference with Tennent. He did remember a short visit by Tennent in New Brunswick, but he claimed that he "could not understand Mr. Gilbert [Tennent], because he spoke in such Latin as was very strange for a German, and . . . [he] could not find expressions which were plain enough [for] Mr. Gilbert." Zinzendorf also charged that "he had not a mind to confer with [Tennent] . . . being convinced by long experience, that he must not discourse with any Presbyterian reprobate, except in a company of different principles."[34]

If one trusts this comment, then Zinzendorf considered the interchange with Tennent inconsequential because the language barrier prevented serious discussion. Zinzendorf's judgment of the degree to which he and Tennent understood each other is probably correct, but his expressed bias against Presbyterians was not likely a part of the original meeting. Such a polemical remark might have been expected from any other middle colony religious leader. The Great Awakening had generated a great deal of friction between local denominational leaders by 1741, but Zinzendorf was known and sometimes hated for his willingness to speak with churchpeople of all types. Consequently, one must ask why such an antagonistic response from an ecumenist who regarded the interchange as insignificant in the first place?

The most likely answer to this query is Tennent's own negative reaction to the New Brunswick meeting. If Zinzendorf interpreted the encounter as unimportant, Tennent certainly did not. In 1742 Tennent published a 110–page diatribe against the Moravian leader and his church. Entitled *The Necessity of holding fast the Truth*, the work publicly declared Tennent's objections to Moravian doctrine as he had received it from Zinzendorf.

Although Tennent shared Zinzendorf's pietistic concern for spiritual rebirth, practical piety, and interdenominational cooperation, these interests were strictly circumscribed by his confessional allegiance to

Calvinism. Therefore, Tennent leveled particularly heavy criticism at Zinzendorf's views on conversion, the possibility of Christian perfection, the role of the biblical law in a Christian's life, and the likelihood of universal salvation.

Tennent could not accept the idea of universal redemption because in his view it suggested that God lacked sufficient knowledge or power to predict and effect his eternal plan. "If he [God] intended the salvation of all by the Redeemer's death and knew not in the mean time, that the most would not attain it; then," asked Tennent, "is not the knowledge of the Almighty finite and imperfect? . . . If the Lord intended the salvation of all, must it not argue great impotency, and dependence on creatures, to fail of compassing his designs?"[35]

As for the converted's ability to live a perfect life, Tennent conceded that Adam and Eve were capable of total obedience, but through their transgressions he believed "they lost this for themselves and us." Those who proposed that perfection was attainable in this life were, in Tennent's opinion, guilty of moderating God's commandments so that it seemed that fallen humanity could fulfill the biblical law. Such softening of the law's requirements was based upon the false assumption that God must have matched his moral law to his creatures' capacities. In actual fact, God's commands were

not the measure of our ability, but of our duty. . . . Can it be supposed with any reason, that creatures' trespass[es] should lessen the Creator's claim . . . to their obedience; or that he should be obliged to model his laws, which are grounded upon the unalterable nature of things, according to the measure of their contracted weakness. No surely. If a person should lend another a sum of money, and he should play the wilfull bankrupt with it, might not full payment be legally demanded and in case of failure, imprisonment inflicted?[36]

The fallacy of Moravian thought in this area was obvious to Tennent, but to reinforce his critique of perfectionist doctrine, he charged that it also undermined the perseverance of the "saints." Any individual who recognized the deep and abiding stain left by original sin would surely not be shocked by his or her continued failures to reach the Christian ideal. But those who expected perfection could only be disheartened by their persistent inability to achieve that goal.[37]

With regard to the moral law, Tennent found Zinzendorf claiming that gracious conversion made the ethical commands of the Old Testament obsolete since the newborn Christian naturally tended toward the "good." Tennent's Reformed background told him otherwise. The moral rules found in Scripture convinced sinners of their damnable state before an uncompromising holy deity and directed the saints along the path to righteousness.[38]

This difference of opinion about the utility of the law indirectly affected the final point of controversy between Tennent and Zinzendorf, i.e., the nature of spiritual rebirth. One reason Zinzendorf radically discounted the law's role in the Christian life was that it had no place in his model for conversion. Like Tennent, Zinzendorf sought the new birth of the human "heart," but his appeals to the heart were more direct than Tennent's. F. Ernest Stoeffler has observed that Zinzendorf believed personal religion was "a matter of feeling, not of reasoning. Its locus is not the head, but the 'heart.' It has nothing to do with theoretical judgements, but with a mode of religious apprehension which involves the whole man, and preeminently his affective nature. It is, therefore, not thinking about God, but 'experiencing' God.'"[39] These views led Zinzendorf to exclude conviction from his paradigm for Christian rebirth. Rather than convict sinners with a careful exposition of their legal guilt before God, the Moravian leader persuaded the sinful to accept grace through a direct appeal to their emotions. Where Tennent sought to convince, then, Zinzendorf attempted to evoke a sympathetic response by graphically recalling the terrible sufferings that Christ had endured for sinful humanity's sake.

Presbyterian "Old Lights" (as opponents of the Awakening were called) had for some time maintained that Tennent's preaching of terrors was nothing more than a similar call to the passions. Tennent viewed his methods quite differently, though. According to his own peculiar account of contemporary "faculty" psychology, the human psyche had three components: the understanding, the will, and the passions. The understanding represented human reasoning; the will, human intention; and the passions, human feeling or desire. Prior to the Fall of Adam, these three faculties were ordered in perfect hierarchical harmony so that the understanding informed the will as to what was the "good," and the will obeyed by directing the passions to their appropriate objects. The Fall destroyed this natural cooperation by reversing the order of priority so that the passions ruled both reason and intention.[40]

Because Tennent's sermons prompted emotional outbursts, his critics charged that revival homiletics only perpetuated the human psyche's fallen condition. But Tennent insisted that such affective responses were merely the secondary consequences of his primary object, which was to convince the understanding through a logical explication of the biblical law's requirements that an infinite gap existed between human righteousness and the holiness demanded by God. If he accomplished this goal, Tennent was not surprised to see strong feelings openly expressed. The human faculties were so closely connected that the understanding's rational conviction that it stood in a damnable state inevitably filtered down to inform the will and arouse the emotions.[41]

While evoking the passions could not be avoided in the work of conversion, Tennent nevertheless rejected direct appeals to the emotions because they impeded the restoration of pre-Fall cooperation among the faculties and encouraged religious enthusiasm. Tennent believed the Moravians were enthusiasts of the worst sort, and this greatly troubled him. Tennent was not the only clergyman to express doubts about Zinzendorf's heavy emphasis upon religious feelings, but his concern was compounded by several other factors. In recent months, the Presbyterian Church had been divided by schism, Tennent's party split by the Covenanters, and the revivalists' reputation blemished by the excesses of New England lay exhorters and James Davenport's itinerations. The last thing the Awakening needed was further division, but Zinzendorf's entrance into the colonies offered just that prospect since it presented an entirely new pietistic formulation of experiential religion for the movement's supporters to squabble over.

Tennent was convinced that the Moravian system represented the greatest challenge to the Awakening's integrity to date because it threatened to capsize the revival's previous balance between a fervent experimental piety and sober theological reflection. But many Awakening supporters did not see these dangers in the Moravians' theology. Indeed, they regarded the Unitas Fratrum as the truest expression of the movement.

The growing success enjoyed by Zinzendorf's followers in attracting revival converts soon threw Tennent into a period of soul searching. The Awakening leader began to ask himself if the movement he had promoted was not the spur to doctrinal error and emotional enthusiasm that his opponents had claimed it to be from the start. Tennent expressed his inner turmoil over this question in a letter to Jonathan Dickinson during February 1742.

I have had many afflicting Thoughts about the Debates which have subsisted for some Time in our Synod; I would to God, the Breach were healed, if it was the Will of the Almighty. As for my own Part, wherein I have mismanaged in doing what I did;—I do look upon it to be my Duty, and should be willing to acknowledge it in the openest Manner.—I cannot justify the *excessive heat of Temper*, which has sometimes appear'd in my Conduct.—I have been of late (since I return'd from New-England) visited with much spiritual Desertions, Temptations, and Distresses of various kinds, coming in a thick, and almost continual Succession; which have given me a greater Discovery of myself than I think I ever had before: These Things, with the Trials I have had of the *Moravians*, have given me a clear view of the Danger of every Thing which tends to ENTHUSIASM and DIVISION in the Church.[42]

By a circuitous route, this private communication between Tennent and Dickinson found its way into the hands of Thomas Clap, the rector of Yale College and a fierce opponent of the Awakening. Clap immediately recognized that its apparent confession of mismanagement and error could damage the revival cause. Therefore, he had the letter published in a prominent New England paper.[43]

Clap's action accomplished its intended purpose, but the letter had already persuaded Jonathan Dickinson that Tennent was sincerely interested in denominational peace. Writing to an associate in April 1742, Jonathan Dickinson revealed his hope that the recent schism would be healed through the intervention of the New York Presbytery. Dickinson based his optimism on Tennent's new attitude, which he described as "a cool and Catholick Spirit . . . ready to submit to proper Terms of Peace."[44]

The peace that Dickinson expected never materialized, even though he correctly evaluated his New Brunswick colleague's state of mind. When the Synod met in May, Dickinson was elected moderator, and he used his position to maneuver the formation of a committee to meet with the ejected brethren. After conferring with the New Lights, the delegation proposed that the Synod conduct discussions with the expelled members in closed session. The motion passed, but its intent failed when the two sides could not agree on who should arbitrate the original issues of the schism. The New Lights demanded that only those who had not signed the Cross protestation or been purged on June 1, 1741, should serve as judges. The Old Lights rejected this proposal. They were eager to explain their reasons for ousting the revivalists, but they would not withdraw their protest, nor would they relinquish their right to determine the Synod's final decision.[45]

Angered by the intransigence of Synod Old Lights, Dickinson voiced a formal objection. Five clergymen from the New York Presbytery and one from the Philadelphia Presbytery joined Dickinson in his complaint. Together they denounced the 1741 expulsion of the New Lights without a trial, the obstruction of a judicial review to the case, and all publications that placed the late "work of divine power and grace" in a negative light. They renounced all divisive, irregular measures currently practised by Synod members, and they declared that the New Brunswick Presbytery and their adherents were in their opinion still members of the Synod despite the 1741 *Protestation*.[46]

Synod Old Lights were for the most part unmoved by the Dickinson protest. The offenses they had suffered at the hands of the Awakeners were too fresh in their minds to allow compromise, and since their party retained control of the church's highest judicatory, they felt no pressing need to make concessions.[47]

His New York friends' abortive attempt at reunion marked the beginning of another long year of troubles for Tennent. During May 1742 James Davenport was arrested in Hartford, Connecticut, for breaking a new law that restricted itinerant preaching. His trial before the General Assembly ended with Davenport's being declared "disturbed in the rational faculties of his mind" and deported to his parish in Southhold, Long Island. Rather than accept his fate, however, Davenport traveled next to Boston. There he was summoned before the "associated Pastors in the Towns of Boston and Charlestown." After a close examination, this group found Davenport a "pious" man but his methods questionable. When the association published their findings in the press, Davenport turned on his examiners by describing them as the prophets of Ahab's court. This earned Davenport an arrest by local authorities and another trial during which he was labeled *non compos mentis*.[48]

Gilbert Tennent's objections to Davenport's practice were by now well known to the public because he had included them in a postscript to the same letter to Dickinson that Thomas Clap had published.[49] Yet Tennent quickly discovered that many misinterpreted his comments as a critique of the Awakening in general and his ministry in particular. To correct this misunderstanding, Tennent produced an explanation which was subsequently printed in local papers. He insisted that his note to Dickinson had been penned in haste without any intention of publication. His declared self-doubts had concerned his former "manner of performing" and in no way should have been interpreted as a criticism of or a retreat from the "matter or substance of what I contended for."

Tennent also stated that he had not wished to blemish the reputation of Davenport's piety or integrity, but had hoped to correct some of his friend's methods.[50]

Unfortunately for Tennent, his explanation did not quiet the controversy over his confession. According to his critics, his second letter was full of "fox-like shifts" that hid his enthusiastic principles. In order to insure that these maneuvers would not be missed by the untrained laity, several rebuttals to Tennent's apology were published in the late fall of 1742.[51]

WHITEFIELD—A MORAVIAN?

During the same autumn, Tennent began to have grave doubts about George Whitefield. The source of these misgivings was the internal politics of the New Building in Philadelphia. This combined church and charity school had been constructed for Whitefield during his second tour through the middle colonies, and on November 9, 1940, Whitefield preached his first sermon in the new structure. Five days later, the four men who owned the land on which the New Building stood legally transferred the property to the building's nine trustees. The trustees included George Whitefield, William Seward, John Stephen Benezet, Thomas Noble, Samuel Hazard, Robert Eastburn, Jr., James Read, Edward Evans, and Charles Brockden. All of these individuals were Awakening supporters, but their backgrounds were quite different. Seward was Whitefield's traveling companion and his most faithful English financial backer. Benezet and Hazard were merchants in Philadelphia. Noble was a New York tradesman with important business connections in Philadelphia. Eastburn was a Philadelphia blacksmith; Brockden, a recorder of deeds for the Philadelphia Company; Evans, a cordwainer; and Read, a gentleman of unknown occupation.[52]

The legal transfer for the New Building's property included a description of the structure's intended purposes. Its builders planned to establish a "house of Publick Worship" and to provide a charity school where poor children could receive a free education "in usefull Literature and the Knowledge of the Christian Religion." The trustees were assigned the task of introducing "such Protestant Ministers to preach the Gospel in the Said House as they shall judge to be sound in their Principles, Zealous and Faithful in the Discharge of their Duty and acquainted with the Religion of the Heart and Experimental Piety with-

out any regard to those Distinctions or different Sentiments in lesser
Matters which have to the Scandal of Religion unhappily divided real
Christians.''[53]

This statement of purpose implied that the building's pulpit was to
be open to colonial clergy of every experimental sort, but Whitefield
restricted access to Calvinist Awakeners by formulating ten theological
statements to which all trustees and ministers connected with the New
Building had to subscribe. Nine of the articles in this summary of
Whitefield's theology were unobjectionable, but the tenth clause read
as follows: ''10. We do also give our Assent and Consent to the 9th.
10th. 11th. 12th. 13th. & 17th. Articles of the Church of England as
explained by the Calvinists in their literal & gramatical sence without
any Equivocation, whatsoever we mention therein particular, because
they are a summary of the foregoing Articles. We believe all that are
sound in the Faith agree in these whatever Points they may differ in.''[54]
By subscribing to this statement, a trustee or minister declared his
support of a strict Calvinist interpretation of original sin, free will,
justification, good works before and after justification, predestination,
and election. This was perfectly acceptable to New Light clergymen,
but it excluded Moravian leaders from participating in the New Building's ministry.

Had the trustees been staunch Calvinists themselves, no problem
might have arisen over Whitefield's articles. But such was not the case.
Many of the trustees had been attracted to the Awakening because of
its emphasis upon spiritual rebirth and interdenominational cooperation.
Therefore, they soon began to view the subscription requirement as
antithetical to the spirit that had prompted the New Building's
construction.

In December 1741 Thomas Noble confessed his doubts about the
articles in this way:

I am really of the mind that the Obligation I laid myself under was not right
and that the making of so many Articles for Terms of Union is not of God but
rather a winning Strategem of the Devil to keep Gods People a Part and so to
prevent the progress of the Gospel. I am more and more convinced in my Heart
that the Moravians are the dear children of God and do believe they Preach the
true Gospel of Jesus Christ. Therefore [I] do give my full consent that they
may have the Use of the New Building. I well know and find that for my thus
judging of these Brethren I shall give Offense to some that are real Brethren
of another Mind, but [I] cannot help it.[55]

Several other trustees shared Noble's sympathy for the Moravians. John Stephen Benezet, Charles Brockden, Edward Evans, and James Read became increasingly enamored with the Unitas Fratrum's ecumenical approach. Indeed, their contacts with Zinzendorf, Bohler, or the Moravian church in Philadelphia led them to suspect that the confessional pietism represented in the New Building's ten articles was an unnecessary obstruction to the perfect fellowship of converted Christians.

During the early months of the New Building's existence, its pulpit was filled exclusively by Calvinist Awakeners.[56] These revivalists strongly opposed the introduction of Moravian leaders into the church. Yet they realized that the balance of power on the trustee board was shifting against them. By June 1742 Whitefield had returned to England and William Seward was dead. This left only seven trustees available to vote on pulpit supplies. Of these seven, only two, Hazard and Eastburn, remained convinced that the New Building should remain under Calvinist control.[57]

Fearful that the board might alter the Whitefield articles so that Moravian preachers could be introduced, Gilbert Tennent and his allies among the trustees began to attack the Moravians with even greater severity than before. Peter Bohler reported to Zinzendorf on June 24 that Tennent was preaching daily in the New Building against the Unitas Fratrum. Some of these sermons offered a ''piece by piece'' rebuttal of Zinzendorf's published writings. Among the trustees, Bohler also observed, ''Hazard and his colleague, [Eastburn], are trying to use every conceivable practice and also to use force so that the house should not fall into our hands.'' Puzzled as to how he should respond, Bohler asked Zinzendorf for instructions.[58]

Zinzendorf advised his lieutenant to deliver the following message to the Moravian congregation in Philadelphia at his next opportunity.

Whereas you did hear that a certain Minister was here who endeavour'd to make our Doctrines susceptible, whom you could not judge or pay in his own Coin,—when it was to be feared that nothing but Divisions would arise amongst the Souls newly stir'd up; Therefore, the Church of the Lord under whose Directions you are, had order'd you to intermitt your Meetings and to keep Silence, after having in few Words given to your Assembly a short and plain Abstract of our Doctrine.[59]

Following this declaration, Zinzendorf described in copious detail what Bohler should say about the Moravians' theology.

Zinzendorf's decision to cancel all Moravian activities in Philadelphia until further notice was compatible with his general policy not to encourage confusion or division wherever it might seem that he or his followers could gain something from it.[60] Nevertheless, a month after Moravian meetings halted, Zinzendorf's friends on the New Building's trustee board made another attempt to introduce Moravian preachers into the pulpit. In July the trustees voted five to two to allow Bohler to conduct services in the structure. But Samuel Hazard pocket vetoed this decision, so to speak, by refusing to surrender the only key to the building.[61]

As conflict of this sort increased, Gilbert Tennent discovered to his dismay that George Whitefield was not firmly behind the Calvinists. Whitefield never supported those trustees who wanted Moravians to preach in the New Building, but he also rejected Tennent's hostile approach to Zinzendorf's followers. Immediately following his discussions with Zinzendorf in New Brunswick, Gilbert Tennent had penned several letters describing the various errors of Moravian doctrine. One of these reports had been sent to Whitefield in England. Whitefield chose to show Tennent's criticisms to a local Moravian leader, August Spangenberg. Spangenberg explained how Tennent had misinterpreted Zinzendorf, and Whitefield relayed Spangenberg's comments along with his own views to Tennent. Whitefield admitted that he did not agree with most of the Unitas Fratrum's principles, but he could not see why this disagreement should interfere with his or Tennent's cooperation with them. After all, he asked, "Do not you and I preach up and profess a Cath[olic] Spirit." Whitefield was convinced the Moravians were the "Children of God" and their ultimate purpose was the "glory of God and the good of souls." Therefore, he chided his colonial friend for being too confined by his Presbyterian principles. As for himself, Whitefield declared he would continue to attempt to bring "people to Jesus Christ and then let them join with such Congregations as they upon due urging judge to be nearest the Mind of Jesus Christ."[62]

When Tennent answered Whitefield's letter in June 1742, he expressed deep disappointment over his colleague's views. "Your high opinion of the Moravians and attempts to join with them Shocks me Exceedingly and opens a Scene of Terror and distress. Oh my dear brother! I believe in my Soul You never did anything in all your Life of such dreadful Tendency to the Church of God as your favouring that Sect of Enthusiastical Hereticks.''[63]

Whitefield's criticisms of Tennent's narrow-mindedness pained the middle colony Awakener greatly. He denied that he was a ''bigot to any form of Government,'' and noted that many in his own communion accused him of excess in the opposite direction. Nevertheless, Tennent warned that ''there can be no scriptural valuable union without an assent to main Doctrinal Principles [for] any other Union is but a Confederacy against Truth and a betraying the Cause of God into the hands of Enemies.'' Tennent then pleaded with Whitefield to end his unreasonable and dangerous encouragement of the Moravian sect.[64]

Whitefield could not be persuaded to change his policy. Although theologically Whitefield continued to lean toward Tennent's Calvinism, his heart was fundamentally in sympathy with Zinzendorf's ecumenism. In the last analysis, theological systems were not as important to Whitefield as the fellowship of reborn Christians. Therefore, while he differed significantly with Zinzendorf in doctrine, he preferred to cooperate with the Moravians in practice.

Tennent would not accept this strategy. Against the Old Lights of his synod, he had defended theological tolerance because he believed many doctrines were not essential for Christian fellowship or cooperation. But the sort of tolerance required to associate with the Moravians amounted to theological suicide, in his opinion, since it necessitated relinquishing essential tenets of the Reformed tradition.

Unable to convince his English friend of this logic, Tennent was also helpless to prevent the potential damage of Whitefield's views. As news of Whitefield's attitude toward the Moravians spread through the colonies, much of the colonial evangelical community began to believe that Whitefield had become a Moravian.[65] Whitefield had not, but an apparent defection was as embarrassing as a real one and as effective at forcing the New Brunswick Awakener to reorient his ministry.

————————————————— 5

REDEEMING A FALTERING
AWAKENING: THE SEARCH
FOR A NEW BALANCE

By 1743 Gilbert Tennent believed the Great Awakening had been seriously compromised by the events of the past few years. Rather than abandon the movement, however, Tennent tried to repair the damage by balancing his calls for new birth with large doses of doctrinal instruction in his preaching. This led to significant alterations in Tennent's rhetorical methods and his style of dress. Taken together, these modifications signaled a self-conscious retreat from Tennent's previously unyielding stance in favor of the Awakening. But they also facilitated a formal alliance of his party with the New York Presbytery and his assumption of a far more irenic posture toward those Presbyterians who had opposed his experimental approach.

PAINFUL LESSONS, POSITIVE RESULTS

Gilbert Tennent's published attacks on the Moravians proved to be a source of serious embarrassment in the winter of 1743, when John Hancock, a New England revival critic, anonymously published *The Examiner; Or Gilbert against Tennent*. Peter Bohler explained Hancock's methods in a letter to Zinzendorf by saying, "Tennent has been severely censured in Boston where someone took all the arrows which he [Tennent] had sharpened for us and shot them at him."[1]

Bohler's analysis was correct. Although Hancock was no friend of the Moravians, he chastised Tennent for his inconsistent condemnation of the Unitas Fratrum for practices that he himself had advocated in

The Danger of An Unconverted Ministry. Hancock highlighted Tennent's hypocrisy by placing excerpts from *The Necessity of holding fast the Truth* in a column labeled "Gilbert" alongside a parallel column of passages from the Nottingham sermon entitled "Tennent." This permitted Hancock to "set *Gilbert* against *Tennent*, for the Readers ease in finding out the Truth."[2]

Hancock could not have chosen a more graphic means of illustrating Tennent's altered policy following his confrontation with Zinzendorf. The Nottingham sermon was Tennent's most radical pronouncement in favor of pietistic, experiential, "heart" religion. *The Necessity of holding fast the Truth,* in contrast, reflected Tennent's horror when he realized the excesses that men like the Count might commit in the name of the same religious orientation. As a result, the two works did contradict each other on several significant points.

At Nottingham Tennent had denied that unconverted clergymen were profitable to the sinner's soul. He supported the laity's right to leave an unconverted ministry, and he attacked modern day Pharisee-Teachers for their excessive concern for doctrine and reason. In *The Necessity of holding fast the Truth* Tennent declared unregenerate ministers could on occasion be successful at converting sinners. He downplayed the laity's right to separate from their settled pastor, and he chastised the Moravians for promoting an uneducated clergy that stressed the emotional side of conversion.[3]

Hancock believed these shifts in Tennent's policy were easily explained. Quite simply, the Moravians had treated Tennent "in the same uncharitable, censorious, imperious, divisive Manner" that he had treated "the Body of the Clergy." Consequently, the spirit that Tennent had formerly promoted now appeared "to him in a most frightful Shape."[4]

Hancock was partially right. Prior to Zinzendorf's arrival in the colonies, Tennent had made bold claims for experiential knowledge in order to counteract its neglect by conservative church leaders who overemphasized the intellect. During his meeting with Zinzendorf, Tennent discovered the opposite "perversion" of Christianity. Unlike the Old Lights, this Moravian so stressed religious experience that reason and doctrine were practically ignored.

Tennent was appalled at this approach, but many of his supporters appreciated the Unitas Fratrum for its thoroughgoing extension of the Awakening's experimental interests. These individuals interpreted Tennent's reluctance to accept Zinzendorf's followers as a sign that he held to the same pharisaic notions that he had condemned earlier in his Presbyterian opponents. To counteract this unexpected attack from the rear, Tennent assaulted the Moravians as fiercely as he had earlier battled Old Light corruptions, and in the process, he left the impression of advocating conflicting policies. Against the Old Lights, he had preached heart knowledge, conversion, and practical piety, while against the Moravians he had proclaimed the value of head knowledge, doctrine, and ecclesiastical order.

Curiously enough, Hancock did Tennent a service by pointing out the contradictions in his writings. Tennent learned from *The Examiner* that he had left himself open to misinterpretation from both ends of the Awakening spectrum and that the best foundation for responsible evangelical piety was a mixture of the Old Light and Moravian programs. Within months of *The Examiner*'s publication, Tennent would show that he had absorbed this crucial lesson by publicly declaring the balanced policy he intended to pursue in the future. But before this could happen, the dissemination of *The Examiner* throughout the colonial community made his new knowledge an extremely bitter lesson to learn.

Presbyterian politics in the middle colonies shifted in Tennent's favor at the same time that *The Examiner* damaged his reputation in New England. At the 1743 Synod Jonathan Dickinson renewed his efforts to unite the warring parties of his divided church. Dickinson used his prerogative as the outgoing moderator to open the judicatory's meeting with a pointed sermon on I Corinthians 1:10— "Now I beseech you, brethren, by the name of our Lord Jesus Christ, that ye all speak the same thing, and that there be no divisions among you; but that ye be perfectly joined together in the same mind and in the same judgment." The message of Dickinson's sermon was obvious, and to show how it might best be applied to the Synod's current situation, the Elizabethtown pastor proposed a six-part compromise for peace.[5]

Dickinson's scheme demanded concessions from all sides. It asked the Old Lights to withdraw the Cross protestation and reinstate the ejected membership, and it required the New Lights to submit all future complaints against their colleagues through proper channels. With regard to candidates, two paths to Synod membership were allowed. A candidate could either submit to Synod examination or complete a year of study in a New England college. Dickinson knew most New Light candidates refused to be examined by the Synod and were too poor to pay for a year in New England, so he suggested the Synod subsidize the education of needy students. Concerning itinerants, Dickinson suggested that no minister be permitted to refuse another Synod member's request to use his pulpit, but at the same time, itinerants must cease their encouragement of new religious societies within existing communions. Finally, Dickinson proposed that all past differences and debates within the Synod be forgotten and a new petition for reunion be submitted to the ejected brethren.[6]

Despite the evenhandedness of his plan, Dickinson knew the chances of its rejection were high, so he requested the formation of a New York Synod if his overture failed. This new body would contain any members of the Philadelphia Synod and Conjunct Presbyteries who wished to belong, but it would not be a schismatic body. Through an interchange of correspondents the New York and Philadelphia Synod would keep in touch and, thereby, the church would be reunited, albeit in a very informal fashion.[7]

The Synod voted down Dickinson's proposal in its entirety. So a dismayed and angry Jonathan Dickinson joined with three other members of his presbytery to declare they still considered themselves presbyters in the Synod but could not see their way clear ''to sit and act as tho' we were the Synod of Philadelphia'' because they could not condone its treatment of the revivalists.[8]

The Synod avoided responding to this statement and, instead, chose to offer its own terms for the return of the purged New Lights. Their conditions were anything but generous, in that they demanded that the Tennent party renounce its *Apology* of 1740 and submit to the majority's will in all future controversies. The Conjunct Presbyteries were to cease their licensing and ordaining of men without prior Synod examinations and submit to the Synod's scrutiny all men who had already been licensed. Itinerations into other presbyteries, the development of new societies, and the supply of existing churches were to end. The New Lights were not to judge their fellow clergy either publicly or privately, and in the future, they must follow proper procedure in complaining about Synod members. Finally, the Awakeners were asked to reject the principles expressed in Gilbert Tennent's Nottingham sermon and repent the error included therein.[9]

Since these demands amounted to a call for unconditional surrender, the Conjunct Presbyteries refused to comply. Dickinson recognized how unreasonable the conditions were because he immediately gave Tennent permission to reissue his *A Display of God's special Grace*. *A Display* vigorously defended the revivals as a special act of God, but in its first edition Dickinson had kept his authorship anonymous and requested that seven prominent New England clergymen provide its preface. In the reissued edition Dickinson took full responsibility for the publication and had Gilbert Tennent write a new preface.[10]

This act alone indicates how Old Light intransigence had pushed Dickinson into Tennent's welcoming arms. Although Dickinson still harbored serious reservations about the Awakeners' methods, his recent correspondence with Tennent assured him that his misgivings were shared by the New Lights' leader.

The 1743 Synod also convinced the Conjunct Presbyteries that re-union could not be expected in the near future. Therefore, to clarify their purpose and the principles by which they would be governed, the presbyteries issued a *Declaration*. This document affirmed the membership's allegiance to the Westminster Confession as well as their belief that Christ alone was King, head, and lawgiver of the church. It stated that Christ in his threefold capacity had appointed ministers, elders, and deacons to exercise ministerial and executive authority over his people, but he had not thereby surrendered his singular power to create ecclesiastical law. The *Declaration* observed that the limited prerogatives Christ had given the clergy were held equally among them so that all church government should be executed in a "conjunct collegiate" manner by mutual consent.[11]

With regard to worship, the Conjunct Presbyteries declared the triune God the only appropriate object of Christian worship. The Scriptures, they claimed, described the manner in which he was to be worshipped, and his church should not add any human inventions. The presbyteries also accepted the Westminster Directory as a guide for proper worship but cautioned that some of its directions were optional.[12]

Then, in a noteworthy action, the two judicatories approved the use of the Church of Scotland's *Directory for Family Worship* with but one exception. Where their Scottish brethren had discouraged meetings of one or more families at stated times for worship without the presence of clergy, the presbyteries sanctioned such gatherings. This was important because it officially encouraged the formation of New Light conventicles. Tennent and Whitefield had for some time been promoting conferences among the converted for Bible study and prayer, but they and their associates preferred the more traditional label of "family worship" over the European pietists' title of "conventicles."[13]

After outlining the doctrinal and structural aspects of their new fellowship, the Conjunct Presbyteries concluded their statement with a list of four prerequisites for participation in any reunion plan with the Philadelphia Synod. They insisted, first, that the *Protestation* of 1741 be withdrawn; second, the ejected memberships' full rights and privileges be restored; third, the New Lights' grievances against Robert Cross and his co-conspirators be tried before Synod; and fourth, the aforesaid defendants give satisfaction for their "opposition to and reflection upon the Work of God's grace and success of the Gospel in the land."[14]

These conditions were as unrealistic as those set down by the Philadelphia Synod during the same year, but they allowed the revivalists the opportunity to respond in kind to the unreasonable demands of their opponents.

A NEW MINISTRY OF BALANCED PIETY

Their wounded pride having been somewhat salved by this verbal act of revenge, the Conjunct Presbyteries next turned to a far more practical means of damaging their opposition. The New Lights had received a petition from the New Building's congregation in which aid was requested for the preparation of a call to Gilbert Tennent. This, of course, was a very promising development for the Presbyterian Awakeners. Their party had been struggling with the Moravians for control of "Whitefield's church," and this solicitation proved their efforts had been successful. Philadelphia was also a center of Old Light power. Revivalists occasionally preached in the New Building pulpit, but not one of their number pastored full-time to a congregation in the city. Thus, the invitation from Whitefield's followers offered the opportunity of a double coup against the presbyteries' major opponents in the region.[15]

The Awakeners decided to delay action on Tennent's call until the New Brunswick congregation could offer its objections to the move, but in the meantime, it appointed Tennent to supply the Philadelphia church for a period of one month during the early summer.[16]

In August 1743 the Conjunct Presbyteries met, with representatives of the New York Presbytery attending. The presence of the New York clergy signified the assembly's recognition that their pending decisions had far-reaching implications. In addition to the business of the New Building, the Awakeners had to rule on a request from a church in Milford, Connecticut, for admission into their body. If they approved both petitions, the Presbyterian revivalists would be extending their organizational reach far beyond their present borders, and this might be interpreted as blatant intrusion by their northern colleagues. To prevent such a misunderstanding, the presbyteries' leadership wanted all Awakening elements to be involved in the deliberations.[17]

The final outcome of these discussions might have easily been predicted. Tennent's associates could not afford to ignore such opportunities. Therefore, they agreed to send Samuel Finley to Milford and Gilbert Tennent to Philadelphia. Tennent's willingness to go to Philadelphia aided the passage of the New Building's call, but a further consideration was the apparent decline of the New Brunswick pastor's usefulness in his New Jersey parish.[18]

Since the first years of his ministry, Gilbert Tennent had been a more successful evangelist in churches outside his home town. According to one report, "Gilbert Tennent was regarded as a proud, austere man [by his congregation], and . . . had not the affections of the people in the degree that his brother, William, had." It was also alleged that Gilbert "did not build up the church [in New Brunswick] greatly, and when he went to Philadelphia, the people were well content that he should go." It appears, then, that Tennent's severe style of homiletics carried over into his pastoral work, and what was effective for converting sinners, when taken in the small doses of an occasional sermon, became difficult to endure when imbibed on a daily basis.[19]

By sending Tennent to the City of Brotherly Love, the Conjunct Presbyteries hoped that this pattern would not be repeated. Indeed, they anticipated that Tennent's stature as the foremost Awakener in the region would tilt the current battle for the prestigious Philadelphia laity in the New Lights' favor.

Dickinson's growing support of the revivals and the prospect of a new pastorate prompted Tennent to publish an answer to John Hancock's *Examiner* in the summer of 1743. Entitled *The Examiner, Examined; Or Gilbert Tennent, Harmonious*, this work offered a careful modification of Tennent's earlier views based on the concept of balance. Tennent accepted Hancock's caution against extremes. He admitted that some individuals who had been awakened criticized their clergy too

harshly, while those in a state of "deep security" made too little distinction between ministers. Neither of these options were acceptable,
and in their stead Tennent advocated a middle ground where pastors
were neither slighted nor idolized. As for the place of reason and passion
in religion, Tennent conceded that "passion without knowledge and
judgment" was but "vain Fancy." Yet he noted that "knowledge and
judgment without some degree of passion" made of Christianity a "dead
formality."[20]

These words suggest that Tennent now realized balance was the key
to a vibrant but responsible Christian piety. Tennent had learned in his
battles with the Old Lights that reason without emotion made the religious life an empty legal exercise. But the Moravians had shown the
opposite extreme to be no better. Religion without knowledge made the
pious life little more than muddle-headed fool's play. Therefore, Tennent sought a new middle ground between the head and the heart where
the mind informed and tempered the passions, and the passions in turn
fired the soul to pursue a life of faithful piety.

Tennent prepared to leave New Brunswick in the fall of 1743, but
before his departure, he delivered a farewell sermon to the congregation
he had served for nearly seventeen years. His text for the occasion was
taken from the Apostle Paul's parting words to the church at Ephesus:
"Therefore watch, and remember, that by the space of three years I
ceased not to warn every one night and day with tears. And now,
brethren, I commend you to God, and to the word of his grace, which
is able to build you up, and to give you an inheritance among all of
them which are sanctified." Tennent considered these verses especially
appropriate to his situation because he too had risked much to warn the
New Brunswick congregation against sin and, in several instances, had
mixed his warnings with tears of sorrow. Tennent was not so presumptuous as to equate his call to Philadelphia with Paul's summons
to Jerusalem. But he did anticipate that life in his new pastorate would
be as trying as Paul's career had been after his departure from Ephesus.
As he described his future prospects:

I leave this place with no expectation of worldly comfort. Whither I am going
I know by long experience, that the Disciple of Christ must expect every where
to bear his cross, and that through many tribulations we must enter into the
Kingdom of Heaven. I am fully persuaded that change of place and outward

Circumstances, is very often but a change of miserys and little else is to be expected on this side [of] Eternity.[21]

Tennent's expectations did not miss the mark by much, for the events of his first year in Philadelphia were anything but encouraging. Before his first communion in April 1744, the New Building's congregation was reduced in number by a schism. Because Tennent had played a major role in the conflicts between local Moravian and New Light leaders, those members of the church who favored the Unitas Fratrum found his call totally unacceptable. Consequently, they left the New Building as soon as Tennent began his new duties.[22]

Another defection that clouded Tennent's early Philadelphia ministry was that of George Gillespie. Gillespie lost faith in the Awakening when he learned of Whitefield's sympathies for the Moravians. In 1744 he renounced the movement publicly, first by publishing a tract entitled *Remarks Upon Mr. George Whitefield, Proving Him a Man under Delusion*, and second by appearing before the Old Light New Castle Presbytery to repent his former affiliation with the Conjunct Presbyteries. In the latter recantation Gillespie justified the expulsion of the revivalists, denounced Whitefield for his errors, and chastised his former colleagues for supporting their misguided experimental program.[23]

Despite these early setbacks, Tennent's new parishioners witnessed his official installation in November 1744. A short time thereafter, noticeable modifications in Tennent's clothing and practice began to surface. Tennent had acquired a reputation during the early years of the Awakening for wearing a pulpit costume reminiscent of John the Baptist. Dressed in a great coat bound about the waist with a leather girdle and letting his hair hang loose rather than wearing it gathered under a powdered wig, Tennent appeared to his auditors as an eighteenth-century vision of the New Testament prophet of Christ's coming. In Philadelphia, though, Gilbert abandoned his traditional outfit and replaced it with the polished style of polite society.[24]

One possible reason for this change was Gilbert's rather exalted view of city dwellers' social status. Tennent received criticism in later years for an ornate church that his congregation built after they were ejected from the New Building. At the time, he defended the church's stylish embellishments by noting that churches in prestigious locations should reflect their more refined environment. It is likely that Gilbert believed the same was true for urban pastors, and thus he assumed the more cultured accoutrements of his new position.[25]

Tennent's manner of preaching also changed after his move to Pennsylvania's capital. Contemporary observers noticed that the New Building's pastor became increasingly dependent upon sermon manuscripts in the pulpit. Tennent probably used notes before 1744, but he customarily departed from such aids when the spirit moved him. This gave his rhetoric an animation and fervor similar to that of Whitefield. However, the liveliness of Tennent's oratory diminished significantly after his move to Philadelphia, since he began to read verbatim from full drafts of his homilies.[26]

A clue as to why Tennent altered his practice in this fashion lies in an unpublished essay written late in Tennent's life. In this work Gilbert compared the merits of preaching with notes to the benefits of speaking extemporaneously:

Now that the mode of preaching by notes . . . is generally the best adapted to instruct the mind, . . . in the knowledge of the whole system of truth and Duty, . . . especially in the more sublime and difficult points of the Christian constitution, . . . will appear to any unprejudiced mind; if it be consider'd that a person in his private Studies has an opportunity . . . to exert all the force of his genius in the composition and that not only in respect of the matter but of the form, . . . whereby much is clearly expressed in a little. . . . In the mean tyme, the mode of preaching without notes has peculiar advantages in other respects, and therefore is of excellent use in the church of god, e.g. it is better adapted to command attention, and move the Affections . . . [and] it has a familiarity of address not easie to be initiated in writing, which serves to insinuate experimental and practical Truths into the minds especially of the vulgar.[27]

For Tennent, then, preaching with a manuscript facilitated the communication of complicated doctrinal truths, while impromptu speaking was better suited to convey experimental knowledge.

Tennent once remarked to a friend in Boston that when he first came to Philadelphia, ''there were so many under Soul-sickness in this Place, that my Feet were pain'd with walking from Place to Place to see them.'' By 1744 the situation had changed, for Tennent noted how ''several Persons have lost their religious Impressions and *return'd with the Dog to his Vomit*, and some others have fallen into erronious Sentiments.'' Tennent credited this backsliding to the fact that ''the greater Part of this Place had never had the Benefit of a strict religious Education, and therefore were never well fixed in the thorough knowledge of a *consistent System of Principles*." Tennent believed that none of those who were "well fixed" in such matters had fallen away, so he altered the focus of his ministry. As he put it: "Since I have come *here*, my Labours seem to be chiefly serviceable to instruct and establish [the people] in the great Truths of Religion, and to comfort pious People."[28]

This statement explains a great deal about the new direction of Tennent's Philadelphia pastorate. Tennent had felt in earlier years that conversion was the most pressing need of the local population. Therefore, he adapted his pulpit rhetoric to that goal. For his method Tennent employed a spontaneous style, and in his preaching he highlighted the false hopes of human righteousness. Tennent later discovered, however, that experimental knowledge was not enough to create a steadfast faith. Many who lacked a firm intellectual foundation to their faith surrendered the gains of their conversion either by returning to sinful old habits or succumbing to Moravian delusions. As a corrective to these errors, Tennent introduced more doctrine into his sermons, and as the content of his preaching changed, so too did his delivery. Carefully outlined notes were required to communicate doctrine. Therefore, Tennent began to compose more complete manuscripts and stuck more closely to his prepared texts while in the pulpit.

Prime examples of the shift in Tennent's subject matter were two publications issued in 1744 and 1745 respectively. The first, entitled *Twenty-Three Sermons Upon The Chief End of Man, the Divine Authority of the sacred Scriptures, The Being and Attributes of God, And the Doctrine of the Trinity*, presented an extended defense of systematic theology. Because "the main Doctrines of Religion, have in a Measure, the Same Relation to Piety in Practice as a Foundation to a Superstructure," it was, said Tennent, "like building a Fabrick in the Air to inculcate the one without having regard to the other. It is doubtless a commanded and Important Duty to be Valiant for the Truth upon the Earth, and to contend for the Faith once deliver'd to the Saints: But how," he asked, "shall we be able to comply with this divine Precept, unless we know the Truths we are to be Zealous for?"[29]

The transformation of Tennent's policy is apparent in this comment. Tennent had used the image of building a "Fabrick in the Air" in former times to explain the error of offering comfort to the laity before digging a deep foundation of conviction with the terrors of the law. Now Tennent substituted "the main Doctrines of Religion" for conviction as the proper foundation to experimental piety.

"The main Doctrines of Religion" that Tennent hoped to instill in his congregation were, in a word, Calvinism. In his *Twenty-Three Sermons* Tennent provided a systematic account of the Calvinist God's nature and man's humble relationship to that deity. In his second published collection, *Discourses On Several Important Subjects*, Tennent offered further Calvinist instruction on justification, the proper use of the moral law, and the necessity of good works after conversion.[30]

The group with which Tennent most often contrasted his views in *Discourses* was the Moravians rather than Presbyterian Old Lights. This too indicates Tennent's altered program. Because of his battles with the Unitas Fratrum, Tennent's opinion of his Presbyterian opponents had improved significantly. John Hancock observed how the Moravians treated Tennent to the bitter fruit that he had once served up to the Old Lights and, as a consequence, he was now more sympathetic to his old foes' fears of theological corruption and spiritual pride.

Tennent himself spoke out against "spiritual pride" in 1744. Noting how it caused "rash judging of other [people's] states and conduct for small matters," Tennent remarked that this malady was not new to the church.

Too much of this unhappy Temper and Practise appear'd for a Time among both the Jewish and Gentile converts, in the Apostolick Days. They judg'd and censur'd one another severely for their different Opinions and Practice about Days and Meats; Bigots on both sides of the Question were very positive and Fire-hot, yes to such a Degree of uncharitableness, did indiscreet and disproportion'd Zeal, carry those Ignorant but well meaning Zealots; that they not only condemned one anothers States, but were also dispos'd to despise and reject one another out of Church Communion; on the Account of the aforesaid circumstantial Differences.[31]

Tennent's interest in the early church conflicts of Jewish and Gentile Christians increased over time. Indeed, Tennent began to view these controversies as paradigmatic of the current differences in his own communion and perhaps prescriptive of a solution to the schism. Tennent remained unwilling to admit his party was guilty of overweening pride, nor would he suggest that his colleagues had been responsible for the schism, but he saw that his differences with the Philadelphia Synod were minor when compared with his objections to the Moravians. This made Tennent wonder whether Old and New Light Presbyterians had committed the same error that early Jewish and Gentile converts had fallen into during the first century. That is, they had destroyed their holy fellowship because of "circumstantial Differences."

DIPLOMATIC SUCCESSES

Many in Tennent's new congregation perceived the transformation in their minister as a return to "old Presbyterianism," but the New York Presbytery found his new approach a welcome change. The censorious attitude of the New Lights had always been a stumbling block to cooperation. Therefore, when it began to dissipate, the two groups moved to reunite.[32]

The continued obstinacy of the Philadelphia Synod contributed significantly to this alliance as well. Jonathan Dickinson, John Pierson, and Ebenezer Pemberton asked the Synod in 1745 to formulate an overture that would remove the grounds of difference between their presbytery and the Synod. The committee assigned this task produced, however, a measure that duplicated the uncompromising demands of three years previous. This led Dickinson and company to request the establishment of a synod in New York which would "consult and act in mutual concern" with its Philadelphia counterpart. Their petition received the following grudging approval:

Though we judge they [the New York Presbytery] have no just ground to withdraw from us, yet seeing they propose to erect themselves into a Synod at New York, and now desire to do this in the most friendly manner possible, we declare, if they or any of them do so, we shall endeavor to maintain charitable and Christian affections toward them, and show the same upon all occasions by such correspondence and fellowship, as we shall think duty, and consistant with a good conscience.[33]

Before the New York clergy could act upon this rather equivocal permission to form their own synod, events conspired to make Tennent even more amenable to participating in their new venture. Gilbert Tennent had the peculiar misfortune of being hit by lightning on July 14, 1745, while working in his study. The best account of this curious episode comes from Charles Brockden, a local Moravian sympathizer and a trustee of the New Building. Writing to Thomas Noble, Brockden reported that "in the Afternoon as Mr. Gilbert Tennent was preparing for his Evening Exercise (as I suppose he being alone above Stairs) a Fire from Heaven fell upon his House, struck him down, tore his Shoes, melted a steel Buckle in one of them and scorched both Feet." Tennent did not hear the thunderclap, which was "very sharp," but the lightning "struck off Bricks from the Chimney, and left other Marks of its Fury in the Floor of the Room. . . . "[34]

It was no accident that a Moravian made special note of this event. The Moravians in Philadelphia interpreted the thunderbolt as a "particular warning" from God against one of their greatest enemies.[35] Within a fortnight their interpretation spread so widely through the Philadelphia community that Tennent was forced to refute the rumor with a sermon. Entitled *All Things come alike to All*, Tennent's homily explained that misfortunes of the sort he had recently experienced were visited upon both the good and the wicked. For the evildoer they represented warnings of impending doom, but for the pious they were God's way of purifying his saints' virtues. Tennent admitted that he did not yet understand the exact meaning of his adversity, but he was certain that it did not signify God's special displeasure with his ministry or the Awakening.[36]

Tennent's "lightning bolt" experience left his body shaken and his reputation singed, but he received an even greater jolt from his friend George Whitefield only a few short months later. Whitefield returned to Philadelphia for a two-week visit in September. During his stay, he called a meeting of the New Building's trustees so that they might vote on "whether the Articles they had sign'd should stand good; and the House be still appropriated to the original Design expressed in those Articles. The vote," according to Jonathan Dickinson, "was carried by Mr. *Whitefield* and the Major Part of the Trustees in the Negative and Mr. *Whitefield* accordingly demanded the keys to the House."[37]

This decision placed Gilbert Tennent in a terrible predicament. Although the board of trustees had been stacked against him from its earliest days, Tennent had been able to thwart their plans to introduce Moravians into the building by reminding them of his close relationship with Whitefield and their pledge to uphold the Calvinist articles of subscription. The 1745 vote destroyed both of these supports and left Tennent expecting the imminent eviction of his congregation.[38]

Since his parishioners had contributed nearly £1000 to the building's construction, more than embarrassment was involved in any eviction. Tennent hoped that his congregation could either collect sufficient funds to buy the structure from the trustees or receive an equitable reimbursement for their substantial investment. Unfortunately, neither of these options proved feasible. Tennent's lay supporters lacked both the financial resources to pay off all the building's contributors and the leverage with Whitefield or the trustees to demand compensation for their outlay.[39]

In the midst of this dilemma, Tennent traveled to Elizabethtown, New Jersey, for the first official meeting of the New York Synod. There his party and the presbytery led by Jonathan Dickinson formulated a "plan and foundation" for their fledgling organization's government. The "plan" reflected the common interests of both groups in one area in particular. The assembled membership supported the individual's right to follow his or her conscience in nonessential matters. So when they collectively approved subscription as a means of insuring future orthodoxy, they also stipulated that enforcement would be guided by the looser conditions of the 1729 Adopting Act. In a similar vein, the Synod decided that all controversial matters would be determined by the majority's will. But anyone who could not "actively concur or pacifically acquiesce" to a particular ruling was not obliged to separate unless the judicatory agreed the matter in question was crucial for the church's well-being.[40]

The "foundation" of the Synod demanded some compromise as well. The New York party's concern for ministerial candidates' educational backgrounds led to the requirement that all applicants for ordination prove their mastery of pastoral and doctrinal knowledge. To placate the Conjunct Presbyterians, however, the new Synod avoided the subject of an examining committee above the level of local presbyteries to test such competency.[41]

Tennent and his associates conceded in turn that they would halt all interference in church affairs outside their jurisdiction. This concession included involvement in the judicial hearings of groups that had separated from a Presbyterian congregation within the Philadelphia Synod's boundaries and providing pulpit supplies. Tennent no doubt found this difficult to accept. For some time he had claimed that the extraordinary character of the awakenings necessitated intrusion into ecclesiastical struggles that normally were not his party's responsibility. Nevertheless, he along with his colleagues surrendered the point to the New York

Presbytery because they now believed a common Presbyterian witness was essential to combat the mindless enthusiasm and disorder that the revivals had unleashed.[42]

The formation of the New York Synod represented an alliance of men whose theology and practice had been molded by the intercontinental ferment of Christian Pietism that had begun among the English Puritans and been refurbished in the Netherlands during the seventeenth and eighteenth centuries. The northern contingent of the new body had absorbed their pietistic orientation from their Puritan parents in New England, while their New Jersey and Pennsylvania colleagues had imbibed their experimental views from the instruction of Theodorus Frelinghuysen and William Tennent, Sr. Because of the differing sources of their Reformed Pietism, disagreements had developed in earlier years that prevented open cooperation. Yet recent conflicts with Old Lights and Moravians had shown both groups that their approaches were far more compatible than different.

Their consolidation of resources proved advantageous to both parties. The two groups that constituted the new synod's membership were already the fastest growing segments of the colonial Presbyterian church, and their formal union only magnified their power and attraction. This fact alone spelled doom for the Philadelphia Synod since the phenomenal growth of the New York Synod in the next decade would force Old Light Presbyterians to modify their objections to the Awakening in order to prevent their party's extinction.

After successfully negotiating an alliance with his fellow churchmen in the north, Tennent turned his attention to the south, where New Light activity was threatened by recent legal actions against Presbyterian revivalists. The first Presbyterian clergyman to bring the Awakening message into Virginia was William Robinson. During the winter of 1742–1743, Robinson traveled through the Shenandoah Valley and along the south side of the James River. Robinson's ministry appealed to many local residents in the Virginia and North Carolina colonies, but the clergy of the Church of England resented his presence. On one occasion, the Anglican establishment used its close connections with Virginia officials to have Robinson arrested for preaching without a license, and in 1743 Robinson was forced to leave the colony for good when rumors began to spread that the authorities planned to jail him again.[43]

John Blair and John Roan succeeded Robinson in Virginia. Roan in particular created quite a stir in Hanover County with his inflammatory rhetoric. As one early historian has described the young man, Roan had "the warmth and deep earnestness of Robinson and Blair, with less prudence and caution; . . . He spoke freely of the parish ministers; publicly and privately, inveighed against their delinquency in morals, and their public ministrations; and turned the ridicule and scorn of his hearers against the teachers appointed and supported by law.''[44] These actions led the Anglican Church to ask for Roan's head. The governor of Virginia, Sir William Gooch, had promised to protect the Presbyterians in Hanover, but Roan's excesses so disgusted him that he urged the revivalist's indictment by a grand jury. Roan's supporters in Hanover sent four delegates to request the Conjunct Presbyteries' intercession. The presbyteries agreed and appointed Gilbert Tennent and Samuel Finley to draft and deliver the plea for their associate's acquittal. Tennent and Finley arrived in Williamsburg just in time for Roan's trial in October. They were met cordially by Gooch and, eventually, managed to get Roan's indictment dropped.[45]

MOVES TO RECONCILE FRIEND AND FOE

Upon his return to Philadelphia, Tennent's life returned to normal until his father's death in May 1746. The old man's health had been deteriorating for some time, so his demise could not have been a surprise. Yet it still was a blow to the Presbyterian Awakeners since William Tennent, Sr., had been a father and tutor to most of them.[46]

Within weeks of the elder Tennent's death, George Whitefield returned to Philadelphia. This time the English evangelist's reentry into the middle colonies was not welcomed by his former associates. Whitefield's part in the revocation of the New Building articles the previous year had been final confirmation to Presbyterian revivalists that Whitefield was a deluded Moravian.

Whitefield held several meetings with Tennent during his stay. Exactly what transpired in these conferences is unknown, but it is clear that Whitefield agreed to declare publicly his opposition to Moravian doctrine. This act was the price that Gilbert Tennent exacted for his endorsement of Whitefield. Whitefield needed Tennent's personal guarantee that he was orthodox to redeem his reputation with Presbyterian New Lights.[47] So he yielded to Tennent's demands, and for his reward, Tennent composed a preface to Whitefield's next colonial publication, entitled *Five Sermons*. Gilbert acknowledged that his friend had made "some exceptionable, unguarded Expressions" in some of his former writings. Yet Tennent dismissed these errors for two reasons. First, he considered them to be the unfortunate effects of Whitefield's young years, strong passions, Arminian education, and frenzied schedule. And second, he noted that even Luther, if "put upon the Rack by ingenious Pens, and not compared with other Passages in the same . . . would appear in a Sable Dress, and might easily be burlesqued." Therefore, Tennent advised his readers to give Whitefield the benefit of the doubt in the future, for he was now convinced of Whitefield's orthodoxy. Indeed, he declared that if Whitefield did "not preach the Gospel of Christ . . . it is not in the Bible."[48]

This high praise for Whitefield must have reminded many middle colony residents of earlier days when the two men had worked as a team to promote the Awakening. Yet they could not have missed two subtle changes in the revivalists' relationship. Whitefield had been considered in former years the premier spokesman for the experimental cause and Tennent was his "man Friday." As such, Tennent acquired his notoriety and status from his association with Whitefield. Now the tables had been turned, though, and Tennent's imprimatur certified Whitefield's orthodoxy and character.

Tennent's attitude toward Whitefield's critics had changed as well. Formerly Tennent would have defended Whitefield's every opinion, but now he openly confessed his English friend's shortcomings. Tennent concluded his preface with this accommodating note to those who had always been less taken with Whitefield than he: "I doubt not, but divers who have opposed both the Reverend Mr. *Whitefield* and myself have had a pious and honest Intention in so doing.—I only beg leave to express my own Opinion with all due Deference to such as are otherwise minded."[49] The opinionated belligerence of Tennent's Nottingham sermon is nowhere to be found in this statement, but the toll of recent disappointments over the cause he had championed is clearly evident. Tennent's moderate rhetoric signaled his readiness to make peace with Old Light Presbyterians so long as both sides accorded their former foes the benefit of the doubt.

During the latter half of the 1740s, Tennent's ministry in the New Building gave his enemies very little cause for insult. A survey of his extant sermons shows that Tennent focused his preaching on three subjects—doctrine, politics, and ecclesiastical peace. With regard to doctrine, Tennent added little to what he had preached and published during his first two years in Philadelphia. From the spring of 1746 until his death in 1764, Tennent reused old sermons with increasing regularity. This practice caused his contemporaries to observe that the power of Tennent's pulpit oratory diminished precipitously after his move to Pennsylvania.[50]

Tennent also became deeply involved in the move to establish a private militia in Pennsylvania. When Great Britain declared war against France and Spain in 1744, the governor of Pennsylvania requested contributions from his Assembly for the defense of British North America. The Quaker-dominated Assembly refused to provide money for the procurement of guns or munitions, and its debates over the issue convinced all knowledgeable observers that the Quakers would never approve the formation of a state-supported militia in the colony. In 1747 Benjamin Franklin proposed a privately funded voluntary militia, or "Association for Defense." He directed his appeals for support to Pennsylvania's Irish and Scottish settlers on the frontier, who were, for the most part, Presbyterian. Because their homes were most vulnerable to attack, the Presbyterian laity accepted Franklin's plan.[51]

Tennent had discussed colonial politics from the pulpit on only two occasions prior to 1747. In April 1744 the victory of a British fleet in the Mediterranean led him to preach on *The Necessity of Thankfulness for Wonders of divine Mercies*. Tennent narrated a long sequence of God's "past Mercies . . . for the Protestant Church in general and the British Zion in particular." The recent triumph in the Mediterranean, he claimed, was but the latest example of God's historic protection of his children and, as in previous cases, deserved a special expression of thanksgiving from local Christians. Tennent communicated a similar idea in 1745 when he spoke on the French defeat at Louisburg. In this sermon, *The Necessity of praising God for Mercies receiv'd*, Tennent suggested that a "good plan," "discreet Conduct," and "intrepid Courage" had contributed to the victory, but it was God ultimately who had "directed," "spirited," and "conducted" the British forces to their success.[52]

Although these sermons were promilitary, they did not involve Tennent personally in colonial squabbles over provisions for Pennsylvania's defense. The Association movement was another matter. On December 24, 1747, Tennent preached his first homily in support of the Association. Speaking in the same building in which the militia had been organized, Tennent presented an extended treatment of Christian "just war'' theory. Offensive wars were evil in any circumstances, according to Tennent, but defensive wars were morally acceptable so long as "the Cause is just, the Authority encouraging it legal, the Design honest and honorable, and the Manner of prosecuting it warrantable, and agreeable to the unalterable Laws of Humanity.'' Defensive wars came in three varieties—those against an unjust invasion of one's person or estates, those seeking to recover something of great value that had been taken unjustly, and those undertaken by the magistrate for the punishment of some wrong that affected the credit or interest of a nation or a people.[53]

With the material prerequisites for a just martial defense fully explained, Tennent went on to discuss the necessary spiritual preparations for battle. Military actions were "necessary and excellent in their Place,'' Tennent observed, but they would not "be crown'd with Success, except we look above them to *God* for the Direction and Assistance; except we repent of our Sins, and reform our Lives!'' Consequently, Tennent called upon the people to end their frequent swearing and Sabbath breaking and asked that the magistrates enforce a colony-wide moral reform. By such moral improvement Tennent claimed he and his neighbors would gird themselves with an impregnable armor superior to any temporal weapon.[54]

Tennent's promotion of the Association prompted a Quaker rebuttal which, in turn, caused Tennent to preach and print two further sermons on the necessity of defensive war. The claims and counterclaims of this argument are not so important for our purposes as the consequences of the debate on the Presbyterian schism. For the first time in many years, Old and New Light Presbyterians found themselves on the same side of an issue. Both groups promoted the moral reformation that was to support the martial efforts of the Pennsylvania Association for Defense, and their common interest became a bridge for rapprochement between the two Presbyterian constituencies. The need for a militia would become a more pressing necessity in the 1750s, and at that time both camps of Presbyterian clergy would resume their call for ethical and martial preparations for war. In the process, their differences over experimental knowledge, church government, and clerical discipline would be sufficiently overshadowed to allow an ecclesiastical reunion.[55]

A move toward accommodation with his old enemies was already evident in Tennent's pulpit rhetoric by the late 1740s, when Tennent spoke to his New Building congregation about the character of Christian brotherly love. Tennent believed the laws of nature and the example of

Jesus Christ demanded such affection within the Christian community. But he cautioned that love, like faith, was constantly tried by spiritual desertions, offenses in conduct, and differences in sentiment about the circumstantial points of religion.[56]

Of the first, Tennent remarked that the children of God who suffered long under spiritual desertions often exhibited a less "edifying conversation." They were like a tree in winter that appears quite dead for lack of leaves and verdure. Beginners in the faith frequently looked contemptuously upon such abandoned individuals, censuring them as fallen Christians. Yet Tennent warned that this was both misguided and cruel, for any mature Christian who had endured his or her own "broken bones" in the faith recognized these ordeals as temporary.[57]

Tennent also noted that Satan frequently urged humanity to impute a bad design to any insult. By this method he divided the body of Christ. Tennent advised his parishioners to regard offenses as the consequences of "inadvertancy or mistake or some violent temptation." This would soften the impact of the affront, promote peace within the church, and allow a perfect imitation of the Savior's forgiving spirit.[58]

Tennent suggested that "we should allow to another the same *Liberty* we take ourselves, and consider that *Men* can't alter their Opinions, or retain them according to their Neighbours Pleasure; but must think and believe as Things appear to them from Time to Time." Since "we are bid to *grow in Knowledge*, as well as in *Grace*; we may, by the Increase of Light, be oblig'd to change our *Sentiments* in some *circumstantial Points*, and to need others Charity and *Forbearance* towards us: . . . why, then," asked Tennent, "should we not express . . . [the same charity] towards them?"[59]

The mistake of not extending such tolerance to one's fellows had been made in apostolic times by both Jewish and Gentile Christians. Yet Paul advised "the strong *Gentile* to receive the weak *Jew* to . . . Church-Fellowship, tho' [he was] in some circumstantial *Errors*; and not [to] trouble and plague him with *doubtful Disputations*, or *Debates* about lesser Things, which are comparatively doubtful." Assuming the role of Paul, Tennent advised the same in his own day.[60]

By offering this counsel Tennent perhaps revealed as much about his own recent "Increase of Light" as he did about the Christian Gospel. His remarks on the three trials of brotherly love were the hard-won lessons of his Awakening career. Tennent had been too quick to censure those who lacked the overt signs of grace in the early days of the

Awakening. He had interpreted every offense in the worst possible light, and he had not recognized that toleration was a two-way street. Now he knew better, and he intended to take a different posture toward his former opponents.

A PLEA FOR PEACE IN JERUSALEM

This new policy expressed itself concretely in a series of proposals that he and three other ministers from the New York Synod submitted to the Philadelphia Synod in 1749. Taken together, the suggested measures represented a plan for reunion in five brief articles. The first declared that all names of distinction should be abolished forever to preserve the common peace of a union. The second made subscription to the Westminster standards a prerequisite for membership and left the terms of that subscription negotiable. The third proposed that all decisions of the united synod be made by a majority and anyone who could not obey for conscience' sake should withdraw if the synod agreed that the point of controversy was essential for orthodoxy. The fourth article made all congregations in the two synods members of the reunited church, and the fifth stipulated that no member could accuse another publicly until formal charges were tried by a regular judicatory.[61]

These overtures were most noteworthy for what they did not say. That is, they lacked the customary New Light demands for a retraction of the 1741 *Protestation* and satisfaction for the Old Lights' past opposition to the revivals. There can be no doubt that Tennent and his associates still desired such concessions, but by 1749 they were willing to subordinate their personal desires to the greater goal of church unity.

In order to encourage both synods to accept this plan, Tennent published the strongest plea for peace of his career in 1749. Entitled *Irenicum Ecclesiasticum, Or A Humble Impartial Essay Upon The Peace of Jerusalem*, the work maintained that the present divisions were a scandal to the church's witness. Tennent admitted that for some time he had been troubled by this fact, but he had bided his time in speaking directly to the issue until he knew the opinion of his brethren. He was gladdened by the sympathetic reception of the Philadelphia Synod to the recent overture for peace, but he realized the proposal had occasioned some uneasiness within his own party.[62]

The views expressed by Tennent in *Irenicum Ecclesiasticum* were markedly different from those he proclaimed at the height of the Awakening. Tennent suggested that the opposing sides of the schism had never really disagreed on the substance of the points debated, "viz, the nature and necessity of Conversion." Instead, their controversy revolved around "circumstantials" among which he now included the ability and authority to judge the inward experience of those who sought membership in the church or a place at the communion table. Division over such matters were, according to Tennent, both scandalous and absurd since these issues were small in comparison with the need for peace and unity in the body of Christ.[63]

In contrast to his earlier opinions, Tennent also declared that love, not conversion, was the "badge and cognizance of our Discipleship, the visible Mark of Distinction, between those that profess Christianity, and those that do not. . . . Love, my Brethren, is the LIVERY which the *King* of the *Church* has appointed his Subjects and Servants to wear, that thereby They may manifest to others, who They belong to, [and] who is their Prince and Master." Tennent warned those who opposed a reunion with the Old Lights that "our *Profession* of, and *Stature* in *Christianity*, is to be measured by our *Love*; the Reality of the former by the Sincerity of it; and the *Progress* of the latter by the *Degree* of it." Thus, "while Persons have but little *love* for Those that differ from Them in smaller Things, and are inclined to fierce Controversies, strong Prejudices, *Schisms* and *Factions*, about circumstantial Matters, it is a *Sign* they have learned but little of the *Gospel* of CHRIST, and are of small *Stature* in Christianity."[64]

Tennent acknowledged that immaturity in the faith was not the only reason for the current misgivings about reunion. The zeal of many of his friends for the church's purity also obstructed the path to reconciliation. Tennent did not wish to destroy this admirable concern, but he cautioned that zeal was only "excellent and advantageous, when directed by *Knowledge* and Discretion, temper'd with *Humility*, *Meekness* and *Mercy*, and proportioned in *Degree* to the Importance of Things."[65]

Tennent knew all too well the potential hazards of untempered zeal. Earlier in his ministry he had depended upon the white-hot fervor of his newborn converts to cleanse the church of its tares. More recently Tennent had himself been burned by the overheated enthusiasm of James Davenport in New England and the Moravians in the middle colonies. He discovered at that time that balance was the key to the church's survival. His first attempt at formulating such a balance had been included in his reply to Hancock's *Examiner*. It consisted of only two elements, knowledge to inform piety and zeal to motivate piety. By 1749 Tennent believed it was necessary to add a new factor to the mixture, that being love. His reasons for this alteration were simple. "*Knowledge* without *Love* is cold and ineffectual like the Light of the Moon: And *Zeal* without *Love* is like a fierce Flame, which scorches and devours all before it. But Knowledge and Zeal, with Love, are like the Light of the Sun which yields a gentle, warming, refreshing and fruitful Influence."[66] Love, then, was the cement that harmoniously joined knowledge and zeal in the same human heart, and Tennent hoped that it would likewise reunite Old and New Light Presbyterians into the same body of Christ.

DENOUEMENT TO A CONTENTIOUS CAREER: CONSOLIDATION, REFORMATION, REUNION, AND REJECTION

Although Gilbert Tennent had decided by 1749 that the Presbyterian schism must be ended, a formal reconciliation took nine long years to effect. Two factors caused this delay. First, the scars left by earlier Awakening conflict were still too fresh for either side to forgive or forget, and second, the New York Synod lacked the numerical strength to force compromise on its Old Light opponents. Time and the formation of the College of New Jersey provided the solutions to both of these impediments, but they were aided by the unexpected appearance of a common enemy who diverted the attention of both parties from their former differences.

Gilbert Tennent's career mirrored this denouement to the Awakening experience, since he spent the last twenty-five years of his ministry pacifying tensions within his divided communion, procuring a sound financial base for the New Jersey college, and promoting moral reformation in the midst of the French and Indian War. Ironically, these constructive activities signaled the end of Tennent's leadership in the Awakening, since each task distracted him from his earlier single-minded advocacy of experimental piety. Tennent never entirely surrendered his allegiance to revivals and rebirth, but his new projects so altered his practice that his own parishioners attempted to replace him in the pulpit with a young man who still burned with the experimental fire.

AN AWAKENING CONGREGATION ASSUMES
PRESBYTERIAN AIRS

A process was set in motion during the late 1740s whereby Gilbert Tennent was disassociated from the primary symbol of the Awakening in Philadelphia. In 1745 Tennent had predicted that his congregation would be evicted from the New Building because of the trustees' decision to revoke Whitefield's articles of subscription. His prediction proved only partially accurate, since eviction did come but four years after he expected it and as a result of financial rather than theological difficulties.

The death of Thomas Noble left a seat vacant on the trustee board in 1746, and Benjamin Franklin was chosen as Noble's replacement. Franklin recalled in his autobiography that he was selected because of his honesty and neutrality on sectarian matters, but an equally important contributor to his election was the building's accumulating debts. The trustees had been unable to collect enough contributions in recent months to pay off their "ground rent" and construction costs so they needed a figure with Franklin's connections to help them through their monetary crisis.[1]

Franklin solved the trustees' problems in a fashion his new associates had probably not expected. In 1748 Franklin began to ponder the possibility of establishing an academy in Philadelphia. Before presenting his plan to the public, he approached the trustees about the academy's taking over their facilities. Franklin's proposal was attractive because he agreed that the school should accept full responsibility for the New Building's outstanding debts, and he promised to allow clergymen from all denominations to continue preaching on the premises. This permitted the trustees to solve their fiscal embarrassment while at the same time preserving the building's original purpose.[2]

A decision to accept Franklin's offer necessitated the relocation of Gilbert Tennent's congregation. The trustees notified Tennent and his parishioners on January 25, 1749, that they could continue to use the building for worship until they found another home. In February a committee of the church bought a lot on the northwest corner of Arch and Third streets, but construction was delayed because the congregation's resources were too meager to finance a new structure.[3]

During the weeks and months that followed, Tennent conducted a one-man campaign to solicit the necessary funds. His first stop was

Benjamin Franklin's printing shop. Franklin refused to help Tennent, but he did offer some free advice as to the best method of seeking contributions. The Philadelphia businessman advised Tennent to "apply [first] to all those whom you know will give something; next to those whom you are uncertain whether they will give anything or not; and show them the list of those who have given: and lastly, do not neglect those who you are sure will give nothing; for in some of them you may be mistaken."[4] Tennent followed this counsel to the letter. His solicitations did not always go smoothly because of opposition from his enemies in Philadelphia, but his efforts were rewarded in the end.[5]

In June 1752 Tennent preached for the first time in his new church. Speaking on *The Divine Government over all considered*, he praised God for overseeing the funding and construction of the new meeting-house.[6] There was great cause for thanksgiving because the contributions that Tennent had received far outstripped his original expectations. Consequently, the Second Presbyterian Church, known locally as the Arch Street Church, was both spacious and ornate.[7]

Some of Second Presbyterian's patrons expressed anger over the way the congregation had used donations to build such an elaborate building, but Tennent answered these criticisms by noting that their gifts had been offered for a house of God. According to Tennent, structural embellishments were a pious tribute to God rather than the superfluous extravagances of vain men. Tennent also remarked that the location of the church necessitated a grandiose edifice. As he put the argument, "It appears to me reasonable in itself, and creditable to societies, that in *Cities* where there is a greater Resort of Persons of Honour, Distinction, and polite Taste; The Structures of a religious Kind, should be adorned with greater Beauty and exactness, then in obscurer Places."[8]

These remarks temporarily silenced local complaints, but similar objections were raised only a year later when the congregation held a lottery to pay for a steeple. The steeple lottery made popular in Philadelphia society a satirical couplet which stated:

> The Presbyterians built a church, and fain would have a steeple;
> We think it may become the *church*, but not become the people.[9]

Whatever airs the new Arch Street Church motivated in its congregation, it is evident from the parish records that it was part of a process whereby Tennent's flock became more self-consciously Presbyterian.

When Tennent had accepted the New Building pastorate, he assumed responsibility for a denominationally mixed group of laypeople. Preaching rather than ecclesiastical allegiances had attracted the membership, and before Tennent's call in 1743, no effort had been made to organize the congregation's collective life. During his first six years in Philadelphia, Tennent tried to remedy this situation by introducing presbyterian government and worship. Tennent established a consistory of deacons and elders, formulated procedures for electing officers, enforced church discipline, and placed communion services on a quarterly schedule.[10]

This provided a rudimentary structure for Tennent's laity, but by 1751 the church still had not declared its ecclesiastical affiliation. Technically the membership worshipped under the ecumenical conditions laid down in the New Building's indenture so long as it resided in the house that Whitefield's followers had built. This restriction no longer applied, however, when the congregation moved to Arch Street. In preparation for the relocation, a "Declaration of Trust" was composed and entered into the official minutes. This document openly proclaimed the Presbyterian pedigree of the Arch Street communion. It stated that the new church and its property were to be used by the "Congregation or People call'd PRESBYTERIANS forever who do or shall hold & Continue to hold & Conform to all the Essential Articles of the Westminister Confession of Faith & Directory agreeable to the Present Interpretation of the Synod of New York to which they are now united. . . . "[11]

This self-identification with Presbyterianism represented a significant change in the predilections of the Second Presbyterian Church and its pastor. Tennent and his parishioners now sought to clarify their status both socially (through their impressive church structure) and ecelesiastically (through their church order) and, in the process, they retreated from the open ecumenical cooperation so characteristic of their evangelical relations at the height of the Awakening. These actions did not immediately contribute to Presbyterian reunion since the Arch Street congregation still promoted an experimental ministry, but it aided reconciliation indirectly since the church's new concern to present a visible Presbyterian witness in Philadelphia coincided with the interests of conservative Old Lights.

RIVAL EFFORTS AT ESTABLISHING A SEMINARY

Another influential factor in the reunification of the divided Presbyterian communion was the very different experiences of the Philadelphia Synod and its New Light offspring in creating a college for the education of ministerial candidates in the 1750s. Presbyterian Old Lights had for some time lobbied for stricter educational standards. In 1734 they had urged all presbyteries to examine the proficiency of applicants for ordination in such areas as natural and moral philosophy, theology, and literature. Then in 1736 they established a Synod committee to test the qualifications of privately educated candidates prior to their presbytery examinations. When the Awakeners foiled their efforts to enforce more rigid requirements, the Old Lights tried to establish a seminary. John Thomson asked the Donegal Presbytery in 1739 to present an overture to Synod for such a project. The Synod approved the proposal and appointed a committee to pursue the matter.[12]

King George's War and the controversy surrounding the schism postponed action on the seminary until 1744, when the Philadelphia Synod took Francis Alison's academy in New London, Pennsylvania, under its care. For his services as the school's master, Alison was exempted from all public business in the Synod and allotted a salary of £20 per annum. Eleven trustees were appointed to oversee Alison's conduct, the academy's curriculum, and the examinations of students who had completed their prescribed course of study.[13]

Even though the New London school still lacked an official charter in 1746, the Philadelphia Synod expected formal recognition would be forthcoming, and while awaiting certification, the Old Lights consulted Thomas Clap to arrange an informal relationship with Yale College. The Synod explained in a letter to Clap the nature of its past disputes with the Tennent party over education, how a schism had resulted from that conflict, and the reasons for the New York Presbytery's departure from their association. It also described the current state of Alison's academy and the good prospects of its receiving governmental sanction. Picturing itself as the only local champion of ecclesiastical order and theological probity, the Synod then asked Clap to support their cause by overlooking slight deficiencies in its candidates when he examined them for admission to Yale.[14]

Unfortunately for the Philadelphia Synod, Clap turned a deaf ear to their plea for help and, worse yet, the New London academy lost its prestigious tutor in 1752. The funds for Alison's salary were to be collected by a yearly solicitation in the judicatory's congregations, but sufficient funds were never available. Therefore, when Alison received an offer to become the rector of the new Philadelphia Academy in 1751–

1752, he accepted the post without consulting the Synod. This led to Alison's being officially reprimanded for unilaterally leaving his charge. Alison was not disciplined, however, because he planned to arrange a deal whereby Old Light candidates could receive their education at the academy. Alison's negotiation in the Synod's behalf never achieved their intended goal, so as a substitute the Synod appointed Alexander McDowell to replace his former mentor at New London.[15]

As the Old Lights struggled to establish an educational facility for the training of new ministers, the Awakeners set to work on a similar project. The revival party's need for such an institution was brought home with special force immediately after the schism when seventeen different congregations in New Jersey, Pennsylvania, Delaware, Maryland, and Virginia presented the ejected brethren with petitions for pulpit supplies.[16]

The Conjunct Presbyteries made no effort to create a new school that might replace the Log College of William Tennent, Sr. But Dickinson and his associates in the New York Presbytery were more farsighted. As soon as they decided to leave the Philadelphia Synod, Dickinson and three other New York clergymen began formulating a plan for a chartered college in the province of New Jersey. They realized that the failing health of William Tennent, Sr., jeopardized the survival of the Log College and that Harvard and Yale could not be trusted to teach future candidates the importance of experimental religion.

The authorities at Yale and Harvard had opposed the Awakening when it came to New England, and at Yale, in particular, students awakened by the revival call had been disciplined severely. After Gilbert Tennent's visit to New Haven in March 1741, several young men were fined for following Tennent to Milford, Connecticut, to hear him preach again. In November 1741 David Brainerd was expelled from Yale for stating in a private conversation that one of his tutors had no more grace than a chair, and during Christmas 1744 two more scholars were expelled for attending a separatist meeting with their parents.[17]

Lingering fears about their new associates also may have motivated the New York Presbytery's move to establish a college.[18] Throughout the early Synod battles over candidate examinations, the New York Presbytery had allied itself with the antirevival subscriptionists. The presbytery did not oppose the Tennent party's pietistic orientation. Instead, they sympathized with the Awakener's emphasis on practical piety because of their own Puritan backgrounds. But the New York clergy were concerned that the revivalists' attacks upon ''Pharisee-Teachers'' and empty ''head knowledge'' would lead to a rejection of a learned ministry. Gilbert Tennent's letter to Dickinson in February 1742 dispelled some of these misgivings, but the decision to unite with the Tennent party after the schism moved Dickinson's party to seek concrete assurances that learning would remain a high priority within the Awakening camp.

Before consulting Gilbert Tennent or any of the excluded brethren, Jonathan Dickinson, John Pierson, Ebenezer Pemberton, Aaron Burr, and three prominent laymen from New York sought an official charter for a college in New Jersey. Their original plan was to keep the college firmly in the hands of New Light Presbyterians, but they realized that the Anglican governor of New Jersey, Lewis Morris, would not approve the creation of a dissenter seminary. Therefore, they based their petition for recognition on the broader principles of the Fundamental Concessions that had been signed by the proprietors of New Jersey in 1664. Since this document had promised religious freedom to all New Jersey residents, the proposed college was to provide an education to young men of all denominations.[19]

After soliciting sufficient contributions to show the local population would support such a school, the seven Presbyterians approached Morris with their charter. Morris, however, withheld his approval because he feared reprisals from the Anglican Bishop of London.[20]

The New Lights' attempt to create a college might have ended there had Morris remained in power. But Morris died suddenly in May 1746 and John Hamilton replaced him in the governor's office. Hamilton was also an Anglican, but he was old and sick and depended heavily upon his advisors, who happened to be major contributors to the college project.[21]

Hamilton's counselors persuaded him to sign the charter on October 22, 1746. The seven organizers of the plan became the institution's first trustees and were delegated the task of choosing five more men to serve in the same capacity. Their choice was almost a foregone conclusion. The New York Presbytery had allied itself with the Tennent party in the Synod of New York, and of course the leaders of the Conjunct Presbyteries controlled a large following in the Pennsylvania-New Jersey area. Therefore, their support was essential for the new institution's long-term survival.[22]

In March 1747 Jonathan Dickinson traveled to Philadelphia to enlist

Gilbert Tennent, William Tennent, Jr., Samuel Blair, Richard Treat, and Samuel Finley as trustees of the College of New Jersey. Because the Log College had by now died with William Tennent, Sr., and because the academies of Blair and Finley could not hope to provide the quality of education or the number of candidates that the proposed college could, all five men accepted Dickinson's offer.[23]

Gilbert Tennent had his own personal reasons for putting his prestige behind the school. Despite his reputation, Tennent had never been opposed to an educated clergy. In his battles with the Presbyterian Old Lights over the qualifications of candidates, he had only rejected the notion that book learning was sufficient to qualify a man for the ministry.[24]

Tennent had tried to balance the Old Light's overemphasis on formal training by stressing experimental knowledge during his early ministry. But this inadvertently left him open to promoting uneducated lay exhorters in New England and Moravian sympathizers in the middle colonies. Once Tennent realized that he too had been guilty of exaggeration, he moved gradually toward the New York party's middle-of-the-road approach. He therefore welcomed the opportunity to promote a higher level of doctrinal understanding among the clergy by serving as a trustee for the College of New Jersey, and he regarded the proposed institution as a major step toward neutralizing the evil influence of Awakening "enthusiasm."

Tennent's support of the college quickly dissipated, however, when pressure from colonial dissenters caused the English crown to appoint Jonathan Belcher as the governor of New Jersey in 1747. Belcher had been a fast friend of the Awakening since Whitefield's first tour through New England, and he fiercely opposed the Arminian notions currently being taught at Harvard and Yale. Consequently, local New Lights expected Belcher to provide official encouragement for their new school.[25]

Belcher fulfilled their expectations, but he also created significant dissension when he suggested several modifications in the college's charter. Shrewdly anticipating his political superiors' possible objections, Belcher maintained that the school had a better chance of surviving if the provincial government were more involved in its affairs. He proposed then that the colonial governor be made the permanent chairman of the trustees and at least four other members of the provincial council be included on the board.[26]

Gilbert Tennent accepted Belcher's appointment to the trustees because of his sympathy for the New Lights' cause, but he questioned whether future political officials would be so favorably disposed to experimental religion. If not, Tennent believed Belcher's plan might lead to a radical shift in the college's policy. Jonathan Edwards later reported that it was feared Tennent would withdraw from the trustees because of this issue. Belcher also understood that Tennent opposed his proposal, so he attempted to answer Tennent's objections in a letter written after a second charter had been approved.[27]

Belcher's views were incorporated into the new charter with only slight modifications. In the document that the governor signed on September 14, 1748, only one of the original trustees was removed from the board's roster and eleven more members were added. The new trustees included important laymen from Pennsylvania, several members of the provincial council, the governor, and a few new Presbyterian ministers. The overall number of Log College men was reduced, but the clergy still outnumbered the laymen. This apparently placated Gilbert Tennent sufficiently to keep him on the board.[28]

TENNENT'S CONTRIBUTION TO THE COLLEGE OF NEW JERSEY

The College of New Jersey faced two major difficulties once its articles of incorporation had been set on a sound political footing. One problem involved the presidency. During the first twenty years of the college's existence, five different men served in this capacity. All of these individuals died suddenly, and three of them expired within the span of thirty-six months. As a result, the trustees were constantly occupied with the business of electing or negotiating for a new leader for their institution.[29]

Gilbert Tennent participated in these recurring elections, but he was far more involved in finding a solution to the second troublesome problem of the college. Although the school had been initiated by New Light Presbyterians, the New York Synod's finances were spread too thin by its numerous missionary activities to provide sufficient funds for the college's operation.[30]

The trustees tried to fill this gap through alternative sources of income such as private donations and public lotteries. The New Jersey legislature prohibited lotteries for any purpose in 1748, but college authorities

attempted to persuade the assembly to exempt their institution from this
blanket prohibition since students coming into the colony would bring
financial profit to the region. This effort proved unsuccessful, so the
trustees organized lotteries in Pennsylvania and Connecticut instead.
These produced the intended new revenue, but legal opposition from
Pennsylvania Old Lights minimized the potential assets.[31]

On at least two occasions between 1749 and 1751, Gilbert Tennent
received private inheritances for the college, and in 1750 Tennent and
Richard Treat settled the affairs of the school's lottery in Pennsylvania.
But Gilbert Tennent's greatest service to the New Light institution came
in 1753 when he and Samuel Davies traveled to Great Britain to seek
contributions.[32]

George Whitefield reported to Ebenezer Pemberton in November
1748 that he had solicited donations for the New Jersey College in
Scotland, but he felt that nothing of great note could be accomplished
there unless Pemberton or "some other popular minister come over,
and make an application in person." He therefore urged Pemberton to
make arrangements for a journey to Great Britain and suggested that
he bring along an Indian student to highlight the fact that the New Jersey
College would educate awakened American aborigines.[33]

Pemberton had just completed a trip to New England for the college
and did not believe that another absence would be accepted by his
congregation, so he proposed that Gilbert Tennent make the voyage.
Whitefield's response indicated that Pemberton could do a better job,
although Whitefield acknowledged that Tennent could "do much for
New-Jersey college."[34]

By October 1750 the trustees had still not sent a representative to the
mother country, so Whitefield wrote Governor Belcher to beg him to
send either Pemberton or Aaron Burr, the college's new president, since
he was certain "liberal contributions" could be raised in both England
and Scotland. When no one appeared by December 1752, an exasperated
Whitefield wrote to Belcher again. This time he declared that a "favorable opportunity" had been lost the past summer and fall.[35]

Whitefield was unaware of the difficulties that the trustees were having
in finding someone to accept the responsibility of a trip to Great Britain.
In an effort to capitalize on Whitefield's advice in 1750, the trustees
had approved a motion to send Ebenezer Pemberton, but their plan was
frustrated when Pemberton's New York congregation would not permit
its pastor to leave. In Pemberton's place the trustees assigned the task

to Aaron Burr. Burr reluctantly accepted but made his departure conditional on Caleb Smith's assuming his teaching duties at the college. When Smith declined, plans to send Burr collapsed.[36]

Finally, in May 1753 the trustees found two individuals who were able and willing to attempt the mission. They were Samuel Davies and Gilbert Tennent. Davies was the pastor of a church in Hanover County, Virginia. In order to combat the Church of England's legal control over the ecclesiastical life of Virginia, Davies had become a major advocate of religious toleration. He had never been to England, but his efforts in behalf of toleration had forced him to carry on an extensive correspondence with the British dissenting community. These important connections made Davies a potentially excellent solicitor for the college.[37]

Davies was reluctant to undertake the mission for the trustees because he feared for his family and his congregation during his absence. Tennent, on the other hand, probably welcomed the task. Between March and May 1753, Gilbert's wife, Cornelia, and his mother, Katherine, died. As a result, the journey to England offered a much needed diversion from his grief. For the college the value of Tennent's appointment was his name. Tennent was one of the most prominent colonial New Lights, and some of his published works were known in both England and Scotland.[38]

The college asked in October 1753 that the New York Synod appoint Tennent and Davies to make the voyage to Europe. The Synod unanimously approved the request and armed its emissaries with two documents, a certificate proving they were duly appointed representatives and an address requesting financial assistance from the General Assembly of Scotland.[39]

The two revivalists set sail for London on November 18. Before their voyage Tennent and Davies were not close friends. According to Davies' diary of the trip, Tennent took "some offense" at his young associate's conduct just before the departure because he considered him "too forward and assuming." This initial coolness melted away, however, with more frequent contact and Tennent's solicitous care of Davies during their journey. While on board ship Davies suffered terribly from seasickness and a severe toothache. Tennent, on the other hand, remained healthy and ministered to his sick companion in addition to preaching every Sunday to his fellow passengers. Because of Tennent's service to him, Davies came to regard the older man as his "Spiritual Father."[40]

Tennent and Davies arrived in London on Christmas Day, 1753.

According to Davies, Tennent "was extremely low-Spirited and silent" when they disembarked. Shortly thereafter, the two men received an invitation from Whitefield to stay with him during their visit to the English capital, but they decided that "public intercourse" with Whitefield might alienate potential patrons, so they only met with him briefly. Their conversation with Whitefield greatly revived Tennent's spirits, so that when he and Davies returned to their lodging, Davies noted that Tennent's "Heart was all on Fire."[41]

Davies' observation of Tennent's initial depression after reaching London was never explained, but it is likely that Tennent expected a welcome from the populace similar to that accorded Whitefield when he arrived for the first time in the middle colonies. Tennent's ego was subject to the same overweening pride that Whitefield, Zinzendorf, and many of the other great figures of the contemporary American and English revivals on occasion exhibited. Therefore, he could not help but be pained by the indifference of the London community to his entry into their city.

Fortunately, Tennent's contact with Whitefield healed his dampened spirits. Such rejuvenation was needed for the task that lay ahead, for in the next twelve months Tennent and Davies encountered major obstacles to their mission. The first and most persistent barrier to success was the sheer size of their job. For five months the two men remained in London, where they canvassed the entire ecclesiastical leadership for contributions. Then in April they journeyed to Edinburgh, where they presented the petition of the New York Synod to the General Assembly. After a brief stay in Edinburgh, Tennent set out for Glasgow and later Ireland, where he attended the General Synod in Dublin. Meanwhile, Davies traveled through the principal towns of southern Scotland and northeastern England. Tennent rejoined Davies in London during the month of October, and after another four weeks of solicitations, Davies set sail on one ship bound for Virginia while Tennent took another to Philadelphia.

Davies registered in his diary the fatigue visited upon both men by this trying schedule when he wrote:

'Tis an Honour to be employed in public Service; and I have Cause of grateful Joy rather than Complaint. But I never engaged in such a Series of wasting Fatigues and Dangers as our present Mission is attended with . . . I have walked in the tedious, crowded Streets of London from Morning to Evening, 'till my

Nature has been quite exhausted; and I have been hardly able to move a Limb. It was but seldom that I could release myself in Conversation with a Friend by Reason of incessant Hurries: and when I have had an Opportunity, my Spirits have been so spent that I was but a dull Companion.[42]

Besides the physical demands of the tour, the two men's efforts were further complicated by the schizophrenic condition of the English Presbyterian community. By the first half of the eighteenth century, the Presbyterian Church in Great Britain was divided into two opposing camps. The majority were unitarians, although they continued to use the Presbyterian label to circumvent certain legal liabilities for their beliefs. This group offered the two visiting New Lights a cold reception, and as far as Davies was concerned, the feeling was mutual, for he noted that "the dissenting Ministers here [in England] have so generally imbibed Arminian or Socinian Sentiments, that it is hard to unite Prudence and Faithfulness in Conversation with them." Tennent and Davies were frequently torn between the equally unpleasant options of either remaining silent during their contacts with such men in order to procure contributions or speaking their minds and losing all hope of acquiring gifts for their college.[43]

A second portion of the English Presbyterian communion was composed of what George W. Pilcher, editor of Davies' diary, has called the "Evangelicals." Tennent found this group more receptive to the goals of the New Jersey College, but even here he encountered some difficulty because of his practice of preaching with notes. Many Independents, Calvinist Baptists, and Congregationalists felt that a minister should rely entirely on the promptings of the Holy Spirit when he spoke from the pulpit. For this reason they took exception to Tennent's constant reference to his manuscripts.[44]

The Evangelicals were also troubled by disparaging reports that they were receiving from Tennent's colonial enemies. Quite early in their travels Tennent and Davies realized that their best chance for success depended upon their ability to convince English dissenters that the College of New Jersey would provide an education to youth of all dissenting denominations.[45] With this aim in mind, Tennent and Davies modified a document given to them by the college's trustees that outlined the enrollment policy and curriculum for the school. The central thrust of this prospectus was not altered by Tennent and Davies, but the ecumenical aspects of the college were highlighted.[46]

In England and Scotland Tennent and Davies faced major objections to their portrayal of the college's purpose. The source of these criticisms were several letters sent to both English and Scottish divines by colonial Old Lights. These letters charged that the New Jersey College was controlled by a group of Calvinist bigots and enthusiasts. According to the reports, middle colony Calvinists had duped the New Jersey governor into believing the new institution would serve an ecumenical student body, but their real project was to introduce the attending youth to the unorthodox doctrine of New Light "enthusiasm." To prove this point, copies of Tennent's *Danger of An Unconverted Ministry* and his *Remarks Upon A Protestation* were included in the Old Light correspondence.[47]

The presence of the Anglican priest William Smith encouraged the spread of these malicious reports in London. Smith was not an Old Light, but he sympathized with them and was seeking contributions for the rival College of Philadelphia. Both factors led Smith to feed every negative rumor about the College of New Jersey.[48]

Tennent and Davies overcame the slanderous reports of their college's narrow purposes in two ways. First, Tennent told those who criticized his 1740 attack on an unconverted ministry that he had written it

in the Heat of his Spirit, when he apprehended a remarkable Work of God was opposed by a set of ministers—that Some of the Sentiments were not agreeable to his present Opinion—that he had painted sundry Things in too strong Colours— . . . [that] he had used all his Influences [since] to promote Union between the Synods; of which he produced his Irenicum, as a Witness—[and] that if the Sermon was faulty, it was but the fault of one Man, and should not be charged upon the whole Body.[49]

When this did not dispel the misgivings of the English and Scottish clergy, Tennent decided to leave Davies in Edinburgh and travel to his native Ireland alone. Tennent believed that his Irish background would permit him more success there, and he recognized that Davies would be more effective with the English because he had not participated in the acrimonious debates of the Awakening.[50]

Tennent's decision paid off richly. The amount he and Davies collected is impossible to determine exactly since the General Assembly in Scotland took years to complete its solicitations and because some of the contributions were used to pay the expenses of the trip. Nevertheless, in 1755 the two men handed the Synod of New York £600 for a scholarship fund and another £200 for the education of Indian youth. According to one report, this £800 was later supplemented by late-arriving contributions, so that the total amount of funds received from the mission came to £3000. Whatever the precise amount, it is clear that the efforts of Tennent and Davies put the College of New Jersey on a sound financial basis.[51]

This accomplishment had an important long-term impact. Between 1748 and 1768, 158 of the college's 338 graduates became clergymen, and the vast majority of this number were confirmed New Light advocates.[52] As the supply of experimental ministers increased in the Presbyterian Church, so too did the power of the Awakening party within that constituency. And as New Light power grew, so too did pressure on the Old Lights to accommodate and reunite with their former enemies.

THE PACIFYING EFFECT OF A COMMON ENEMY

One last service that Tennent did for the College of New Jersey was his participation in a student revival during March 1757. According to Gilbert Tennent and William Tennent, Jr., both of whom were involved in this small awakening, the revival was not initiated by "the ordinary Means of Preaching, or promoted by any alarming Methods." Instead, several letters and practical books on "The Necessity and Excellency of internal Religion" that various students received at about the same time that a young scholar at the college was converted prompted the event.[53]

A general leavening of spiritual interest among the seventy pupils at the school occasioned an invitation to William and Gilbert Tennent to come to the college and view the revival firsthand. Gilbert Tennent later interpreted what he saw as a sign of the college's special place in the history of Christian Pietism. Writing to an English benefactor of the institution, Tennent observed that there was "a great resemblance, between this Seat of Learning, and that of Hall[e] in Saxony, begun by pious Dr. Frank, in respect of their rise, progress, and *influence*, especially in respect to *vital* Piety."[54]

To insure the continuance of such pious progress, Tennent offered several sermons to the students during which he discussed the origin and character of humanity's tainted nature; how individuals were saved;

how they could backslide and, on occasion, recover; and why there was a pressing need in the current period of national danger for Christians to practice their belief above and beyond the letter of their duty.[55]

This series of homilies was noteworthy for two reasons. First, it gave Tennent his only opportunity to present his mature theological reflections to the next generation of Presbyterian clergymen that would soon emerge from the College of New Jersey.[56] Moreover, it allowed Tennent to trumpet a call for moral reformation based on the current political crisis. During the 1760s and the 1770s, this rationale for spiritual renewal would be used by many of the students in Tennent's audience to undergird the American Revolutionary movement with a sense of community identity and righteousness over against the colonies' corrupted British foe.[57]

Tennent's use of politics to motivate moral regeneration had surfaced briefly in his sermons during the 1740s, but it blossomed into full form in the 1750s. When Tennent returned from his trip to Great Britain, he found his homeland threatened by another war. This time the foe was the French and the Indians, and the wartime destruction on the frontier was far more extensive.

In the latter half of the 1750s, Presbyterian clergymen became deeply involved in the rising agitation for a suitable defense of the middle colonies' borders. Since a large part of their constituency lived in these areas, this was to be expected. However, the development of a common foe against which Old and New Light ministers could rally together was an unanticipated result of this action.

Nathan Hatch has noted that the Awakening in New England fostered hopes that the Kingdom of God would soon be established in America, but the movement's decline in the late 1740s forced New England Awakeners to reevaluate their overly optimistic expectations. This reassessment prepared the way for a significant shift in New England apocalyptic thought during the French and Indian War. The war with the papist French and the heathen Indians allowed the northern clergy to formulate a new moral dichotomy between their fellow colonials and the French and Indian foe. As this idea took hold, New England Awakeners turned away from the spiritual introspection encouraged by the revivals and emphasized instead their collective role in this "last decisive struggle" with Satan. New England Old Lights, on the other hand, began to proclaim the French menace was the most serious attack by the Antichrist to date. Thus, Old Lights became less concerned about

the dangers of Awakening "enthusiasm" just as the New Light preoccupation with the hazards of an unconverted ministry began to wane.
This allowed a new cooperation among former Awakening enemies as
both groups became "more concerned with their common struggle than
with [the] divisive questions relating to the spread of vital piety."[58]

In the middle colonies a similar shift took place. In the sermons of
Gilbert Tennent there was never any expectation of the millennium's
coming first to America as a result of the Awakening. Not as well versed
in Puritan apocalyptic thought as New England Awakeners, Tennent
misunderstood much that had been written by English Puritan millen-
nialists. There was in Tennent's preaching, however, a definite sense
that the Awakening represented an "extraordinary" period of religious
progress. In his view, the revivals added to the earthly Kingdom of
God in an unprecedented fashion, and before the troubles of 1741–
1742, Tennent saw no end to the accomplishments that the experimental
movement could effect in God's name.

The excesses of his fellow Awakeners and the spread of Moravian
"enthusiasm" tempered Tennent's optimism in the late 1740s. As he
moderated his advocacy of experimental religion and searched for a
new balance that could prevent immoderate expressions of such piety,
Tennent's rhetoric lost its clear, almost simplistic focus of earlier years.
The "Pharisee-Teachers" and unconverted ministers who had served
so well as the targets of his preaching dropped from his vocabulary and
were replaced by the Moravian enthusiast. But Tennent's attacks on the
Moravians' experimental views were always conditional, since he regarded experimental knowledge a valid and essential component of the
balanced piety he wished to promote.

The French and Indian War solved the problem of focus for Tennent
by providing a new enemy against which he could aim his sharp tongue.
In 1758 Tennent preached a series of sermons in which he used the
current afflictions at the hands of the French and the Indians as a
justification for a new reformation in colonial morality.[59] Using images
reminiscent of the traditional New England Puritan jeremiad, Tennent
declared that the current "controversie" was not only with the French
and the Indians. Behind this concrete threat lay the wrath of God. In
Tennent's words, God "has a quarrel with our poor sinful nation, and
therefore has employ'd the French and their savage confederates, as his
servants and sword to distress or destroy . . . [the British nation and its
colonies], for their iniquitys against him." This, Tennent claimed, the

English "overlook entirely" since "they depend upon their comparative righteousness . . . the suppos'd wisdom and military courage of their commanding officers . . . [their] plans of operation as well as . . . [the] suppos'd bravery of their Fleets and Troups." As a consequence, they "do not repent and reform," even though this is "the only thing that can save our nation."[60]

Tennent realized that many colonials assumed God would save them either because the British cause was just or because England was a Protestant bulwark against the forces of papist Rome. But Tennent considered both beliefs to be bogus justifications for a dangerously false security. To those who put their faith in the first of these empty pretensions, Tennent asked if the "cause of the Jews in a civil sense" were not as just "in respect of their right to Jerusalem . . . and the land of Canaan . . . as ours, and yet," he noted, "the King of Babylon and other princes and nations, were sent by the Almighty in just judgement to take . . . [the Jews'] rights" because they did not repent their sins.[61]

As for being a Protestant bulwark, Tennent observed that the English nation was "a very poor Bulwark indeed" since its behavior had "been contrary to the Laws of Religion and good Policy." He warned that "it is foolish and fatal, not only for individuals, but for nations who are made up of such, to magnify their importance beyond any just foundation . . . [for] Jehovah is able to support his cause and preserve his church" without the assistance of the English. The only real hope of protection from God's wrath, Tennent asserted, was moral reformation, since it was "the established constitution of God's moral government over nations and communities that they . . . acknowledge God's sovereignty over them, repent their sins and reform their lives or they can expect national ruin."[62]

Tennent was not alone in taking this position. Old and New Light ministers in the late 1750s spoke of the same divine controversy with the colonies. Their common aim was the improvement of public morality so that God would protect them from the French and Indian infidels. The subject of moral reform was a neutral one. Even before the Awakening all parties in the Presbyterian Church had supported the need for moral probity. Thus, as this refrain became dominant in both Old and New Light rhetoric, the two sides began to warm to each other.

The respective strength of the two parties had also radically changed by the late 1750s. The post-schism Philadelphia Synod contained twenty-seven ministers in 1741, while the Conjunct Presbyteries could muster only thirteen clergymen and the New York Presbytery included only nine ordained members. But by 1758 the Synod of Philadelphia had experienced a net loss of five ministers, while its New York counterpart's membership had jumped to a total of seventy-three pastors.[63]

The Old Light Presbyterians lacked a college in 1758 as well. Therefore, they remained dependent on immigrant clergy to fill their dwindling ranks. The New Lights, on the other hand, had founded a school for the education of their ministerial candidates by the same date and produced sufficient contributions to insure its future growth.[64]

Clearly the Synod of Philadelphia needed an alliance with the New York Synod if it wished to survive, but no real breakthrough in negotiations between the two bodies occurred until 1755. The major stumbling block was the 1741 *Protestation*. The New York Synod continued to demand that this document either be rejected outright or put to a new vote in both synods. Against these suggestions the Philadelphia Synod argued that the protestation had been an act of the full membership and could not be rejected by any but those now belonging to that synod.[65] A significant modification of the Old Lights' position broke this deadlock in 1755. Using an argument that the Awakeners had employed in the late 1740s, the Philadelphia Synod declared that the 1741 *Protestation* had been the act of a few members and not of the entire Synod. However, it refused to remove the protest from its minutes since it claimed all such complaints should be registered even though the majority opposed them. In this way Presbyterian Old Lights kept the *Protestation* on the records but qualified its status as the Synod's official stance.[66]

The New Lights recognized this concession as a conciliatory gesture. Therefore, they decided to meet in 1750 at the same time and place as the Philadelphia Synod in order to facilitate negotiations for reunion. Gilbert Tennent, along with twelve other ministers from the New York Synod, served on a joint commission that formulated the final plan for reconciling the two rival judicatories.[67]

The terms of reunion that eventually passed both bodies represented a compromise weighted slightly in the New Lights' favor. The new Synod of New York and Philadelphia approved and received the Westminster standards as their confession of faith and plan for worship, government, and discipline. The Synod declared that members with scruples about any future actions of the membership had two recourses. One, they could protest after appropriate appeals, or, two, they could withdraw peaceably. Separation would only be required, however, where the Synod determined the issue in question was "indispensable in doctrine or Presbyterian government." As to the 1741 *Protestation*, the Philadelphia Synod conceded that it had never been "judicially adopted" and, therefore, was not accounted a "Synodical act." All future accusations against fellow members were to be lodged through "private brotherly admonition, or by a regular process," and any infraction of this rule would be considered a scandal, as would any presbytery's assigning a minister to preach in another presbytery or any clergyman's doing the same without the permission of the settled pastor or the session of the church. Licensing and ordaining were left to the presbyteries, but each candidate was to give "competent satisfaction as to his learning and experimental acquaintance with religion, . . . skill in divinity and cases of conscience." Presbyteries were to be remodeled as the reunion Synod saw fit, and divided congregations with settled pastors were to remain intact except where they voluntarily agreed to consolidate.[68]

The Synod also sanctioned a list of several signs of a true work of God in the individual soul. Visions of Christ, voices, external lights, or convulsive fits were labeled dangerous delusions, but wherever the agreed upon evidences of God's gracious hand appeared, they were to be recognized as divinely inspired.[69]

Finally, the Synod proclaimed that "all former differences and disputes are laid aside and buried" and that anyone who sought a judicial inquiry on the grounds of any of these past controversies would be censured and rebuked.[70]

All things considered, the reunion was a New Light victory. The revivalists successfully introduced those items that their New York Synod had declared it stood for in its 1745 "foundation." Their only concession was to allow the *Protestation* of 1741 to remain in the Synod's minutes.

For Gilbert Tennent the unification of his divided church was a personal triumph. Before the two synods formally merged in 1758, Francis Alison acknowledged as much in a sermon to the Philadelphia Synod on *Peace and Union Recommended*. In his homily Alison noted that "Gilbert Tennent . . . has written more and suffered more for his writings, to promote peace and union, than any member of this divided church." Since both synods agreed with Alison, the reunited membership chose Tennent as its first moderator.[71]

Tennent continued to speak for reconciliation long after the formal reconciliation had been accomplished. In 1759 he delivered two homilies to the Synod on *The Blessedness of Peace-Makers represented; and the Danger of Persecution considered*. Contrasting peacemaking with persecution, Tennent tried to clarify the parameters of each. Peacemaking, he suggested, was a universal duty achieved through both negative and positive means. Negatively, peace was procured by avoiding rash judgments, unscriptural terms for communion, uncharitable divisions, and pride. Positively, it required that all deal justly and honestly with each other, be clothed in humility, love one another, be candid and charitable in thought and speech, treat all with courtesy, be mindful of one's own business, and maintain the church's government that had been appointed by the Almighty.[72]

Tennent emphasized, however, that the duty of peacemaking did not demand the surrender of the truth. The Christian walked a fine line between unconditional toleration of all opinions for the sake of co-existence and persecution of others for circumstantial reasons. The former extreme was the sin of the Moravians; the latter, the error of the Seceders.[73] Pointedly directing his remarks against those who still found the Moravians an attractive example of Christlike toleration, Tennent declared: "Tho' we are earnestly to prosecute peace, yet not so far as to barter truth and holiness to obtain it." There were certain essential "grand particulars" in religion that must not be compromised.[74]

On the other hand, Tennent also acknowledged that there were many "circumstantials" in religion. Alexander Craighead had rejected the fellowship of other Presbyterians for such matters, and Tennent believed that the sixteenth-century Reformers had suffered from this error as well.[75] In a sermon presented during the same period, Tennent explained this charge by observing that the Protestant Reformation had been founded on the principle of "free inquiry and the liberty of private judgment," but as so often happens in human affairs, men abused this "long sequestered Privilege" by developing "several curious fancys" which were superfluous to the Gospel. These "fancys" were harmless "while held indifferent," but soon they were "made important and the Terms of Church Fellowship" by the Reformers. This mistake proved fatal to the Reformation since it tore the movement into various parties and provided the Church of Rome with the opportunity to charge that the Reformation promoted a spirit of confusion. The Catholics complained that "when men had once left the center of unity, and would seek Truth by a Liberty of thinking, which authoriz'd private judgement, there would soon be as many false opinions as free enquirers; and as many sects as both.'' Smarting from this accusation, the Protestant Reformers assumed it was impractical to go back to the "simplicity of gospel-Faith; and on that simplicity to regulate the Terms of Church-communion; [so] they contented themselves with stopping where they were; which they tho't they should be able to do, by applying just coercion to all such noveltys, as either by their subtilty or plausibility promis'd the Birth of a *new Sect*, or by their grossness & extravagance, reflected dishonor upon reformation itself. This error was not more disgraceful to the beginnings of Reformation,'' Tennent claimed, "[than it was] fatal to the progress of it'' since it brought the imposition of new religious laws and persecution on circumstantial matters.[76]

If this unnecessary persecution were avoided and the grand particulars of religion steadfastly protected, Tennent felt a proper peace could be established in the colonial church. But the reunion Synod found the line between "circumstantials'' and "grand particulars'' difficult to define, and after the reconciliation, internal differences continued to surface over the old questions of candidates' qualifications and ministerial discipline.[77]

During 1760 and 1761 the Philadelphia Presbytery examined Samuel Magaw and John Beard as candidates for the ministry. After inquiring into their experiences of grace, several New Light ministers, including Gilbert Tennent, found the two men's answers inadequate. In the case of Magaw, seven of the eleven ministers in the presbytery requested another opportunity to discuss his experimental knowledge. His second interview left them equally dissatisfied, so they requested that their objections be registered in the minutes.[78]

Another minor skirmish that involved Gilbert Tennent concerned the appointment of James Faires. Faires had been the leader of psalms singing at the First Presbyterian Church in Philadelphia but had lost the post when the church disciplined him for some unnamed offense. Since the Arch Street Church held quite different views on discipline, Tennent's trustees hired Faires. This angered Robert Cross and his First Presbyterian congregation, and the matter was brought before the presbytery. The presbytery decided to condemn the Second Presbyterian Church's pastor and session for their apparent disregard for the opinions of their colleagues across town.[79]

FINAL BATTLES OF A CONTENTIOUS CAREER

Conflict over candidates and discipline continued into the 1760s, but Tennent avoided these internal church squabbles because of his preoccupation with two other matters that troubled him more deeply. In 1759 Philadelphia was visited by an Anglican clergyman named William McClenachan. McClenachan hailed from Ireland but had led the immigration of a number of Presbyterian families to Portland, Maine, in 1736. There he served his migrant parishioners for several years before moving to Georgetown, Maine, and later Chelsea, Massachusetts. At the suggestion of Governor Shirley, McClenachan sailed in 1754 to London, where he was ordained a priest in the Church of England. He returned to the colonies two years later and served as a missionary for the Society for the Propagation of the Gospel in Georgetown, Maine. In 1759 McClenachan became restless again and decided to travel to Virginia in order to investigate the possibility of taking a parish in the south. On his return to New England, he stopped briefly in Philadelphia.[80]

The rector of Christ Church in Philadelphia was the Reverend Robert Jenney. Jenney's failing health had prevented him from fulfilling his many duties, so he applied to the Bishop of London for a second assistant. When McClenachan appeared in Philadelphia, Jenney asked him to preach. The Irishman quickly cultivated a following in the congregation, and they began to agitate for his appointment as Jenney's new subordinate. Their urgings were not well received by either Jenney or William Smith of the College of Philadelphia. Both men strongly objected to McClenachan's extemporaneous style of worship and the content of his sermons, which Smith characterized as a "continual ringing the Changes upon the words Regeneration, instantaneous Conversion, imputed Righteousness, the New Birth etc." Smith had also learned that New England Anglicans had opposed McClenachan because they believed him to be an "avowed Methodist and follower of Whitefield's plan." For all these reasons, Jenney barred McClenachan from his pulpit.[81]

Since McClenachan was a disciple of Whitefield, he attracted Gilbert Tennent's attention and support. To help McClenachan get the assistantship at Christ Church, Tennent along with seventeen other New Light Presbyterian ministers requested his appointment in a letter to the Archbishop of Canterbury.[82] Tennent had received word through some of John Brainerd's correspondence that the Archbishop was well disposed toward experimental religion and dissenters. Therefore, he and his associates addressed their letter to the Archbishop rather than the Bishop of London, who had formal jurisdiction over Anglican missions in the colonies.[83]

Their letter backfired on the New Lights, however, when Smith asked his colleague at the Philadelphia College, Francis Alison, to seek the Synod's opinion of its members' actions. Old Lights like Alison found their associates' behavior objectionable because it represented the same type of interference in the affairs of another communion that had occurred during the Great Awakening. When considered in Synod, that body declared the eighteen Presbyterians had "acted without due consideration and improperly in that affair."[84]

During the same period, the eighteen ministers were further embarrassed by a series of pamphlets that not only pictured their support of an Anglican priest as a renunciation of their Presbyterian affiliation but also used the opportunity to rehash the past ecclesiastical sins of the Awakeners. These works were answered by anonymous defenders of the New Lights. Nevertheless, the whole affair served to aggravate old grievances and animosities.[85]

The last and most poignant controversy of Tennent's contentious career followed swiftly upon the McClenachan fiasco. By 1762 Tennent had accomplished a great deal in his life. In the Synod and its presbyteries his party held a dominant position. In Philadelphia his Arch Street Church enjoyed a respected place in the religious community, and at home he had acquired a new family. Sometime after his return from Great Britain, Tennent had remarried. His new spouse was Sarah Spofford, the widow of a captain in the Royal Navy. Sarah brought a daughter from her first marriage to live with her in the Tennent household, and during the last decade of Tennent's life, she gave Gilbert his first natural children.[86]

Despite these many public and private successes, Tennent's health began to fail in 1762. During the next two years, the Second Presbyterian Church made frequent requests for pulpit supplies. One of the first men to provide such assistance was George Duffield. Duffield had graduated from the College of New Jersey in 1752 and thereafter served a brief time as a tutor at his alma mater. In 1756 the New Light Presbytery of New Castle ordained Duffield, and for the next three years he traveled among the churches of Virginia promoting revivals. These journeys ended in 1759, when churches at Carlisle and Big Spring, Pennsylvania, called Duffield to be their minister.[87]

Tennent's congregation decided in October 1762 that their pastor needed an assistant. Tennent consented to a congregation meeting for preparing such a call because he thought the church would choose a young man without a settled position to act as a fixed supply. He did not expect his illness to continue indefinitely, so he saw no need for a permanent associate.[88]

During the church's deliberations Tennent discovered that he had incorrectly read the congregation's will. A group of his parishioners liked Duffield's extemporaneous style of preaching and they rigged the final vote by introducing a number of nonvoting members into the tally. Thus, the meeting ended with Duffield's being chosen as Tennent's new assistant.[89]

Tennent was quite ill as he moderated the discussions, and his ailment worsened when he realized what was happening. As he later described his mood, "I was very far from expecting such . . . as had hap[pen]ed, the sight of which astonished and distressed me, for it look'd like burying me while I was alive in a House under which God I had built."[90]

When the congregation presented their call to Duffield, first at the Philadelphia Presbytery and later at his Presbytery of Donegal, Tennent presented two different remonstrances against the proposed action. Tennent declared that the recent election had been "disorderly" in at least three ways. First, it had been "antiscriptural" because the group that had manipulated the vote had usurped his right as pastor to influence the congregation's deliberations. Second, it had been "unconstitutional" because the tally had included a number of unqualified voters. And third, it had been "ungrateful" because, as Tennent put it,

not only this society but many other persons in City and Country know the pains . . . I have undergone to get a Church etc. for this Society. . . . I have procured more, yea perhaps manifold more, for that and its apendages in different ways than this whole society together . . . while in the mean tyme I have supported my Familie in this Place now almost 20 years in a considerable degree every year upon my own private substance: it is therefore strange after all this, to see an attempt made . . . to introduce without my consent any gentleman into that Pulpit . . . [and] Church which originally in some sense is much more mine than theirs.[91]

Tennent noted that he approved of Duffield's practice as a minister, but he found his young associate an unsuitable candidate for the Arch Street Church at the present time for several reasons. Tennent believed that Duffield's departure from his current congregations would "demoralize the ministers of his presbytery and leave many of the churches he served open to no ministry." Also he felt that Duffield's extemporaneous preaching would only encourage a dangerous bias of the Philadelphia congregation. Tennent admitted that a portion of his flock had developed a prejudice against his ministry because "they reckon preaching with notes . . . to be no preaching at all." If Duffield accepted the call, Tennent feared that this opinion would gain a wider currency, and the minds of his congregation would thereby "be more and more contracted and their charity or Love lessened in proportion." Since charity and love was "the Substance and Scope of all Religion both natural and revealed," Tennent felt compelled to oppose Duffield's election.[92]

Unfortunately for Tennent, this line of reasoning left his congregation unmoved. But his objections did create enough doubt in Duffield and the Donegal Presbytery for the call to be refused. This controversy took almost a year to settle, and when it was finally resolved all parties were dissatisfied because the church still had an ailing pastor whose health had been further weakened by the prolonged debates that the conflict had generated.[93]

During his battles over the Duffield call, Tennent compared himself to Moses being persecuted by a host of ungrateful Israelites. Although a bit pretentious, the image was apt. Tennent had led his people out of the bondage of formal orthodoxy into the promised land of awakened practical piety. When he became aware of the dangers of this new theological terrain, he tried to warn his followers. But his warnings were not always appreciated.[94]

The pain caused by his congregation's action was mercifully cut short when Gilbert Tennent died on July 23, 1764. Shortly thereafter the church that Tennent believed had rejected his ministry paid a belated tribute to their pastor's service by placing his tomb in the center aisle of their sanctuary and inscribing the following words in a marble slab above his coffin.

> Under this marble are buried the remains of
> Gilbert Tennent,
> first Pastor of this Church;

by whose agency chiefly,
this building,
sacred to God,
was erected.
The son of William Tennent;
born in Armagh, Ireland,
on February 5th, 1702;
elected Pastor at New Brunswick,
in 1725;
then called to Philadelphia,
in 1743;
he died on July 23d, 1764,
in the 62nd year of his age.
He was a prudent, experienced, venerable man;
in manners and piety eminent;
as a Husband, Brother, Father and Friend,
among the most excellent:
a bold, learned, faithful, successful
Defender of true religion;
and finally,
a Christian without guile.
The congregation, his former hearers,
have caused his name
to be commemorated by this eulogy.[95]

CONCLUSION

When one surveys the entirety of Gilbert Tennent's career, a number of significant shifts in his public stance become evident. Yet Tennent believed in the last years of his life that he had consistently supported the program of experimental reform that he had begun so many years before in his first pastorate. Indeed, Tennent maintained that the so-called "new" elements that were introduced into his ministry during the 1740s and 1750s were not corrections of his own course but rather clarifications of his longstanding policy.

In order to understand how Tennent could consider himself free of contradiction despite the significant movement in his public proclamations, it must be remembered that Tennent learned from Frelinghuysen that he should constantly adapt his ministrations to the changing spiritual state of his congregation. Tennent discovered in New Brunswick that the needs and the understanding of his parishioners did not remain the same as they progressed toward salvation. Individuals not yet convicted of their sin needed to hear the terrors of God's righteous law. Those fully humbled by their iniquity required the application of the Gospel balsam, and Christians filled with grace demanded the presentation of a solid doctrinal system to found their faith on firm ground. Consequently, Tennent altered the style and content of his pulpit rhetoric to suit his auditors' level of spiritual development.

What was valid on the congregational level Tennent assumed to be appropriate for a denomination or for a nation. Tennent did not expect the methods that had been effective in promoting ecclesiastical or national renewal in the 1730s to be appropos for the same task in the 1760s. Modifications in both the manner and substance of his Awakening gospel were required as the nation and the church progressed spiritually. Such revisions, in Tennent's view, did not create a fundamentally different revival message. Instead, they transposed the same proclamation to a new key in order to meet the unique demands of the ever-changing colonial religious situation.

Recognizing this fact, one can divide Tennent's career into three periods. In each Tennent offered a slightly different rendition of his experimental program, and for each he employed a new biblical image to symbolize the current problems and potentials of the contemporary church.

During the first stage of his ministry, from 1726 (the year of Tennent's ordination in New Brunswick) to 1741 (the year of the Presbyterian schism), Tennent was preoccupied with the dangers of pharisaic piety. Under the influence of William Tennent, Sr., and Theodorus Frelinghuysen, Tennent learned to abhor all forms of shallow, hypocritical Christianity. He believed that modern-day "Pharisee-Teachers" threatened to corrupt the faithful with their pretensions to righteousness much as Jewish Pharisees had done in Jesus' day, so he mounted an attack on two fronts.[1] Against individual sinners he sent forth the terrors of the biblical law to expose the rotten foundations of human self-righteousness, and against the church's pharisee-infested clergy he leveled a withering assault on unconverted ministers. Tennent planned to rejuvenate the ordained leadership of the Presbyterian communion by introducing experimental candidates into its ranks. On occasion this effort demanded that Tennent protect the sovereignty of his presbytery over the examination and ordination of candidates. This, of course, generated stiff opposition from those in his denomination who believed piety would be better served by an educated ministry backed by a powerful ecclesiastical hierarchy. Conflict over these two opposing programs for reform led to the schism of the Presbyterian Church.

The second period of Tennent's career began with his meeting with Zinzendorf in New Brunswick and ended just prior to his call for Presbyterian reconciliation in 1749. Over this span of years Tennent counseled his supporters to "hold fast to the truth" that they had received much as John of Patmos had advised his beleaguered brothers and sisters in the faith to stand firm against second-century Roman persecution.[2]

Tennent envisioned his own situation as similar to that of Nehemiah rebuilding the walls of Jerusalem.[3] With one hand he wielded a literary sword against the enemies of experimental piety, and with the other hand he built up the faithful's theological understanding. Tennent realized that colonial Awakeners had been thrown on the defensive. The Moravians' ''enthusiasm,'' Craighead's intolerance, Davenport's intemperance, and Whitefield's ecumenism had divided the Awakening community as well as provided a wealth of ammunition for antirevival criticism. As a result, Tennent set to work formulating a conceptual balance that could anchor experimental piety on a sound doctrinal foundation and thereby protect it from the winds of uninformed passions and the decay of pharisaic formality.

Tennent's new concern for stability expressed itself concretely in three ways. In the pulpit, the fire of Tennent's spontaneous rhetoric gave way to methodical expositions of doctrine read from prepared manuscripts. In his Philadelphia parish, the relatively unstructured, ecumenical New Building congregation was transformed into a self-conscious Presbyterian organization. And in his dress, Tennent replaced the symbolic garb of John the Baptist with the more refined accoutrements of a city gentleman. These changes signaled Tennent's retreat from the Awakening but not from the experimental interests that had led him into the movement in the first place. The revivals had spawned an outburst of conversions and a renewal of piety, but they had also given birth to wild enthusiasm. Therefore, Tennent attempted to distance himself from the latter while at the same time consolidating the Awakening's gains by giving them a social and theological respectability.

In 1749 (the year of his call for peace in the divided Presbyterian communion), Tennent entered the third and last stage of his career. During this period, Tennent invoked the example of first-century Jewish and Gentile Christians in order to heal the scars left by Presbyterian Awakening conflict.[4] Tennent believed his church had repeated a mistake of early Christian disciples by allowing itself to be split by ''circumstantial,'' nonessential differences. Presbyterians on both sides of the revival issue had forgotten during the heat of battle their fundamental agreement on the ''grand particulars of Religion.'' Recent conflict within the Awakening camp proved that Presbyterian revivalists shared more in common with their denominational opponents than with revival supporters like the Moravians or the Seceders. So Tennent called for peace among Presbyterians on the basis of the same tolerant terms that

Jewish and Gentile Christians had been reconciled in the early church. Of course, the growing power of the New York Synod and the onset of the French and Indian War encouraged a friendly reception to this summons for peaceful coexistence, but equally, if not more, important was Tennent's own acknowledgement that doctrine and education were as necessary for a converting ministry as experimental knowledge. Unfortunately for Tennent, many of his supporters interpreted the irenic posture of his last years as an unconditional surrender to his former enemies and, as a result, the final battle of Tennent's career was fought with his own Philadelphia congregation over their right to call a man who could arouse the same experimental zeal that Tennent once, but no longer, inspired in his parishioners.

For the Awakening historian, Gilbert Tennent's life can be quite instructive. As much as any individual's biography can, Tennent's reveals the multiple factors that shaped his time and place, and as such, it cautions the student of the First Great Awakening not to take the movement's title too literally. The first major religious revival in American history was "great" in its scope and impact, but its theological foundations and ecclesiastical politics differed significantly in various colonial regions. Consequently, the traditional search for the social and religious threads that made the Awakening an intercolonial event should be matched by equally intensive investigations into the critical variations among the colonists' revival experience.

APPENDIX: TENNENT'S HOMILETIC DECLENSION

A chart of Gilbert Tennent's extant manuscript sermons indicates that Tennent created an impressive number of sermons for his new congregation during his first two years in Philadelphia. But Tennent's output declined dramatically after 1746 as he began to reuse old sermons with increasing regularity.

	Ms. Sermons Preached for the First Time	Ms. Sermons Preached More Than Once Before
1743	4	–
1744	54	–
1745	41	6
1746	29	22
1747	25	41
1748	20	37
1749	7	31
1750	14	27
1751	3	36
1752	1	28
1753	5	17
1754	–	–
1755	5	38
1756	3	38
1757	12	29
1758	8	42
1759	7	30

	Ms. Sermons Preached for the First Time	Ms. Sermons Preached More Than Once Before
1760	1	42
1761	1	24
1762	1	9
1763	4	28
1764	–	5
No date	9	

NOTES

ABBREVIATIONS

DCP   James Tanis, *Dutch Calvinistic Pietism in the Middle Colonies: A Study in the Life and Theology of Theodorus Jacobus Frelinghuysen.* The Hague: Martinus Nijhoff, 1967.

DH   *Documentary History of William Tennent and the Log College.* Edited by Thomas C. Pears, Jr. Department of History, General Assembly of the Presbyterian Church in the United States of America, 1940.

ER   *The Ecclesiastical Records (of the) State of New York.* Edited by Hugh Hastings. 7 vols. Albany, N.Y.: J. B. Lyon, 1902.

FAT   Leonard J. Trinterud. *The Forming of an American Tradition: A Re-examination of Colonial Presbyterianism.* Philadelphia: Westminster Press, 1949.

GWJ   George Whitefield. *George Whitefield's Journals.* Edited by William V. Davis. Gainesville, Fla.: Scholars' Facsimile and Reprints, 1969.

MPC   *Minutes of the Presbyterian Church in America 1706–1788.* Edited by Guy S. Klett. Philadelphia: Presbyterian Historical Society, 1976.

ACKNOWLEDGMENTS

1. Milton J Coalter, Jr., "The Radical Pietism of Count Nicholas Zinzendorf as a Conservative Influence on the Awakener, Gilbert Tennent," *Church History* 49 (March 1980): 35–46; and Milton J Coalter, Jr., "Gilbert Tennent, Revival Workhorse in a Neglected Awakening Theological Tradition," in *Religion in New Jersey Life Before the Civil War.* Edited by Mary R. Murrin. Trenton: New Jersey Historical Commission, Department of State, 1985.

INTRODUCTION

1. Despite the voluminous research dedicated to the First Great Awakening, no published work has had Gilbert Tennent as its central focus and only one dissertation has dealt with Tennent in any depth. That dissertation by Miles Douglas Harper approaches Tennent as though he were a systematic theologian and, consequently, misses the principal characteristic of his ministry, i.e., Tennent's adaptation of his theology and techniques to the changing religious conditions of his region. For this reason, Harper's analysis is quite different from that offered in this study. Miles Douglas Harper, "Gilbert Tennent, Theologian of the 'New Light' " (Ph.D. diss., Duke University, 1958).

2. Martin Ellsworth Lodge, "The Great Awakening in the Middle Colonies" (Ph.D. diss., University of California, Berkeley, 1964), pp. 124–125.

3. The most recent example of this approach is William Howland Kenney's "George Whitefield and Colonial Revivalism: The Social Sources of Charismatic Authority, 1737–1770" (Ph.D. diss., University of Pennsylvania, 1966).

4. Examples of this approach are too numerous to mention in full, but a few of the most important works are the following: Richard L. Bushman, *From Puritan to Yankee: Character and the Social Order in Connecticut, 1690–1765* (Cambridge, Mass.: Harvard University Press, 1967); Edwin Scott Gaustad, *The Great Awakening in New England* (New York: Harper and Row, 1957); C. C. Goen, *Revivalism and Separatism in New England: Strict Congregationalists and Separate Baptists in the Great Awakening* (New Haven: Yale University Press, 1962); Alan Heimert and Perry Miller, eds., "Introduction," in *The Great Awakening: Documents Illustrating the Crisis and Its Consequences* (Indianapolis: Bobbs-Merrill, 1967); and Alan Heimert, *Religion and the American Mind: From the Great Awakening to the Revolution* (Cambridge, Mass.: Harvard University Press, 1966).

5. Heimert and Miller, "Introduction," p. xxx.

6. *FAT*, pp. 54–56, 170 (see list of abbreviations).

7. For descriptions of this international cross-fertilization of theology, see F. Ernest Stoeffler, *The Rise of Evangelical Pietism* (Leiden: E. J. Brill, 1965); Heinrich Heppe, *Geschichte des Pietismus und der Mystic in der Reformierten Kirche* (Leiden: E. J. Brill, 1879); Wilhelm Goeters, *Die Vorbereitung des Pietismus in der Reformierten Kirche der Niederlande* (Leipzig: J. C. Inrichs, 1911); and Martin Schmidt, "England unter der deutsche Pietismus," *Evangelische Theologie* 4/5 (1953): 205–224.

8. *DCP*, pp. 4–7 (see list of abbreviations).

1. INSTRUCTION IN THE EXPERIMENTAL MINISTRY

1. For the best biographies of William Tennent, Sr., see Archibald Alexander, *Biographical Sketches of the Founder and Principal Alumni of the Log*

College (Philadelphia: Presbyterian Board of Publications, 1851); George H. Ingram, "Biographies of the Alumni of the Log College, II: William Tennent, Sr., the Founder," *Journal of Presbyterian History* 14 (March, 1930): 1–27; and Mary A. Tennent, *Light in Darkness: The Story of William Tennent, Sr., and the Log College* (Greensboro, N.C.: Greensboro Printing, 1971).

2. Mary A. Tennent, *Light in Darkness*, p. 27.

3. *Records of the General Synod of Ulster, from 1691 to 1820*, 3 vols. (Belfast, 1890), I:52.

4. The other Tennent children were born in 1705 (William Jr.), 1706 (John), 1708 (Ellenor), and 1711 (Charles). Thomas C. Pears, Jr., "History by Hearsay or New Light on William Tennent: A Footnote on the 'Documentary History of William Tennent,' &c.," *Journal of Presbyterian History* 19 (1940): 73–75.

5. *Ibid.*, pp. 73–74; extract from the Kennedy Family Book, Miscellaneous Data, William Tennent, Sr., Collection, Presbyterian Historical Society, Philadelphia; Thomas Witherow, *Historical and Literary Memorials of Presbyterianism in Ireland* (London: William Mullan and Son, 1879), p. 230; and *DH*, p. 63b (see list of abbreviations).

6. Pears, "History by Hearsay," pp. 73–75.

7. *DH*, p. 39a.

8. John M. Barkley, "The Presbyterian Church in Ireland: Part I," *Journal of Presbyterian History* 44 (1966): 258–259; and James C. Leyburn, *The Scotch-Irish* (Chapel Hill, N.C.: University of North Carolina Press, 1962), p. 166.

9. Before mentioning Tennent in his letter to Greenshields, James Logan congratulated Greenshields for his new benefice worth £250. *DH*, p. 39a.

10. *MPC*, p. 34; and Pears, "History by Hearsay," p. 75.

11. *MPC*, p. 34.

12. Pears, "History by Hearsay," p. 75; and *DH*, pp. 15, 18.

13. In 1722 the rector of Yale College, Timothy Cutler, along with the school's only tutor resigned their offices because of their newfound conviction that ordination without a bishop was invalid. Shortly thereafter, they sailed for England, where they were ordained by an Anglican bishop. This defection to the Church of England by the faculty of Yale surprised and appalled the Puritan trustees of the college. In the wake of Cutler's resignation, several candidates were considered for the rectorship. *DH*, p. 39a; and Richard Warch, *School of the Prophets: Yale College, 1701–1740* (New Haven: Yale University Press, 1973), pp. 130–131.

14. Tennent's money problems continued in Bedford despite a salary of £40 per annum, various donations of land from Bedford, permission from nearby towns for him to receive the minister's rate from their inhabitants, and a loan of £30 from the Synod's "Fund for Pious Uses." *DH*, pp. 24, 26–29, 32, 35, 39, 43–44.

15. *Ibid.*, pp. 45–46, 52; and Ingram, "William Tennent, Sr.," p. 6.

16. *DH*, p. 53.

17. Thomas Clinton Pears, Jr., "The American Wilderness: A Study of Some of the Main Currents in Colonial American Presbyterianism" (Lectures for the L. P. Stone Foundation, Princeton Theological Seminary, 1942), p. 41; and Ingram, "William Tennent, Sr.," p. 10.

18. *DH*, p. 53 and Pears, "American Wilderness," p. 42.

19. *GWJ*, p. 351 (see list of abbreviations); Before the Log College building was completed, Gilbert Tennent, Samuel Blair, William Tennent, Jr., and John Tennent finished their studies under the elder Tennent. *DH*, p. 174; and Pears, "American Wilderness," pp. 42–43.

20. Tennent delivered this sermon on several occasions while he was still a minister of the Church of Ireland. William Tennent, Sr., Ms. Sermon I, Presbyterian Historical Society, Philadelphia.

21. *Ibid.*

22. *Ibid.*

23. *Ibid.*

24. Tennent used this sermon while he was a clergyman in the Church of Ireland and later when he became a Presbyterian pastor in the colonies. Thomas C. Pears, Jr., ed., "William Tennent's Sacramental Sermon," *Journal of Presbyterian History* 19 (March, 1940): 81–82.

25. *Ibid.*, pp. 77–78.

26. *Ibid.*, pp. 78–80.

27. William Tennent, Sr., Ms. Sermons IV and V, Presbyterian Historical Society, Philadelphia.

28. William Tennent, Sr., Ms. Sermons IV, VIII, and X, Presbyterian Historical Society, Philadelphia. See Sermon VIII for source of quote.

29. William Tennent, Sr., Ms. Sermon XII, Presbyterian Historical Society, Philadelphia.

30. William Tennent, Sr., Ms. Sermon VIII.

31. William Tennent, Sr., Ms. Sermons VI and XIV, Presbyterian Historical Society, Philadelphia.

32. William Tennent, Sr., Ms. Sermons XI and XIII, Presbyterian Historical Society, Philadelphia.

33. Samuel Finley, *The Successful Minister of Christ Distinguished in Glory* (Philadelphia: William Bradford, 1764), app., p. 11.

34. In his reference to the "New Lond[on] College," Logan probably meant the New Haven College or Yale. *DH*, p. 39a.

35. Franklin B. Dexter, *Biographical Sketches of the Graduates of Yale College*, 6 vols., 2nd series (New York: H. Holt, 1885–1912), I:312; and Warch, *School of the Prophets*, pp. 267–268.

36. Warch, *School of the Prophets*, pp. 126–132.

37. Mary A. Tennent, *Light in Darkness*, p. 72; and "Minutes of the Presbytery of New Castle," *Journal of Presbyterian Historical Society* 15 (1932): 108.

38. "Minutes of the Presbytery of New Castle," pp. 114–115.

39. MPC, p. 68; "Minutes of the Presbytery of the Presbytery of New Castle," p. 116.

40. Finley, *The Successful Minister*, p. ii; Richard Webster, *A History of the Presbyterian Church in America, from its Origin until the Year 1760* (Philadelphia: Joseph M. Wilson, 1857), p. 387.

41. *ER*, IV:2557, 2588–2589 (see list of abbreviations).

42. *DCP*, pp. 27–29; and James Tanis, "Reformed Pietism in Colonial America," in *Continental Pietism and Early American Christianity*, ed. F. Ernest Stoeffler (Grand Rapids, Mich.: Wm. B. Eerdmans Publishing, 1976), p. 48.

43. *DCP*, pp. 36–37; and Tanis, "Reformed Pietism," p. 48.

44. *DCP*, p. 37

45. Reordination was required since the Classis of Amsterdam was not formally associated with the German Reformed Church in which Frelinghuysen was originally ordained. *Ibid.*, pp. 38–40.

46. John P. Luidens discusses the real dangers to the Dutch Church that New York's English government represented in his dissertation on "The Americanization of the Dutch Reformed Church" (Ph.D. diss., University of Oklahoma, 1969), chapter 2, "The Colonial Church in New York, 1664–1720: Political Pressure and Ecclesiastical Loyalty."

47. *DCP*, pp. 44–49; and Tanis, "Reformed Pietism," pp. 43–46.

48. Without a trace of shame, Frelinghuysen admitted to Boel that he was so caught up in his "howling prayer" that he had not heard what he had spoken. *ER*, IV: 2259; and *DCP*, p. 43.

49. *ER*, IV:2260.

50. *DCP*, p. 43

51. *Ibid.*, pp. 49–50.

52. [Tobias Boel], "Klagte van eenige Leeden der Nederduytse Hervormde Kerk, woonende op Raretans, etc., in de Provincie van Nieu Jersey," in *ER*, III:2250, 2260–2261, 2274–2276.

53. *Ibid.*, III:2250, 2269–2270, 2279–2280.

54. Jean de Labadie developed a separatist form of Pietism in the Netherlands during the latter half of the seventeenth century that precipitated a schism in the Dutch Reformed Church. Frelinghuysen was neither a Labadist nor a separatist, but he did emphasize the need for conversion and a converted clergy as Labadie had done. For treatments of Labadism, see Stoeffler, *Rise of Evangelical Pietism*, pp. 162–169; Heppe, *Geschichte des Pietismus*, pp. 240–274; and Goeters, *Vorbereitung des Pietismus*, pp. 139–286.

55. The Raritan controversy was finally laid to rest in August 1738, when a letter of settlement was signed by all the parties involved. This compromise was effected by Dominie Du Bois of New York, who grew more sympathetic to Frelinghuysen during the Great Awakening. *DCP*, p. 62. Coens's activities against Frelinghuysen are chronicled in *ER*, IV:2460, 2557.

56. From letters sent to the Classis of Amsterdam during the Raritan controversy, it appears that Frelinghuysen's enemies were not trying to use Tennent to undermine Frelinghuysen's hold over the Raritan. Only one of Frelinghuysen's lay opponents contributed to Tennent's salary, and he claimed that his donation was given to satisfy the local custom of aiding one's neighbors in their religious enterprises. *ER*, IV:2557, 2588–2589.

57. Thomas Prince, ed., *The Christian History Containing Accounts of the Revival and Propagation of Religion in Great Britain and America for the year 1744, 5* (Boston: S. Kneeland and T. Green, 1745), pp. 292–293.

58. *ER*, III:2260; and *DCP*, p. 51.

59. Prince, *Christian History . . . 1744, 5*, p. 293.

60. In time Tennent's cooperation with Frelinghuysen became so common that Frelinghuysen's opponents began to demand that it must cease if reunion among the Dutch was to occur. *ER*, IV: 2466, 2538–2540, 2542, 2553–2554, 2557, 2567, 2585, 2587.

61. *ER*, III:2275–2276.

62. It should be noted that this three-stage *ordo salutis* is a distillation of the different descriptions of the conversion process given by various pietist thinkers. This pattern of conversion was never rigidly interpreted as the only manner by which an individual might be saved. For representative views of the conversion process by German pietists, see F. Ernest Stoeffler, *German Pietism During the Eighteenth Century* (Leiden: E. J. Brill, 1973), chapter 1, "August Herman Francke"; and Dale W. Brown, *Understanding Pietism* (Grand Rapids, Mich.: Eerdmans Press, 1978), pp. 116–119; by Puritan theologians, see Norman Pettit, *The Heart Prepared: Grace and Conversion in Puritan Spiritual Life* (New Haven: Yale University Press, 1966), pp. 1–21; and by the Dutch Reformed Frelinghuysen, see *DCP*, pp. 114–132.

63. *DCP*, p. 108.

64. Theodorus Jacobus Frelinghuysen, *Sermons*, trans. by William Demarest (New York: Reformed Protestant Dutch Church, Board of Publication, 1856), p. 378.

65. Lodge, "Great Awakening," pp. 117–120.

66. Theodorus Jacobus Frelinghuysen, "A Mirror that Flattereth Not . . . ," in *DCP*, p. 168.

67. Ezekiel 3:17–19.

68. Frelinghuysen, *Sermons*, p. 380.

69. Frelinghuysen, "A Mirror," in *DCP*, p. 169.

70. Frelinghuysen, *Sermons*, pp. 79–81, 90–95.

71. *Ibid.* pp. 83–85, 90–95.

72. *Ibid.* pp. 92–95; 374.

73. *DCP*, p. 72.

74. Lodge, "Great Awakening," p. 128.

75. For an excellent summary account of the New England Puritans' view

of the clergy, see David D. Hall, *The Faithful Shepherd: A History of the New England Ministry in the Seventeenth Century* (New York: W. W. Norton, 1972). Norman Pettit provides the best treatment of Puritan conversion theology in his *Heart Prepared,* and F. Ernest Stoeffler offers a synthesis of the Puritan perspective on the "practice of piety" in his *Rise of Evangelical Pietism,* pp. 24–108.

76. Hall, *Faithful Shepherd,* p. 54–55.

2. SOURCES OF PRE-AWAKENING PRESBYTERIAN DIVISIONS

1. Because the first page of the Philadelphia Presbytery's 1706 minutes is lost, it is impossible to know whether a church constitution or creed was discussed. However, in subsequent meetings of the presbytery, and later the Synod, there is no reference to any official documents of this kind, and John Thomson justified his subscription overture in 1729 by noting the lack of such standards. *Records of the Presbyterian Church in the United States of America . . . 1706–1788* (Philadelphia: Presbyterian Board of Publication and Sabbath School Work, 1904), p. vi; *FAT,* p. 30; and (John Thomson), *An Overture Presented to the Reverend Synod of Dissenting Ministers, Sitting in Philadelphia, in the Month of September 1728* [Philadelphia]: printed for author, 1729), pp. 28–29.

2. For a more complete discussion of the theological and ecclesiastical differences between presbyterianism in New England, Scotland, and Ireland, see *FAT,* pp. 16–20.

3. *Ibid.*

4. *MPC,* pp. 46, 47, 50, 51.

5. Jonathan Dickinson, *A Sermon Preached at the Opening of the Synod At Philadelphia, September 19, 1722* (Boston: T. Fleet, 1723); Charles Robert Reed, "Image Alteration in a Mass Movement: A Rhetorical Analysis of the Role of the Log College in the Great Awakening" (Ph.D. diss., Ohio State University, 1972), p. 47; Barkley, "Presbyterian Church in Ireland," pp. 260–261; Frederick W. Loetscher, "The Adopting Act," *Journal of the Presbyterian Historical Society* 13 (December 1929): 339; and James H. Nichols, "Colonial Presbyterianism Adopts Its Standards," *Journal of Presbyterian History* 34 (March 1956): 55–56.

6. Webster, *History of the Presbyterian Church,* p. 98.

7. Dickinson, *Sermon . . . September 19, 1722,* pp. 1, 2.

8. *Ibid.,* pp. 12–20.

9. *Ibid.,* p. 18.

10. Martin E. Lodge has carefully documented the negative effects of middle colony pluralism on local religious life just prior to the Great Awakening. See Martin E. Lodge, "The Crisis of the Churches in the Middle Colonies,

1720–1750," in *Interpreting Colonial America: Selected Readings*, 2nd ed., ed. James Kirby Martin (New York: Harper and Row, 1978), pp. 410–427.

11. John Thomson expressed this rationale for subscription in his *Overture . . . 1728*, pp. 28–29.

12. "Minutes of the Presbytery of New Castle," p. 100; Jedidiah Andrews to Benjamin Colman, 7 April 1729, Beinecke Library, Yale University, New Haven; and *MPC*, p. 98.

13. Jedidiah Andrews to Benjamin Colman, 30 April 1722, Beinecke Library, Yale University, New Haven.

14. Thomson, *Overture . . . 1728*, p. 4.

15. [Jonathan Dickinson], *Remarks Upon A Discourse Intituled An Overture, Presented to The Reverend Synod of Dissenting Ministers sitting in Philadelphia, in the Month of September, 1728* (New York: John Peter Zenger, 1729).

16. Thomson, *Overture . . . 1728*, pp. 8ff.

17. *Ibid*, pp. 15–16, 18–19.

18. *Ibid.*, pp. 20–21.

19. [Dickinson], *Remarks Upon . . . An Overture*, pp. 27–28.

20. Thomson, *Overture . . . 1728*, pp. 28–29.

21. [Dickinson], *Remarks Upon . . . An Overture*, pp. 7–11.

22. [Dickinson], *Remarks Upon . . . An Overture*, pp. 16–18.

23. Howard Miller, *The Revolutionary College: American Presbyterian Higher Education, 1707–1837* (New York: New York University Press, 1976), p. 11.

24. *MPC*, pp. 103–104; and Nichols, "Colonial Presbyterianism Adopts Its Standards," pp. 56, 59.

25. *MPC*, pp. 103–104.

26. *Ibid.*, p. 104.

27. *Ibid.*, p. 105.

28. "Minutes of the Presbytery of New Castle," p. 175; Donegal Presbytery, "The Records of the Proceedings of the Presbytery of Dunagal, 1732–1750," vol. I, 11 October 1732, Presbyterian Historical Society, Philadelphia; Nichols, "Colonial Presbyterianism Adopts Its Standards," p. 60; and *MPC*, pp. 141–142.

29. *MPC*, pp. 120–121.

30. Benjamin Franklin, *The Autobiography of Benjamin Franklin*, ed. Leonard W. Labaree et al. (New Haven: Yale University Press, 1964), pp. 147, 167; and Merton A. Christenson, "Franklin on the Hemphill Trial: Deism Versus Presbyterian Orthodoxy," *William and Mary Quarterly*, 3rd series, 10 (July 1953): 429–430.

31. Other than short articles published in the *Philadelphia Pennsylvania Gazette*, Franklin issued the following pamphlets on the Hemphill affair: *Some Observations on the Proceedings Against The Rev. Mr. Hemphill; With A*

Vindication of his Sermons (Philadelphia: B. Franklin, 1735); *A Letter to a Friend in the Country, Containing the Substance of a Sermon Preached at Philadelphia, in the Congregation of The Rev. Mr. Hemphill, Concerning the Terms of Christian and Ministerial Communion* (Philadelphia: B. Franklin, 1735); and *A Defense Of the Rev. Mr. Hemphill's "Observations: Or, An Answer to The Vindication of The Reverend Commission"* (Philadelphia: B. Franklin, 1735). Although his interpretation of internal Presbyterian politics is untrustworthy, Melvin Buxbaum provides an excellent treatment of Franklin's changing attitude toward the Presbyterian Church during the last half of the eighteenth century. See Melvin H. Buxbaum, *Benjamin Franklin and the Zealous Presbyterians* (University Park, Pa.: Pennsylvania State University Press, 1975).

32. [Jonathan Dickinson], *Remarks Upon a Pamphlet, Entitled, A Letter to a Friend in the Country, containing the Substance of a Sermon preached at Philadelphia, in the Congregation of the Rev. Mr. Hemphill* (Philadelphia: Andrew Bradford, 1735), pp. 134–135.

33. *MPC*, pp. 141–142.

34. Nichols, "Colonial Presbyterianism Adopts Its Standards," p. 61.

35. *MPC*, pp. 136, 146.

36. *Ibid.*, pp. 104, 141–142, 152; "Minutes of the Presbytery of New Castle," p. 180.

37. For Gilbert Tennent's own account of John Tennent's illness, see Gilbert Tennent, "A Prefatory Discourse to the following Sermons with Relations of some Memoirs of the Author's Conversion and Character," in John Tennent, *The Nature of Regeneration opened, and its absolute Necessity, in order to Salvation, demonstrated. In a Sermon From John III. 3* (London: J. Oswald, 1741), pp. iii–viii. The earliest printed description of William Tennent, Jr.'s, illness can be found in Elias Boudinot's *Memoirs of the Life of the Reverend William Tennent* (Philadelphia, 1827), pp. 12–21.

38. Gilbert Tennent, "Prefatory Discourse," pp. iii–viii.

39. Boudinot, *Memoirs,* pp. 12–21.

40. *Ibid.*

41. Gilbert Tennent to Thomas Prince, 24 August 1744, in *Christian History . . . 1744, 45,* p. 295.

42. *MPC*, pp. 122–123.

43. *Ibid.*, p. 123.

44. *Ibid.*

45. Gilbert Tennent, "Prefatory Discourse," pp. xi–xii.

46. Gilbert Tennent, *A Solemn Warning To The Secure World, From The God of terrible Majesty. Or, The Presumptuous Sinner Detected, his Pleas Consider'd, and his Doom Display'd* (Boston: S. Kneeland and T. Green, 1735).

47. *Ibid.*, pp. 12, 15–19, 34, 50, 85, 87–88, 97, 102.

48. *Ibid.*, pp. 2, 19–32.

49. *Ibid.*, pp. 97–102.

50. *Ibid.*, p. 99.

51. *Ibid.*, pp. 72–73.

52. *Ibid.*, pp. 70–71.

53. The Maidenhead pulpit had recently fallen vacant when the church's pastor, Joseph Morgan, had been suspended from the ministry for drunkenness. Gilbert Tennent, "The Solemn Scene Of The Last Judgment. Open'd in a Sermon, On 2. Thes. i. 6, 7, 8, 9, Preach'd at Maiden-Head in New Jersey, May the 23d, 1737," in *Sermons on Sacramental Occasions by Divers Ministers* (Boston: J. Draper, 1739), pp. 217–218.

54. Part of the Philadelphia Presbytery's opposition to Tennent's visit may have been caused by a contemporary debate between David Cowell and Gilbert Tennent. For the past few months, Tennent and Cowell had exchanged several long letters in which each attacked the other's view of man's chief end. The debate between these two men would surface at the 1738 Synod when Tennent asked the Synod for its judgment. In a paper apparently prepared by Tennent for the Synod's deliberations, Tennent quoted Cowell's opinion that "self love is the foundation of all the love we owe or pay to God." Tennent strongly objected to this view, since he maintained that humanity's highest end was the glorification of God. Tennent did not deny that God had "graciously so ordered . . . (creation) that man shall obtain his chief good in the end which he is obliged to seek." But he did reject the notion that self-love could lead humanity to its chief end. According to Tennent, self-love was an egocentric affection that tempted the individual to commit "spiritual idolatry" by giving priority to the self. Therefore, it could never lead individuals to glorify God with all their heart, mind, and body. The 1738 Synod did not rule on the controversy. Instead it referred the matter to its committee. This committee deferred the matter to the next Synod. In 1739 the Synod decided that the debate was the result of the two participants' unclear notions on the subject. The Synod declared that the "designs of the glory of God and our own happiness are so inseparably connected that they must never be placed in opposition to each other." Tennent was dissatisfied with this conclusion. Therefore, he continued to agitate for a review of the case. However, the 1740 Synod ruled against Tennent and the matter was closed. Gilbert Tennent, Ms. Reply to David Cowell, n.d., Presbyterian Historical Society, Philadelphia; and *MPC*, pp. 150, 156–160, 165, 169.

55. Gilbert Tennent, "The Duty of Self-Examination, Considered In a Sermon, On I Cor. 11.28. Preach'd at Maiden-Head in New Jersey, October 22, 1737. Before the Celebration of the Lord's Supper," in *Sermons on Sacramental Occasions By Divers Ministers* (Boston, 1739).

56. *MPC*, pp. 153–154.

57. The three Log College graduates in the New Brunswick Presbytery were Gilbert Tennent, Samuel Blair, and William Tennent, Jr. *MPC*, p. 154.

58. *GWJ*, p. 351 (see list of abbreviations).

59. *MPC*, p. 157.

60. Although the subscriptionists were sincerely concerned about the educational qualifications of candidates, their concern could on occasion be embarrassingly selective. At the 1738 Synod George Gillespie strongly protested the Donegal Presbytery's recent treatment of Richard Zanchy. Zanchy was the son-in-law of the staunch subscriptionist John Thomson, but he plagiarized his ordination sermon. When called before the Donegal Presbytery, he was rebuked rather than suspended and mention of his plagiarism was omitted from the presbytery's minutes. In response to Gillespie's protest, the subscriptionist-dominated Synod did little more than slap the hand of the Donegal Presbytery for not mentioning Zanchy's offense. *MPC*, p. 155; and *FAT*, pp. 70, 74–75.

61. *MPC*, p. 157.

62. Philadelphia Presbytery, "Minutes 1733–1746," 29 June 1736, Presbyterian Historical Society, Philadelphia; and [Francis Alison], *An Examination and Refutation of Mr. Gilbert Tennent's Remarks Upon the Protestation Presented to the Synod of Philadelphia, June 1, 1741* (Philadelphia, 1742), p. 21.

63. New Brunswick Presbytery, "Minutes 1738–1756," vol. I, 8 August 1738 and 7 September 1738, Presbyterian Historical Society, Philadelphia.

64. *Ibid.*, 7 September 1738.

65. Philadelphia Presbytery, "Minutes," 19 September 1738.

66. *MPC*, pp. 161–162. The paper of objections presented by the New Brunswick Presbytery was published in 1741 under the title "The Apology of the Presbytery of New-Brunswick, for their Dissenting from Two Acts or New Religious Laws, which were made at the last Session of our Synod." See Gilbert Tennent, *Remarks Upon A Protestation Presented To The Synod Of Philadelphia, June 1, 1741* (Philadelphia: B. Franklin, 1741), pp. 37–68.

67. *Ibid.*, pp. 40–46.

68. *Ibid.*, pp. 47–52.

69. *Ibid.*, p. 53.

70. *Ibid.*, pp. 57–63.

71. *Ibid.*, p. 67.

72. *Ibid.*, p. 51.

73. Bryan F. LeBeau, "The Subscription Controversy and Johnathan Dickinson," *Journal of Presbyterian History* 54 (Fall 1976): 328.

74. In the Synod's 1738 itineracy act, a minister who complained about an itinerant's preaching had to be a member of the vacant congregation's presbytery. In 1739 the Synod decided that a clergyman from any presbytery could warn away an itinerant. Also, once a complaint had been registered, the itinerant was obliged to appear before the presbytery that had received a complaint. *MPC*, p. 163.

75. *Ibid.*

76. *Ibid.*, pp. 147–148.

3. THE GREAT AWAKENING

1. *MPC*, p. 164.

2. *Ibid.*, p. 142; Philadelphia Presbytery, "Minutes," 1 July 1736 and 15 September 1736.

3. Philadelphia Presbytery, "Minutes," 19 September 1738 and 25–26 October 1738.

4. *Ibid.*, 15–18 September 1739.

5. New Brunswick Presbytery, "Minutes," 11 October 1739.

6. *Ibid.*

7. *Ibid.*

8. *Ibid.*, 1 April 1740; *DH*, p. 174.

9. George Whitefield, *Letters of George Whitefield, for the period 1734–1742* (1771; reprint ed., Carlisle, Pa.: Banner of Truth Trust, 1976), p. 109. For the best biography of George Whitefield, see Arnold A. Dallimore, *George Whitefield: The Life and Times of the Great Evangelist of the Eighteenth-Century Revival*, 2 vols.(Westchester, Ill.: Cornerstone Books, 1970–1979).

10. William Howland Kenney, "George Whitefield, Dissenter Priest of the Great Awakening, 1739–1741," *William and Mary Quarterly*, 3rd series, 26 (January 1969): 46–47.

11. Dallimore, *Whitefield*, II:543.

12. *GWJ*, p. 341 (see list of abbreviations).

13. *Ibid.*, pp. 342–343.

14. Jonathan Dickinson, *Danger of Schisms and Contentions With Respect to The Ministry and Ordinances of the Gospel, represented In a Sermon Preached at the Meeting of the Presbytery at Woodbridge, October 10th, 1739* (New York: J. Peter Zenger, 1739), pp. 6–14.

15. *Ibid.*, pp. 28–29.

16. *Ibid.*, p. 20.

17. *Ibid.*, pp. 20–21.

18. *Ibid.*, pp. 20–27.

19. *Ibid.*

20. *Ibid.*, p. 22.

21. *GWJ*, pp. 344–347.

22. *Ibid.*, pp. 347–348.

23. *Ibid.*, p. 134.

24. Gilbert Tennent, Benjamin Colman, and William Tennent, *Three Letters To The Reverend Mr. George Whitefield* (Philadelphia: Andrew Bradford, [1739]), p. 8. Tennent's sermon at Nottingham was first issued by Benjamin Franklin in 1740. The first edition quickly sold out, so Franklin published a second edition in 1740. In addition to Franklin's editions, Christopher Sauer of Germantown issued a German edition of the sermon in 1740, and a Boston

edition based on Franklin's second edition was published in 1742. Gilbert Tennent, *The Danger of An Unconverted Ministry, Consider'd In A Sermon On Mark VI, 34. Preached at Nottingham, in Pennsylvania, March 8, Anno. 1739, 40*, 2nd ed. (Philadelphia: B. Franklin, 1740).

25. Elizabeth A. Ingersoll, "Francis Alison: American "Philosophe," 1705–1799" (Ph.D. diss., University of Delaware, 1974), p. 339; and *FAT*, pp. 88–89.

26. Tennent, *Danger of An Unconverted Ministry*, pp. 6–7.

27. *Ibid.*, pp. 8–9.

28. Tennent tempered this radical suggestion somewhat by attaching two conditions to separations from one's regular pastor. Before leaving a parish, laypeople were to seek "benefit" from their pastor's ministry, and when departing, they were to make a regular application for their separation. The last of these conditions was hardly practical since most clergymen who were unacceptable to lay revival supporters would not have admitted their own unconverted state as a valid reason for an orderly dismissal. *Ibid.*, p. 12.

29. *Ibid.*, pp. 13, 18–19.

30. *Ibid.*, p. 20.

31. *Ibid.*, p. 17.

32. *Ibid.*, p. 16–17.

33. In his sermon Tennent specifically attacked the idea that remaining in one's church automatically put one "in God's way." *Ibid.*, pp. 12, 14, 18–19.

34. Whitefield informed Tennent as early as January 22, 1740 that he would return to the middle colonies in time for the 1740 Synod. Whitefield, *Letters*, pp. 141–142.

35. *GWJ*, pp. 402–427.

36. *Ibid.*, pp. 423–424.

37. Jonathan Dickinson to Thomas Foxcroft, 24 May 1740, Thomas Foxcroft Correspondence, Firestone Library, Princeton University, Princeton, N.J.

38. *GWJ*, p. 419; *Philadelphia Pennsylvania Gazette*, 12 June 1740; C. H. Maxson, *The Great Awakening in the Middle Colonies* (1920; reprint ed., Gloucester, Mass.: Peter Smith, 1958), p. 62. At one point during the Society Hill revival, Gilbert Tennent refused to let Jonathan Dickinson preach on the Whitefield stage. He would later regret this decision. Nevertheless, he justified his action by the rather lame excuse that the absent Whitefield had not agreed to let Dickinson preach on the stage. See Gilbert Tennent, *Remarks Upon a Protestation*, pp. 7–8.

39. *MPC*, pp. 169–170.

40. *Ibid.*, p. 171; Gilbert Tennent, *Remarks Upon A Protestation*, pp. 3–6; *Examination . . . of . . . Tennent's Remarks*, pp. 11–12, 15–17; [Robert Cross], *A Protestation Presented To the Synod of Philadelphia: June 1, 1741* (Philadelphia: B. Franklin, 1741), pp. 2–3.

41. *MPC*, p. 171; and Samuel Blair, "A Vindication of the Brethren," in *The Works Of The Reverend Mr. Samuel Blair* (Philadelphia: William Bradford, 1754), pp. 205, 225–226; John Thomson, *The Government of the Church of Christ* (Philadelphia: Andrew Bradford, 1741), pp. 28–31, 35–38, 45–46.

42. *MPC*, p. 171; Blair, "Vindication," pp. 205, 225–226; and Thomson, *Government of the Church*, pp. 9–10, 16–17, 19–21.

43. Thomson, *Government of the Church*, p. 21.

44. Gilbert Tennent, *A Discourse Upon Christ's Kingly-Office, Preached at Nottingham, In Pennsylvania, Sept. 24th, 1740* (Boston: C. Harrison, 1741), pp. ii–iii.

45. Thomson, *Government of the Church*, pp. 8, 24, 28; and Blair, "Vindication," pp. 225–226.

46. *MPC*, p. 171.

47. *GWJ*, p. 488.

48. The churches at Christiana Bridge, White Clay Creek, and Bohemia Manor were served by Charles Tennent, George Gillespie, and Alexander Hutcheson, respectively. All these men were supporters of Tennent's program at the time. *Ibid.*; Maxson, *Great Awakening*, pp. 63–65.

49. Donegal Presbytery, "Records," 6 September 1740; Maxson, *Great Awakening*, pp. 66f.; *FAT*, pp. 99–101; and *The Querists, Or An Extract of Sundry Passages taken out of Mr. Whitefield's printed Sermons, Journals and Letters: Together With Some Scruples propos'd in proper Queries raised on each Remark. By some Church-Members of the Presbyterian Persuasion* (Philadelphia, 1740).

50. Maxson, *Great Awakening*, pp. 66f.

51. *GWJ*, p. 491.

52. *Ibid.*, p. 344.

53. *Boston Weekly News-Letter*, 5 June 1740; *FAT*, p. 88; Reed, "Image Alteration in a Mass Movement," p. 250; Dietmar Rothermund, *The Layman's Progress: Religious and Political Experience in Colonial Pennsylvania, 1740–1770* (Philadelphia: University of Pennsylvania Press, 1961), p. 24; and Dallimore, *Whitefield*, I:521.

54. *GWJ*, p. 491.

55. Whitefield explained to Belcher that Tennent's purpose in coming to New England was "to blow up the divine fire lately kindled there." He also recommended Tennent to Belcher as "a solid, judicious, and zealous minister of the Lord Jesus Christ," Whitefield, *Letters*, p. 221. The Harvard tutor was Daniel Rogers. Rogers had accompanied Whitefield on his return from New England. At the meeting with Tennent, Rogers gave Gilbert an invitation from several pastors in Boston to come to New England. Mary A. Tennent, *Light in Darkness*, p. 82.

56. *Boston Weekly News-Letter*, 1–8 January 1741, 22–29 January 1741, 26 March–2 April 1741; *The General Magazine and Historical Chronicle, For*

All the British Plantations in America, vol. I (1741; reprint ed., New York: Columbia University Press, 1938), I:144–145.

57. There are only three references to Tennent in extant copies of New England papers during the winter of 1740–1741. The first simply reports Tennent's arrival in Boston. The second announces the publication of a Tennent sermon, and the third reports Tennent's departure from Boston. Included with the last notice is a complimentary poem on Tennent's visit. *Boston Weekly Post–Boy*, 19 January 1741; *Boston Weekly News-Letter*, 12–19 February 1741, 27 February–5 March, 1741. Other brief comments on Tennent's activities may have circulated in New England papers, since a few were reprinted in middle colony papers. See *Philadelphia Pennsylvania Gazette*, 15 January 1741; *General Magazine*, 9, 15 January 1741; and *Philadelphia American Weekly Mercury*, 16 July 1741. Gilbert Tennent, *The Examiner, Examined, Or Gilbert Tennent, Harmonious* (Philadelphia: William Bradford, 1743), pp. 38–40.

58. John Nichols, *Illustrations of the Literary History of the Eighteenth Century*, 2 vols. (London, 1822), II:304; and [Charles Chauncey], *A Letter from a Gentleman in Boston, to Mr. George Wishart . . . Concerning The State of Religion in New-England* (1742; reprint ed., Edinburgh: Clarendon Historical Society, 1883), 7–8.

59. Prince, *Christian History . . . 1744, 5*, p. 384.

60. Hopkins did not complete his plans to study with Tennent because the following September he heard Jonathan Edwards speak at commencement. Impressed with Edwards, Hopkins decided to apprentice under Edwards. Sereno E. Dwight, "The Life of President Edwards," in *The Works of President Edwards*, ed. Sereno Dwight, 9 vols. (New York: S. Converse, 1829), I:156. For further documentary evidence of Tennent's effect on the Yale student body, see Stephen Nissenbaum, ed., *The Great Awakening at Yale College* (Belmont, Calif.: Wadsworth Publishing, 1972), pp. 143–145.

61. The reports that credited Tennent with reaping the harvest Whitefield's first New England tour had sown were the most numerous. *The Weekly History: or, An Account of the Most Remarkable Particulars relating to the present Progress of the Gospel* (London: J. Lewis, 1743), nos. 16 and 26; Thomas Prince, ed., *The Christian History Containing Accounts of The Revival and Propagation of Religion in Great-Britain and America for the year 1743* (Boston: S. Kneeland and T. Green, 1743), pp. 397–399; Prince, *Christian History . . . 1744, 5*, pp. 105–106, 125, 126–127, 133–134.

62. "The Glasgow Weekly History, 1743," *Massachusetts Historical Society, Proceedings* 53 (October 1919–June 1920): 194–196.

63. "Biography [of] . . . Gilbert Tennent," *Evangelical Intelligencer* 3 (1807–1808): 244–245n.

64. Gilbert Tennent, *The Righteousness of the Scribes and Pharisees considered* (Boston: J. Draper, 1741), pp. 7–8, 12.

65. Reports of Tennent's New England tour that were published in England

or Scotland may be found in *The Weekly History*, nos. 9, 11, 16, 17, 26; and "The Glasgow Weekly History, 1743," pp. 194–198, 201, 202. Several documents also show that Whitefield's Scottish supporters wanted Tennent to come to Scotland and that Whitefield asked Tennent to make such a trip. See *The Weekly History*, no. 42; and Gilbert Tennent to George Whitefield, 5 June 1742, Box: "Pennsylvanica 1740s + Lischy," Folder: "Pennsylvania Controversies," Moravian Archives, Bethlehem, Pa.

66. Gilbert Tennent to George Whitefield, 5 June 1742.

67. *Ibid.*; Genealogical information, Gilbert Tennent: Trustee, Mudd Library, Princeton University, Princeton, N.J.; and Mary A. Tennent, *Light in Darkness*, p. 94.

68. Jonathan Dickinson to Colonel Alford, 12 April 1742, Thomas Foxcroft Correspondence, Firestone Library, Princeton University Princeton, N.J.

69. By August 1740 the *Philadelphia Pennsylvania Gazette* had published five pro-Whitefield articles and only one negative item on Whitefield's ministry. See the *Philadelphia Pennsylvania Gazette*, 13 December 1739, 27 December 1739, 18 January 1740, 28 March 1740, 1 May 1740, and 6 May 1740. The *Philadelphia American Weekly Mercury*, on the other hand, had published three articles in favor of Whitefield and only one in opposition to him. See the *Philadelphia American Weekly Mercury*, 6 December 1739, 27 December 1739, 8 January 1740, and 15 January 1740. For the accounts of the Society Hill revivals, see the *Philadelphia Pennsylvania Gazette*, 12 June 1740, 6 July 1740, 15 July 1740 and 11 August 1740.

70. *The Querists*, pp. 23, 40–43; and Maxson, *Great Awakening*, p. 67.

71. *Philadelphia Pennsylvania Gazette*, 16 October 1740.

72. George Whitefield, *A Letter From the Reverend Mr. Whitefield, To some Church Members of the Presbyterian Persuasion, in Answer to certain Scruples and Queries relating to some Passages in his printed Sermons and other Writings* (Boston: S. Kneeland and T. Green, J. Edwards and S. Eliot, 1740), pp. 56–67.

73. *A Short Reply to Mr. Whitefield's letter which he wrote in answer to the Querists* (Philadelphia, 1741); Samuel Blair, *A Particular Consideration Of A Piece, Entitled, "The Querists"* (Philadelphia: B. Franklin, 1741).

74. *General Magazine*, p. 121.

75. *Ibid.*, pp. 272–276.

76. *Boston Weekly Post-Boy*, 12 January 1741, quoted in *General Magazine*, pp. 123–124.

77. *New England Weekly Journal*, 27 January 1741, quoted in *General Magazine*, pp. 124–126.

78. *The Querists, Part III, Or, An Extract of sundry Passages taken out of Mr. G. Tennent's Sermon preached at Nottingham, of The Danger of an Unconverted Ministry* (Philadelphia: B. Franklin, 1741), pp. 11, 38.

79. *Ibid.*, pp. 32, 37, 95.

80. *Ibid.*, pp. 69–70.

81. *Ibid.*, p. 112.

82. *Ibid.*, pp. 99–103.

83. Ingersoll, "Alison," pp. 361–362; and Donegal Presbytery, "Records," 10 October 1740 and 10–11 December 1740.

84. Donegal Presbytery, "Records," 10–11 December 1740.

85. *Ibid.*

86. *Ibid.*, 9 April 1741; and Ingersoll, "Alison," pp. 365–366.

87. Donegal Presbytery, "Records," 9 April 1741.

88. *MPC*, p. 173. An extant letter by Jedidiah Andrews suggests that the New York Presbytery members planned their absence and urged their Synod associates prior to the 1741 meeting to avoid debate because of their absence. See Jedidiah Andrews to Unidentified Recipient, 25 June 1741, Simon Gratz Autograph Collection, American Colonial Clergy, Pennsylvania Historical Society, Philadelphia.

89. *MPC*, pp. 173–174.

90. George Gillespie, *A Letter To The Rev. Brethren of the Presbytery of New-York, or of Elizabeth-Town* (Philadelphia: B. Franklin, 1742), p. 15; and Maxson, *Great Awakening*, p. 74.

91. The protestors of 1740 who were to be ejected by this new protestation included the following ministers and elders: ministers—Samuel Blair, Alexander Craighead, John Cross, George Gillespie, John Henry, Alexander Hutchinson, Charles Tennent, Gilbert Tennent, William Tennent, Jr., William Tennent, Sr., and Eleazer Wales; elders—David Chambers, James Cockran, Robert Cummings, William Emmitt, Daniel Henderson, James McCoy, William McCrea, Robert Mathews, James Miller, Hugh Lynn, Joseph Steel, Richard Walker, John Weir and Thomas Worthington. *MPC*, pp. 163, 170; and [Cross], *Protestation*, pp. 6–8.

92. [Cross], *Protestation*, p. 15; *Examination . . . of . . . Tennent's Remarks*, pp. 133–149.

93. Gilbert Tennent, *Remarks Upon A Protestation*, pp. 32–35.

94. Historians disagree as to the exact numbers on each side at the 1741 Synod, but all agree the antirevivalists controlled the majority of those present. *FAT*, p. 104; Maxson, *Great Awakening*, p. 75; and Richard Cartwright Austin, "The Great Awakening in Philadelphia" (B.A. thesis, Swarthmore College, 1956), p. 115.

95. Jedidiah Andrews to Unidentified Recipient, 15 June 1741.

96. Gillespie, *Letter to the New York Presbytery*, p. 3.

97. *Ibid.*, pp. 3, 5.

98. New Brunswick Presbytery, "Minutes," 2 June 1741.

99. *Ibid.*

100. [Cross], *Protestation*, p. 3; Thomson, *Government of the Church*.

101. Thomson, *Government of the Church*, pp. 59–60, 64.

102. *Ibid.*, pp. 62–63.
103. *Ibid.*, p. 61.
104. Blair, "Vindication," p. 205, 218–219.
105. *Ibid.*, pp. 211–212.
106. Gilbert Tennent, *Remarks Upon A Protestation*, p. 9.
107. *Ibid.*, pp. 14–16.
108. *Examination . . . of . . . Tennent's Remarks*, p. 35.
109. *Ibid.*, p. 67.

4. TROUBLES WITHIN THE REVIVAL CAMP

1. For the most complete accounts of the arrests and trials of John Rowland and William Tennent, Jr., see G. H. Ingram, "History of the Presbytery of New Brunswick: The Trials of Rev. John Rowland and Rev. William Tennent Jr., 1741–1742," *Journal of Presbyterian History* 8 (September 1915): 114–122; Boudinot, *Memoirs of William Tennent*, pp. 38–51; Henry W. Green, "The Trial of the Rev. William Tennent," *Princeton Review* 40 (July 1868): 322–344; and Carl Bridenbaugh, *Early Americans* (New York: Oxford University Press, 1981), pp. 121–149.

2. Ingram, "History of Presbytery of New Brunswick: Trials of Rowland and Tennent," pp. 116–122; and Boudinot, *Memoirs of William Tennent*, pp. 43–58.

3. *FAT*, p. 169.

4. Webster, *History of the Presbyterian Church*, pp. 185–186; and Nichols, "Colonial Presbyterianism Adopts Its Standards," pp. 63–64.

5. Tennent quoted Whitefield as his authority for judging Craighead's views to be too narrow. Whitefield had encountered the same "covenanting scheme" in Scotland when he met the Erskine brothers. As quoted from Gilbert Tennent, *Examiner, Examined*, pp. 120–121. See also Gilbert Tennent, "Fragment on (Alexander) Craighead," Presbyterian Historical Society, Philadelphia; and Whitefield, *Letters*, p. 141.

6. Webster, *History of the Presbyterian Church*, p. 186; and Nichols, "Colonial Presbyterianism Adopts Its Standards," pp. 64–65.

7. Goen, *Revivalism and Separatism*, pp. 28–31.

8. Gilbert Tennent to Rev. Mr. Benjamin Lord, n.d., Pennsylvania Historical Society, Philadelphia; and Gilbert Tennent to Rev. Mr. Stephen Williams, n.d., Pennsylvania Historical Society, Philadelphia. The same letter was also sent to Jonathan Edwards, according to Edwards's biographer, Sereno E. Dwight. Dwight, "Life of President Edwards," I:153.

9. Webster, *History of the Presbyterian Church*, pp. 536, 537.

10. The best chronological account of Davenport's revivals can be found in Webster, *History of the Presbyterian Church*, pp. 537–541; and Goen, *Revivalism and Separatism*, pp. 20–25.

11. Gilbert Tennent to Jonathan Dickinson, 12 February 1742 in *Boston Weekly News-Letter*, 15–22 July 1742.

12. *Ibid.*

13. *New York Weekly Journal*, 12 July 1742.

14. For the early history of the Unitas Fratrum in America, see John R. Weinlick, "Moravianism in the American Colonies," in *Continental Pietism and Early American Christianity*, ed. Stoeffler, pp. 123–163; Vernon Nelson, "The Moravian Church in America," in *Unitas Fratrum*, eds. Mari P. van Buijtenen, Cornelius Dekker, and Huib Leeuwenberg (Utrecht: Rijksarchief, 1975), pp. 145–176; and Adelaide Lisetta, *The Moravians in Georgia, 1735–1740* (Raleigh, N.C.: Edwards and Broughton, 1905).

15. Peter Bohler to Nicholas Zinzendorf, 20 April 1740, Peter Bohler Papers, trans. Albert F. Jordan, Moravian Archives, Bethlehem, Pa.; *GWJ*, p. 410; William Seward, *Journal of a Voyage from Savannah to Philadelphia and from Philadelphia to England, 1740* (London, 1740), p. 13; and Dallimore, *Whitefield*, I:503.

16. Peter Bohler to Nicholas Zinzendorf, 20 April 1740.

17. Peter Bohler to Nicholas Zinzendorf, 25 March 1741, trans. Albert F. Jordan, Peter Bohler Papers, Moravian Archives, Bethlehem, Pa.; and Dallimore, *Whitefield*, I:594–596.

18. Whitefield, *Letters*, pp. 227–229, 251–253.

19. It should be noted that Philip Molther, the Moravian leader of the Fetter Lane Society in London, was the originator of the doctrine of "stillness." For a treatment of Moravian "stillness," see Clifford Towlson, *Moravian and Methodist: Relationships and Influences in the Eighteenth Century* (London: Epworth Press, 1957), pp. 84–104.

20. *Ibid.*

21. Whitefield, *Letters*, pp. 251–253.

22. The letter sent by the Amsterdam Classis was titled "Pastoral and Fatherly Letter, for the Discovery of and warning against the Dangerous Errors of those People who are known under the Name of Moravians." *ER*, IV:2723. The book conveyed to the Dutch Reformed clergy in the colonies was Gerardus Kulenkamp's *Treu-Vatterlicher Hirten-Brief an die Reformirte Gemeine der Stadt Amsterdam auf Veranlassung der Entdeckten und Gefahrlichen Irrthumen der Zinzendorf und Herrnhuthischen Bruderschafft, zur Warnung geschrieben von denen Predigern und Altesten des Amsterdammer Kirchen-Raths* (Amsterdam, 1739).

23. For discussions of the pietist *ecclesiolae in ecclesia*, see Stoeffler, *Rise of Evangelical Pietism*, pp. 237–238; and Brown, *Understanding Pietism*, pp. 60–62.

24. For a general history of the Unitas Fratrum under Zinzendorf's leadership, see J. T. Hamilton and K. G. Hamilton, *History of the Moravian Church: The Renewed Unitas Fratrum, 1722–1957* (Bethlehem, Pa: Interprovincial Board of Christian Education, Moravian Church in America, 1907).

25. The best treatments of Zinzendorf's ecumenical views can be found in Theodor Wettach, *Kirche bei Zinzendorf* (Wuppertal: Rolf Brockhaus, 1971), pp. 59–71; Stoeffler, *German Pietism*, pp. 156–159; and A. J. Lewis, *Zinzendorf, The Ecumenical Pioneer* (Philadelphia: Westminster Press, 1962), pp. 138–160.

26. Wettach, *Kirche*, pp. 59–71; Stoeffler, German Pietism, pp. 156–159; Lewis, *Zinzendorf*, pp. 138–160.

27. A good example of the way Moravian rhetoric could promote suspicion is a reported comment by Peter Bohler in 1754. Speaking to an assembly of Moravian sympathizers, Bohler declared: "We wish that all [Moravian] society members would continue in their respective churches as bait, . . . It is not our way to draw people from the Churches in which they have been brought up, and we earnestly wish the ministers of other denominations would be friendly to us, for in that way they would not lose so many members." Despite Bohler's protestations, many religious leaders felt Moravian "bait" in their congregations was a fifth column undermining the allegiances of all members in their denomination. John R. Weinlick, "Colonial Moravians, Their Status among the Churches," *Pennsylvania History* 26 (July 1959): 220.

28. Jacob John Sessler, *Communal Pietism Among Early American Moravians* (New York: Henry Holt, 1933), p. 24; and Lewis, *Zinzendorf*, pp. 138–160.

29. John B. Frantz, "The Awakening of Religion among the German Settlers in the Middle Colonies," *William and Mary Quarterly*, 3rd series, 33 (April 1976): 274, 281–282.

30. Gilbert Tennent, *Some Account Of The Principles Of the Moravians* (London: S. Mason, 1743), p. iii. This work was originally published as an appendix to Gilbert Tennent's *Necessity of holding fast the Truth* (Boston: S. Kneeland and T. Green, 1743). However, the preface in which this quotation appears was included only in the London edition.

31. Gilbert Tennent, "Some Account Of The Principles Of the Moravians," in *Necessity of holding fast the Truth*, p. 73.

32. Peter Bohler to Nicholas Zinzendorf, 25 March 1741.

33. Quoted in John F. Watson, *Annals of Philadelphia* (Philadelphia: E. L. Carey and A. Hart, 1830), p. 521.

34. "Desaven des Herrn Gilbert Tennents Pfarrers in Neu Braunschweig, inserirt in die Philadelphischen Zeitungen," in *Budingische Sammlung* 3 (Budingen, Germany, 1744): 309.

35. Gilbert Tennent, *Necessity of holding fast the Truth*, p. 31.

36. *Ibid.*, p. 34.

37. *Ibid.*, p. 35.

38. *Ibid.*, p. 10.

39. Stoeffler, *German Pietism*, p. 144.

40. This rendition of faculty psychology was peculiar to Tennent. Classical

thinkers considered the "understanding" and the "will" to be the only true "faculties," for they alone distinguished the human from all other animals. Norman S. Fiering, "Will and Intellect in the New England Mind," *William and Mary Quarterly*, 3rd series, 19 (October 1972): 517–521. For Tennent's unique conception of faculty psychology both before and after the Fall, see Gilbert Tennent, *A Solemn Warning*, pp. 113, 121–123; Gilbert Tennent, *The Necessity of keeping the Soul* (Philadelphia: William Bradford, 1745), pp. 7–8; and Gilbert Tennent, *Sermons on Important Subjects* (Philadelphia: James Chattin, 1758), pp. 164–165.

41. Gilbert Tennent, *Examiner, Examined*, pp. 46, 48–49, 56; and Gilbert Tennent, "De Sanctificatione," 10 February 1744/5, Gilbert Tennent Ms. Sermons, Presbyterian Historical Society, Philadelphia, Pa.

42. Gilbert Tennent to Jonathan Dickinson, 12 February 1742. After its first appearance in the *Boston Weekly News-Letter*, it was reprinted in both the *Philadelphia Pennsylvania Gazette* and the *Philadelphia American Weekly Mercury*. *Philadelphia Pennsylvania Gazette*, 12 August 1742; and *Philadelphia American Weekly Mercury*, 5–12 August 1742.

43. *Ibid.*

44. Jonathan Dickinson to Colonel Alford, 12 April 1742.

45. *MPC*, pp. 176–178.

46. *Ibid.*, pp. 177–178.

47. Only one Old Light was swayed by the New York Presbytery's protest. That was Francis Alison. Alison did not join in the Dickinson protest, but he did enter a statement into the minutes that stated his belief that the ejected brethren should be given a fair trial. *MPC*, p. 178.

48. Webster, *History of the Presbyterian Church*, p. 540; "The Declaration of a Number of the associated Pastors in Boston and Charles-Town, with Regard to the Rev. Mr. Davenport, and his Conduct," In *Philadelphia Pennsylvania Gazette*, 17 August 1742; Goen, *Revivalism and Separatism*, pp. 20–25; *Boston Weekly News-Letter*, 19–26 April 1742; and *Philadelphia American Weekly Mercury*, 9–16 September 1742.

49. Gilbert Tennent to Jonathan Dickinson, 12 February 1742, in *Philadelphia Pennsylvania Gazette*, 12 August 1742; and *Philadelphia American Weekly Mercury*, 5–12 August 1742.

50. Gilbert Tennent to Benjamin Franklin, 19 August 1742, in *Philadelphia Pennsylvania Gazette*, 2 September 1742; and *Boston Weekly News-Letter*, 16–23 September 1742.

51. [John Hancock], *The Examiner, Or Gilbert against Tennent* (1743; reprint ed., Philadelphia: B. Franklin, 1743), p. 11. In September 1742, David Evans criticized Tennent's letter to Dickinson, and in December he critiqued the logic of Tennent's letter of explanation to Benjamin Franklin. To redeem Tennent's sagging reputation, Samuel Finley defended Tennent against Evans's commentary. David Evans to Mr. Franklin, in *Philadelphia Pennsylvania Gazette*,

2 September 1742; David Evans to Mr. Franklin, in *Philadelphia Pennsylvania Gazette*, 8 December 1742, postscript; and Samuel Finley to Mr. Franklin, in *Philadelphia Pennsylvania Gazette*, 8 December 1742, postscript.

52. "Indenture for the New Building in Philadelphia," 14 November 1740, Box: "Pennsylvanica 1740s + Lischy," Folder: "Pennsylvania Controversies," Moravian Archives, Bethlehem, Pa.; Charles P. Keith, *Chronicles of Pennsylvania*, 2 vols. (Philadelphia: Patterson and White, 1917), I:361–362.

53. "Indenture for the New Building," 14 November 1740.

54. "Articul. darauf sich die Trustee der New-building in Philad. unterschrieb haben," n.d., Box: "Pennsylvanica 1740s + Lischy," Folder: "Pennsylvania Controversies," Moravian Archives, Bethlehem Pa.

55. Thomas Nobel to Edward Evans, 28 December 1741, Box: "Letters: L–Z," Folder: "N," Moravian Archives, Bethlehem, Pa.

56. Gilbert Tennent, William Tennent, Jr., John Rowland, Samuel Blair, and Samuel Finley led worship at one time or another during the first three years that the congregation of the New Building held services. For information on their early ministry in the New Building, see "An Account of the origin, progress and present State of the Second Presbyterian Church in the city of Philadelphia," Presbyterian Historical Society, Philadelphia.

57. Between the time Gilbert Tennent met with Zinzendorf in November 1741 and the summer of 1742, Presbyterian New Lights had several meetings with Moravian representatives to discuss their respective theologies. Each of these conferences convinced another New Light that the Moravians were a dangerous sect and, therefore, should be kept out of the New Building at all cost. Meetings between Samuel Finley and Nicholas Zinzendorf, Gilbert Tennent and August Spangenberg, Samuel Hazard and Christopher Pyrleus, and Theodorus Frelinghuysen and Nicholas Zinzendorf are described in Gilbert Tennent, "Some Account Of the Moravians," pp. 76–77, 99, 109–110. Robert Eastburn, Jr., also provided a report of a stormy encounter with Christopher Pyrleus in a letter to Whitefield. See Robert Eastburn to George Whitefield, 7 June 1742, Box: "Pennsylvanica 1740s + Lischy," Folder: "Pennsylvania Controversies," Moravian Archives, Bethlehem, Pa. One other New Light account of a conference with Moravians is by Samuel Finley. See Samuel Finley to Unidentified Recipient, 18 January 1742, Hazard Papers, Miscellaneous, Pennsylvania Historical Society, Philadelphia.

58. Peter Bohler to Nicholas Zinzendorf, 13/24 June 1742, trans. Albert F. Jordan, Peter Bohler Papers, Moravian Archives, Bethlehem, Pa.

59. "Br. Lewis's Letter to Br. Boeler in Philadelphia when Mr. Gilbert Tennent was preaching very severely against the Brethren. A. 1742," Nicholas Zinzendorf Letters, Box A, Folder IV, Moravian Archives, Bethlehem, Pa.

60. Kenneth G. Hamilton, ed., *The Bethlehem Diary* (Bethlehem, Pa.: Archives of Moravian Church, 1971), p. 109.

61. Peter Bohler to Nicholas Zinzendorf, 28 July 1742, trans. Albert F. Jordan, Peter Bohler Papers, Moravian Archives, Bethlehem, Pa.

62. George Whitefield to Gilbert Tennent, 27 February 1742, Box: "Pennsylvanica 1740s + Lischy," Folder: "Untitled," Moravian Archives, Bethlehem, Pa.

63. Gilbert Tennent to George Whitefield, 7 June 1742, Box: "Pennsylvanica 1740s + Lischy," Folder: "Pennsylvania Controversies," Moravian Archives, Bethlehem, Pa.

64. *Ibid.*

65. Whitefield, *Letters*, p. 441; and Jonathan Dickinson to Thomas Foxcroft, 21 January 1745/6.

5. REDEEMING A FALTERING AWAKENING

1. [Hancock], *Examiner*; and Peter Bohler to Nicholas Zinzendorf, 4/15 June 1743, Peter Bohler Papers, trans. Albert F. Jordan, Moravian Archives, Bethlehem, Pa.

2. [Hancock], *Examiner*, p. 11.

3. *Ibid.*, pp. 12–15, 16–17, 25, 29.

4. *Ibid.*, p. 31.

5. *MPC*, pp. 179, 181–183.

6. *Ibid.*

7. *Ibid.*

8. *Ibid.*, p. 183.

9. *Ibid.*, pp. 183–185.

10. [Jonathan Dickinson], *A Display of God's special Grace* (Boston: Rogers and Fowle, 1742); and Jonathan Dickinson, *A Display of God's special Grace* (Philadelphia: William Bradford, 1743).

11. *A Declaration of the Presbyteries of New-Brunswick and New Castle met together at Philadelphia, May 26, 1743* (Philadelphia: William Bradford, 1743), pp. 7–11.

12. *Ibid.*, pp. 11–12.

13. *Ibid.*

14. *Ibid.*, p. 13.

15. New Brunswick Presbytery, "Minutes," 26 May 1743.

16. *Ibid.*

17. *Ibid.*, 10 August 1743.

18. *Ibid.*

19. Robert Davidson, *Historical Sketch of the First Presbyterian Church . . . of New Brunswick* (New Brunswick: Terhune and Son, 1852), pp. 12–13.

20. Gilbert Tennent, *Examiner, Examined*, pp. 23, 132.

21. Gilbert Tennent, "Sermon valedictoria pred. N[ew] B[runswick]," n.d., Gilbert Tennent Ms. Sermons, Presbyterian Historical Society, Philadelphia.

22. Tennent's congregation at his first communion service numbered 335 people. This included 203 white females, 104 white males, and 28 blacks. One-

fourth of the white females were young girls, and the same proportion of white males were young boys. Kenney, "Whitefield and Colonial Revivalism," pp. 151–157; Second Presbyterian Church, Philadelphia, "(List of) Communicants . . . Memorandum of persons spoken with in order to Communion of, 2 April 1744," Presbyterian Historical Society, Philadelphia; and "An Account of the origin, progress, and present state of the Second Presbyterian Church in the City of Philadelphia, 2 May 1792."

23. George Gillespie, *Remarks Upon Mr. George Whitefield, Proving Him a Man under Delusion* (Philadelphia: B. Franklin, 1744); *Philadelphia Pennsylvania Gazette*, 9 March 1744; and *Philadelphia American Weekly Mercury*, 16–23 February 1744.

24. Davidson, *Historical Sketch of First Presbyterian Church*, pp. 11, 13; Mary A. Tennent, *Light in Darkness*, p. 88; *FAT*, pp. 119–120; and Alexander, *Biographical Sketches*, pp. 52, 58–59.

25. Gilbert Tennent, *The Divine Government over all considered* (Philadelphia: William Bradford, [1752]), p. 64.

26. Davidson, *Historical Sketch of First Presbyterian Church*, p. 13; Mary A. Tennent, *Light in Darkness*, p. 88; *FAT*, pp. 119–120; and Alexander, *Biographical Sketches*, pp. 53, 58–59.

27. Gilbert Tennent, "Thoughts on extempore preaching," n.d., Presbyterian Historical Society, Philadelphia.

28. Prince, *Christian History . . . 1744, 5*, pp. 295–296.

29. Gilbert Tennent, *Twenty-Three Sermons Upon the Chief End of Man. The Divine Authority of the Sacred Scriptures, The Being and Attributes of God, And the Doctrine of the Trinity* (Philadelphia: William Bradford, 1744), p. i.

30. Gilbert Tennent, *Discourses, On Several Important Subjects* (Philadelphia: William Bradford, 1745).

31. Gilbert Tennent, *The Danger of Spiritual Pride represented* (Philadelphia: William Bradford, [1745], p. 19.

32. [Herman Husbands], *Some Remarks on Religion, With the Author's Experience in Pursuit thereof* (Philadelphia: William Bradford, 1961), p. 37.

33. *MPC*, pp. 200, 204–207.

34. Charles Brockden to Thomas Noble, 21 July 1745, Box: "PhB:Phila: Varia + Letters 1743–1782," Folder: "PhB II," Moravian Archives, Bethlehem, Pa.

35. "Philadelphia Diary [of the English Congregation], 1745–1746," 14 July 1745, Moravian Archives, Bethlehem, Pa.

36. Gilbert Tennent, *All Things come alike to All* (Philadelphia: William Bradford, 1745), pp. 22, 34–39.

37. Jonathan Dickinson to Thomas Foxcroft, 21 January 1745/6.

38. *Ibid.*

39. *Ibid.*

40. *MPC*, pp. 263–264.

41. *Ibid.*

42. *Ibid.*

43. For an account of the Virginia mission and Tennent's activities, see William Henry Foote, *Sketches of Virginia: Historical and Biographical*, 2 vols. (Philadelphia: Wm. S. Marten and J. D. Lippincott, 1850–1855), I:118, 133–142.

44. *Ibid.*, I:134.

45. *Ibid.*, I:134–135.

46. Ingram, "William Tennent, Sr.," p. 21.

47. Whitefield clearly realized that he needed Tennent's endorsement because he notified his friends throughout the colonies as soon as he had made peace with Tennent. Whitefield to Rev. Mr. Prince, 28 May 1746, in "George Whitefield's Letterbook 1745–1746," Presbyterian Historical Society, Philadelphia, Pa.; and George Whitefield to Rev. Mr. Smith, 30 May 1746, "George Whitefield's Letterbook 1745–1746."

48. Whitefield completed his part of the bargain after much delay by attacking Zinzendorf in 1753 under the title "An Expostulatory Letter, Addressed to Nicholas Lewis, Count Zinzendorf, and Lord Advocate of the Unitas Fratrum." See George Whitefield, *The Works of the Reverend George Whitefield*, 4 vols. (London, 1771), IV:251–261; and Gilbert Tennent, "Preface," in George Whitefield, *Five Sermons*, (Philadelphia: B. Franklin, 1746), pp. ix, x, xi.

49. Gilbert Tennent, "Preface," pp. xi–xii.

50. See Appendix.

51. Benjamin Franklin, *Plain Truth* (Philadelphia: [B. Franklin], 1747).

52. Gilbert Tennent, *The Necessity of Thankfulness for Wonders of divine Mercies* (Philadelphia: William Bradford, 1744), pp. 5, 12–16; and Gilbert Tennent, *The Necessity of praising God for Mercies receiv'd* (Philadelphia: William Bradford, [1745]), pp. 10–11, 36–40.

53. Gilbert Tennent, *The late Association for Defence, encourag'd, Or The lawfulness of a Defensive War* (Philadelphia: William Bradford, [1748]), pp. 6–8.

54. *Ibid.*, pp. 39–41.

55. [John Smith], *The Doctrine of Christianity, As held by the People called Quakers, Vindicated* (Philadelphia: B. Franklin, 1748); Gilbert Tennent, *Late Association for Defence Farther Encouraged: Or, Defensive War Defended* (Philadelphia: B. Franklin and D. Hall, 1748); and Gilbert Tennent, *The late Association for Defence, Farther encourag'd, Or The Consistency of Defensive War, with True Christianity* (Philadelphia: William Bradford, [1748]).

56. Gilbert Tennent, *Brotherly Love recommended, by the Argument of the Love of Christ* (Philadelphia: B. Franklin, 1748), pp. 3–4, 6.

57. *Ibid.*, pp. 6–7.

58. *Ibid.*, pp. 7–8.
59. *Ibid.*, p. 8.
60. *Ibid.*, p. 9.
61. *MPC*, pp. 220, 269–270.
62. Gilbert Tennent, *Irenicum Ecclesiasticum, Or A Humble Impartial Essay Upon The Peace of Jerusalem, Wherein The Analogy between Jerusalem and the visible Church is in some Instances, briefly hinted* (Philadelphia: William Bradford, 1749), p. iii.
63. *Ibid.*, pp. v–vi.
64. *Ibid.*, p. 138.
65. *Ibid.*, p. 140.
66. *Ibid.*

6. DENOUEMENT TO A CONTENTIOUS CAREER

1. Franklin, *Autobiography*, pp. 194–195.
2. *Ibid.*, pp. 193–195.
3. Second Presbyterian Church, Philadelphia, "Congregational and trustee minutes, January 1749–August 1772," 25 January 1749 and 8 February 1749, Presbyterian Historical Society, Philadelphia.
4. Franklin, *Autobiography*, pp. 201–202.
5. Tennent's subscription list contained 169 names, including those of the governor, chief justice, and secretary of the province as well as the mayor and recorder of Philadelphia and members of the council and assembly. Gilbert Tennent, "Subscription List," Presbyterian Historical Society, Philadelphia; and Gilbert Tennent to Rev. Philip Doddridge, 20 July 1752, Presbyterian Historical Society, Philadelphia.
6. Gilbert Tennent, *Divine Government*, pp. 51–53.
7. According to one report, the Arch Street Church was quite large and elegant. Inside there were 140 pews, each of which could seat half a dozen people. J. Thomas Scharf and Thompson Westcott, *History of Philadelphia, 1609–1884*, 2 vols. (Philadelphia, 1884), II:1266.
8. Gilbert Tennent, *Divine Government*, pp. 64, 66–69.
9. Watson, *Annals of Philadelphia*, pp. 391–392.
10. The consistory began to record its meetings on January 16, 1745. The first discipline case was heard by the consistory on May 10, 1745. Ground rules for electing officers were established on September 25, 1746, and communion services were set on a quarterly basis on July 5, 1748. Second Presbyterian Church, Philadelphia, "Consistory Book, 16 January 1744/5–24 January 1798," 16 January 1745, 10 May 1745, 25 September 1746, and 5 July 1748, Presbyterian Historical Society, Philadelphia.
11. Second Presbyterian Church, "Congregational and trustee minutes," 7 January 1751.

12. *FAT*, p. 137; and *MPC*, pp. 165–166.

13. *MPC*, pp. 197–198.

14. *Ibid.*, pp. 211–214.

15. *Ibid.*, pp. 233–234, 236.

16. New Brunswick Presbytery, "Minutes," 2 June 1741.

17. In later years, Aaron Burr claimed: "If it had not been for the treatment received by Mr. Brainerd at Yale College, New Jersey College never would have been erected." Quoted in Thomas Jefferson Wertenbaker, *Princeton, 1746–1896* (Princeton, N.J.: Princeton University Press, 1946), p. 18; Jonathan Edwards, ed., *An Account of the Life of the late Reverend Mr. David Brainerd* (Boston: D. Henchman, 1749), pp. 19–21; and Nissenbaum, *Great Awakening at Yale*, pp. 219–250.

18. Sloan, *Scottish Enlightenment*, p. 59.

19. Wertenbaker, *Princeton*, pp. 15–16, 19–20.

20. *Ibid.*, pp. 20–21. For further information on the early politics of the College of New Jersey, see Alison B. Olson, "The Founding of Princeton University: Religion and Politics in Eighteenth Century New Jersey," *New Jersey History* 87 (Autumn 1969): 133–150.

21. Wertenbaker, *Princeton*, pp. 21–22.

22. *Ibid.*, pp. 396–404.

23. *Ibid.*, pp. 23–24.

24. Miller, *Revolutionary College*, pp. 50–53.

25. Wertenbaker, *Princeton*, pp. 24–25. For Belcher's political reasons for supporting the New Jersey College, see Olson, "Founding of Princeton University," pp. 133–150.

26. Wertenbaker, *Princeton*, pp. 26–27.

27. *Ibid.*, p. 27; and Dwight, "Life of President Edwards," I: 275; (Princeton, N.J.: Princeton University Press, 1947), p. 33.

28. The only trustee who was excluded from the board by the second charter was Samuel Finley. Wertenbaker, *Princeton*, pp. 397–398.

29. Howard Miller, "The 'Frown of Heaven' and 'Degenerate America': A Note on the Princeton Presidency," *The Princeton University Library Chronicle* 31 (Autumn 1969): 38–46.

30. Miller, *Revolutionary College*, p. 72.

31. *Ibid.*, pp. 73–74; *FAT*, pp. 125–127.

32. "The Minutes of the Proceedings of the Trustees of the College of New Jersey, Agreeable to ye Royal Charter obtain'd of his Excellency Governor Belcher Esqr. Anno Domini 1748," 27 September 1749, 15 May 1751, and 26 September 1750, Mudd Library, Princeton University, Princeton, N.J.

33. Whitefield, *Works*, II:206.

34. *Ibid.*, II:266.

35. *Ibid.*, II:384–462.

36. The trustees were painfully aware of the fact that the college could ill

afford to miss any favorable opportunity for new contributions. As Governor Belcher once described the college's promise and dilemma: "By the Smiles of Heaven upon this Undertaking [the College of New Jersey], the Students are become so Numerous as that the Bed is Shorter than a Man can't stretch himself upon it, and the Covering narrower than that he can wrap himself in it, . . . " "Minutes . . . of the Trustees of the College of New Jersey," 27 September 1752; see also "Minutes . . . of the Trustees of the College of New Jersey," 25 September 1941, 14 May 1752; and Dwight, *Life of President Edwards*, p. 498.

37. "Minutes . . . of the Trustees of the College of New Jersey," 23 May 1753; and George W. Pilcher, ed., *The Reverend Samuel Davies Abroad: Diary of a Journey to England and Scotland, 1753–1755*. (Urbana, Ill.: University of Illinois Press, 1967), p. x.

38. Pilcher, *Davies Abroad*, pp. x, 4. Several letters either from Tennent or about him had been published in the serial accounts of the international revivals that were printed in Scotland and England during the 1740s. Also, a portion of Tennent's attack on Moravian errors had been issued in London by the time of his trip. Gilbert Tennent, *Some Account Of The Principles Of the Moravians* (London,1743); "Glasgow Weekly History," pp. 194–198, 201–202; and *The Weekly History*, nos. 9, 11, 16, 17, 26, 29.

39. *MPC*, pp. 285, 289, 327–329.

40. Pilcher, *Davies Abroad*, pp. 18, 23, 28–43.

41. *Ibid.*, pp. 43–44.

42. *Ibid.*, p. 88.

43. *Ibid.*, p. 113.

44. *Ibid.*, p. 55.

45. *Ibid.*, pp. 49–50, 55, 57.

46. Before the departure of Tennent and Davies for Great Britain, the college's trustees published a prospectus of their institution. Included in this pamphlet was a history of the school's origins, an explanation of the need for such an institution in the colonies, its intended purpose, and the curriculum that would be followed. Tennent and Davies were given a copy of this prospectus to use in their fund-raising activities, but once in England they realized certain modifications were necessary to increase the college's appeal. In London, Tennent and Davies published a new edition of the pamphlet with the required changes. The trustees' version was *A General Account Of The Rise and State Of The College, Lately Established In The Province of New-Jersey, In America: And Of the End and Design of its Institution* (New York: James Parker, 1752). Tennent's edited version was entitled *A General Account of the Rise and State of the College, Lately Established in the Province of New-Jersey, in America: And of the End and Design of its Institution* (London, 1754) (Hereafter cited as *General Account . . . of the College* (1754).

47. Pilcher, *Davies Abroad*, pp. 59–61, 75–76, 86, 89, 93–94, 145.

48. *Ibid.*, pp. 50–52, 59–61, 145.

49. *Ibid.*, p. 60.

50. George W. Pilcher, *Samuel Davies: Apostle of Dissent in Colonial Virginia* (Knoxville, Tenn.: University of Tennessee, [1971]), p. 144.

51. *MPC*, pp. 289–299; Pilcher, *Davies: Apostle*, pp. 156–157.

52. James McLachlan, *Princetonians, 1748–1768: A Biographical Dictionary* (Princeton, N.J.: Princeton University Press, 1976), p. xxi.

53. Gilbert Tennent, *Sermons on Important Subjects*, p. v.

54. Gilbert Tennent to Reverend Dr. (John) Guise near Moorfields, 15 November 1757, Firestone Library, Princeton University, Princeton, N.J.

55. Gilbert Tennent, *Sermons on Important Subjects*, pp. v–xi.

56. At least thirty-one students subscribed to the publication of these sermons so that they could have a copy of Tennent's presentations. *Ibid.*, p. xii.

57. Perry Miller has described the characteristic revolutionary jeremiad based on this theme. See Perry Miller, "From the Covenant to the Revival," in *The Shaping of American Religion*, eds. James Ward Smith and A. Leland Jamison (Princeton, N.J.: Princeton University Press, 1961), pp. 322–368.

58. Nathan O. Hatch, "The Origins of Civil Millennialism in America: New England Clergymen, War with France, and the Revolution," *William and Mary Quarterly*, 3rd series, 31 (1974): 407–430.

59. Gilbert Tennent, Ms. Sermon on Jonah 3:5, Firestone Library, Princeton University, Princeton, N.J.; Gilbert Tennent, Ms. Sermon on Isaiah 1:19–20, Firestone Library, Princeton University, Princeton, N.J.; Gilbert Tennent, Ms. Sermon on Jeremiah 13:15–26, Firestone Library, Princeton University, Princeton, N.J.; and Gilbert Tennent, Ms. Sermon on Jeremiah 13:17, Firestone Library, Princeton University, Princeton, N.J.

60. Gilbert Tennent, Ms. Sermon on Jonah 3:5.

61. *Ibid.*

62. *Ibid.*

63. *FAT*, pp. 150–151.

64. *Ibid.*

65. *MPC*, pp. 246–247.

66. *Ibid.*

67. *Ibid.*, p. 254.

68. *Ibid.*, pp. 340–341.

69. *Ibid.*, pp. 341–342.

70. *Ibid.*

71. Francis Alison, "Peace and Union Recommended," in Francis Alison and David Bostwick, *Peace and Union Recommended; And Self disclaim'd, and Christ exalted* (Philadelphia: W. Dunlap, 1758), p. 51; and *MPC*, p. 339.

72. Gilbert Tennent, *The Blessedness of Peace-Makers represented; and the Danger of Persecution considered* (Philadelphia: William Bradford, 1765), pp. 4–14.

73. *Ibid.*, pp. 46–47. Tennent did not mention Craighead or his Seceders' movement specifically in these sermons, but his reference to "separatists" was clearly directed at that group. The Seceders were a threat to Tennent because a number of New Light supporters found the new reunion difficult to accept. They began to believe the Seceders were right when they accused the New Lights of capitulating to the Old Lights. Alexander, *Biographical Sketches*, pp. 161–162.

74. Gilbert Tennent, *Blessedness of Peace-Makers*, pp. 4–5.

75. *Ibid.*, pp. 42–43.

76. Gilbert Tennent, Ms. Sermon on James 4:12, Presbyterian Historical Society, Philadelphia.

77. Leonard Trinterud discusses at length the various internal battles within the Synod that followed the reunion. See *FAT*, Chapter 9, "Union Without Love."

78. Philadelphia, First Presbytery, "Minutes 1758–1781," vol. III, 12–14 August 1761, Presbyterian Historical Society, Philadelphia.

79. *Ibid.*, 7 April 1762, 18 May 1762, and 12 May 1763.

80. Horace Wemyss Smith, *Life and Correspondence of the Rev. William Smith, D.D.*, 2 vols. (Philadelphia: Ferguson Bros., 1880), I:215–219; and *FAT*, p. 155.

81. Smith, *Life of William Smith*, p. 225.

82. *Ibid.*, pp. 227–236.

83. Dwight, "Life of President Edwards," pp. 277–278.

84. *MPC*, pp. 371–372.

85. *A True Copy of a Genuine Letter, Sent to the Archbishop of Canterbury by Eighteen Presbyterian Ministers, in America* (New York, 1761); *The Mechanick's Address to the Farmer* (Philadelphia: Andrew Steuart, 1761); *The Conduct of the Presbyterian Ministers who sent the Letter to the Archbishop of Canterbury Considered* (Philadelphia: Andrew Steuart, 1761); and *A Second Letter to the Congregations of the Eighteen Presbyterian (or New Light) Ministers, who wrote the Late Contradictory Letter to the Archbishop of Canterbury* (Philadelphia: Andrew Steuart, 1761).

86. Tennent had three children with Sarah Spofford Tennent. The oldest was a son, Gilbert, who was lost at sea while a young man. The second was Cornelia Tennent, who later married Dr. William Smith, a successful physician in Philadelphia, and the third was Elizabeth Tennent, who died very young. Mary A. Tennent, *Light in Darkness*, pp. 94–95; "Biographical Sketch . . . of Gilbert Tennent," p. 224.

87. Second Presbyterian Church, Philadelphia, "Congregational and trustee minutes," 8 March 1762; and Webster, *History of the Presbyterian Church*, p. 672.

88. Second Presbyterian Church, "Congregational and trustee minutes," 21 October 1762; and Gilbert Tennent, "Draft of remonstrance 22 February 1762," Presbyterian Historical Society, Philadelphia.

89. Gilbert Tennent, "Draft of remonstrance"; Gilbert Tennent, "Remonstrance and Remarks, December 15, 1762," Speer Library, Princeton Theological Seminary, Princeton, N.J.

90. Gilbert Tennent, "Draft of remonstrance."

91. *Ibid.*; and Gilbert Tennent, "Remonstrance and Remarks."

92. Gilbert Tennent, "Draft of remonstrance"; Gilbert Tennent, "Remonstrance and Remarks."

93. Philadelphia, First Presbytery, "Minutes," 9–11 November 1762, 14–15 December 1762; Donegal Presbytery, "Minutes," 12–13 April 1763, 18 May 1763, and 29 June 1763.

94. Gilbert Tennent, "Thoughts on extempore Preaching."

95. The year of Tennent's birth was incorrectly inscribed on his tombstone. He was born in 1703. "Biographical Sketch . . . of Gilbert Tennent," p. 225.

CONCLUSION

1. Tennent used the image of "Pharisee-Teachers" in his two most famous sermons during this period. Gilbert Tennent, *Danger of An Unconverted Ministry;* and Gilbert Tennent, *Righteousness of the Scribes and Pharisees considered.*

2. In Tennent's sermons on the *Necessity of holding fast the Truth*, the text was taken from Revelations 3:3, where John of Patmos recorded an angel's instructions to "remember . . . how thou has heard, and received, and hold fast." Gilbert Tennent, *Necessity of holding fast the Truth*, p. 1.

3. Tennent observed in his work *The Examiner, Examined* that "our Case of late . . . seems very much to resemble that of *Nehemiah*, and the other Builders of the Wall of *Jerusalem*." Thus, he expressed the hope that his supporters would "work on the Wall with one Hand, and hold a Weapon in the other" like those "primitive Builders." Gilbert Tennent, *The Examiner, Examined*, pp. 6–7.

4. The reconciliation of early Jewish and Gentile Christians was employed as a paradigm for Presbyterian reunion in several of Tennent's sermons. Gilbert Tennent, *Danger of Spiritual Pride*, p. 19; Gilbert Tennent, *Brotherly Love recommended*, p. 9; and Gilbert Tennent, *Irenicum Ecclesiasticum*, pp. 82–83.

BIBLIOGRAPHY

GILBERT TENNENT: MANUSCRIPTS

Bethlehem, Pa. Moravian Archives. Gilbert Tennent to George Whitefield, 5 June 1742. "Pennsylvanica 1740s + Lischy."

Montreat, N.C. The Historical Foundation of the Presbyterian and Reformed Churches. "Tennent Family Records."

Newark, N.J. New Jersey Historical Society. Gilbert Tennent to (Ebenezer) Pemberton, November ult. 1741.

Philadelphia. Pennsylvania Historical Society. Gilbert Tennent Papers.

Philadelphia. Presbyterian Historical Society. Gilbert Tennent Papers.

Princeton, N.J. Princeton University, Firestone Library. Gilbert Tennent to Reverend Dr. (John) Guise, 15 November 1757. Gilbert Tennent Ms. Sermons.

Princeton, N.J. Princeton University. Mudd Library. Gilbert Tennent, Trustee.

Princeton, N.J. Princeton Theological Seminary. Speer Library. Gilbert Tennent Ms. Sermons. "Remonstrance and remarks."

GILBERT TENNENT: PUBLISHED WORKS

All Things come alike to All: A Sermon, on Eccles. IX, 1, 2, and 3 Verses. Occasioned by a Person's being struck by the Lightning of Thunder. Preached at Philadelphia, July the 28th, 1745. Philadelphia: William Bradford, 1745.

The Blessedness of Peace-Makers represented; and the Danger of Persecution considered; In Two Sermons, on Mat. v. 9 Preach'd at Philadelphia, the 3d Wednesday in May, 1759, before the Reverend the Synod, of New-York and Philadelphia. Philadelphia: William Bradford, 1765.

Brotherly Love recommended, by the Argument of the Love of Christ: A Sermon, Preached at Philadelphia, January 1747–8. Before the Sacramental Solemnity. With some Enlargement. Philadelphia: B. Franklin, 1748.

The Danger of An Unconverted Ministry, Consider'd In A Sermon On Mark VI. 34. Preached at Nottingham, in Pennsylvania, March 8. Anno 1739, 40. 2nd edition. Philadelphia: B. Franklin, 1740.

The Danger of forgetting God, describ'd. And the Duty of considering our Ways explain'd. In A Sermon on Psalm L. 22. Preach'd at New-York, March 1735. New York: John Peter Zenger, 1735.

The Danger of Spiritual Pride represented. A Sermon Preach'd At Philadelphia, December the 30th, 1744. On Romans XII. 3. With Some Enlargements. Philadelphia: William Bradford [1745].

The Dark Depths of Divine Providence, Opened and Vindicated from the impertinent Cavils of foolish Men. In A Sermon, On 2 Thes. II. 11,12. Preached at New Brunswick, in New Jersey, August 17th, 1735. With Enlargements. New York: John Peter Zenger, 1735.

Discourse Upon Christ's Kingly-Office. Preached at Nottingham, in Pennsylvania, Sept. 24th, 1740. Boston: C. Harrison, 1741.

Discourses, On Several Important Subjects. Philadelphia: William Bradford, 1745.

The Divine Government over all considered, And The necessity of Gratitude, for Benefits conferred, (by it,) Represented, in two Sermons, Preach'd June the 7th, 1752. in the Presbyterian Church lately erected in Arch-Street, in the City of Philadelphia. On Occasion Of the first Celebration of religious Worship there. Philadelphia: William Bradford, [1752].

"The Divinity of the Sacred Scripture Considered; And the dangers of Covetousness Detected: In A Sermon, On Jeremiah 22. 29. Preach'd at New Brunswick in New-Jersey, April ult. 1738." In *Sermons On Sacramental Occasions by Divers Ministers.* Boston: J. Draper, 1739.

"The Duty of Self-Examination, Considered In a Sermon, On 1 Cor. 11. 28. Preach'd at Maiden-Head in New Jersey, October 22, 1737. Before the Celebration of the Lord's Supper." In *Sermons On Sacramental Occasions by Divers Ministers.* Boston: J. Draper, 1739.

The Espousals Or a Passionate Perswasive. To a Marriage with the Lamb of God, Wherein The Sinners Misery And The Redeemers Glory is Unvailed in A Sermon upon Gen. 24 49. Preach'd at N. Brunswyck, June the 22d, 1735. New York: J. Peter Zenger, 1735.

The Espousals: Or, a passionate Perswasive To a Marriage with the Lamb of God, &c. In A Sermon Upon Gen xxiv. 49. Boston: Thomas Fleet, 1741.

The Examiner, Examined, Or Gilbert Tennent, Harmonious. In Answer To a Pamphlet entitled, The Examiner, Or Gilbert against Tennent: Being a

Vindication of the Rev. Gilbert Tennent and his Associates, together with six Rev. Ministers of Boston, from the unjust Reflections cast upon them by the Author of that Anonymous Pamphlet, together with some Remarks upon the Querists, the third Part, and other of their Performances. The Whole being an Essay to vindicate the late Glorious Work of God's Power and Grace in these Lands, from the unreasonable Cavils and Exceptions of the said Pamhphlet, and others of like Nature. The whole Essay is submitted to the Decision of Truth and Common Sense. Philadelphia: William Bradford, 1743.

"An Expostulatry Address to Saints and Sinners." Appendix of *The Nature of Regeneration opened, and its absolute Necessity, in order to Salvation, demonstrated, In A Sermon from John iii. 3.* By John Tennent. 2nd edition. London: J. Oswald, 1741.

A Funeral Sermon, Occasion'd by the Death of the Reverend Mr. John Rowland, Who departed this Life, April the 12th, 1745. Preach'd at Charles-Town, in Chester County, April the 14th, 1745. Philadelphia: William Bradford, 1745.

A General Account Of The Rise and State Of The College, Lately Established In The Province of New Jersey, In America: And Of the End and Design of its Institution. Originally published in America, anno. 1752, by the Trustees of the said College; and now republished, in pursuance of their order, with some alterations and additions, adapted to its present state, for the information of the friends of learning and piety in Great Britain. By Gilbert Tennent and Samuel Davies. Edinburgh, 1754.

The good Mans Character and Reward represented, and his Loss deplor'd, together with Reflections on the Presages of approachinq Calamities. In A Funeral Discourse, with some Enlargements Occasioned by the Death of Captain William Grant of this City, who departed this Life, September 30.1756. Preached in Philadelphia on the following Sabbath. And now published, at the Desire of the Hearers. Philadelphia: William Bradford, [1756].

The Gospel a Mystery. A Sermon Preach'd At Philadelphia, December 1749. Upon I Corinthians ii, 7. Philadelphia: William Bradford, [1750].

The Happiness of Rewarding the Enemies of our Religion and Liberty, Represented In A Sermon Preached in Philadelphia, February 17, 1756, to Captain Vanderspiegel's Independent Company of Volunteers, at the Request of their Officers. Philadelphia: James Chattin, 1756.

Irenicum Ecclesiasticum, Or A Humble Impartial Essay Upon The Peace of Jerusalem, Wherein The Analogy between Jerusalem and the visible Church is in some Instances, briefly hinted. The Nature, the Order, the Union, of the visible Church, together with her Terms of Communion, are particularly considered, and their Excellency opened. Moreover the following important Points are largely explain'd. 1. What is to be under-

stood by the Peace of Jerusalem. 2. What by Praying for the Peace of Jerusalem. 3. How, and why should we pray for its Peace and Prosperity. Under the aforesaid General Heads, the following Particulars are discuss'd, viz. The Nature, Kinds, Hindrances, Means and Motives, of Peace and Union, together with an Answer to Objections. Also A Prefatory Address to the Synods of New-York & Philadelphia. Philadelphia: William Bradford, 1749.

The late Association for Defence, encourag'd, Or The lawfulness of a Defensive War. Represented In A Sermon Preach'd At Philadelphia December 24, 1747. Philadelphia: William Bradford, [1748].

Late Association for Defence Farther Encouraged: Or, Defensive War Defended; And Its Consistency with True Christianity Represented. In A Reply To Some Exceptions against War, in a late Composure, intituled, The Doctrine of Christianity, as held by the People called Quakers, vindicated. Philadelphia: B. Franklin and D. Hall, 1748.

The late Association for Defence, farther encourag'd, Or The Consistency of Defensive War, with True Christianity. Represented In Two Sermons Preach'd at Philadelphia, January 24, 1747–8. Philadelphia: William Bradford, [1748].

"*The Legal Bow bent, Or, Arrows on the String, Against the King's Enemies. In Two Discourses On Psal. 45. 3, 4, 5. Wherein The natural Enmity of secure Sinners against Christ; and the Manner of their Reduction to his Obedience, by a Work of Conviction, is described. Preach'd at New-Brunswick in New Jersey, April 23, 1738.*" In *Sermons On Sacramental Occasions By Divers Ministers.* Boston: J. Draper, 1739.

Love to Christ a necessary Qualification in Order to feed His Sheep. A Sermon Preach'd at Neshaminie, December 14, 1743. Before the Ordination Of the Reverend Mr. Charles Beatty. Philadelphia: William Bradford, 1744.

The Necessity of holding fast the Truth represented in Three Sermons on Rev. iii. 3. Preached at New-York, April, 1742. With an Appendix, relating to Errors lately vented by some Moravians in those Parts. To which are added, A Sermon on the Priestly-Office of Christ, And another, On The Virtue of Charity. Together with A Sermon of a Dutch Divine on taking the little Foxes; faithfully translated. Boston: S. Kneeland and T. Green, 1743.

The Necessity of keeping the Soul. A Sermon Preach'd At Philadelphia, December the 23d, 1744. On Deuteronomy IV. 9. Philadelphia: William Bradford, [1745].

The necessity of praising God for Mercies receiv'd. A Sermon Occasion'd, By the Success of the late Expedition, (under the Direction and Command of Gen. Pepperel and Com. Warren) in reducing the City and Fortresses of Louisburgh, on Cape-Breton, To the Obedience of His Majesty King George the Second. Preached at Philadelphia July 7, 1745. Philadelphia: William Bradford, [1745].

The Necessity Of Receiving the Truth in Love, Considered in A Sermon On 2 Thes. 2. 10. Preached at New-Brunswick in New Jersey, August 17, 1735. With enlargements. New York: John Peter Zenger, 1735.

The Necessity of Religious Violence in Order to Obtain Durable Happiness. Open'd and Urg'd in a Sermon Upon Mat. 11. v. 12. Preach'd at Perth-Amboy, June 29, 1735. New York: William Bradford, [1735].

The necessity of studying to be quiet, and doing our own Business. A Sermon Preach'd at Philadelphia, September the 30th, 1744 on I Thessalonians iv. 11. With some Enlargement. Philadelphia: William Bradford, n.d.

The Necessity of Thankfulness for Wonders of divine Mercies. A Sermon Preached at Philadelphia April 15th 1744. On Occasion of the important and glorious Victory obtain'd by the British Arms in the Mediterranean, under the Conduct of Admiral Matthews, Over the united Fleets of France and Spain, And likewise the Frustrating a detestable Attempt to Invade England, By A Popish Pretender. Philadelphia: William Bradford, 1744.

A Persuasive, To The Right Use of the Passions in Religion; Or, The Nature of religious Zeal Explain'd, its Excellency and Importance Open'd and Urg'd, In A Sermon, On Revelations iii. 19. Preached at Philadelphia, January 27th, 1760. Philadelphia: W. Dunlap, 1760.

"The Preciousness of Christ To Believers, Consider'd In A Sermon, On 1 Pet. ii. 7. Preach'd at New-Brunswick in New-Jersey The First Sabbath in August, before the Celebration of the Lord's Supper, Anno Domini, 1738." In *Sermons on Sacramental Occasions by Divers Ministers.* Boston: J. Draper, 1739.

"Preface." In *A Faithful Narrative of the many Dangers and Sufferings, as well as the wonderful Deliverances of Robert Eastburn, during his late Captivity among the Indians.* By Robert Eastburn. Philadelphia: W. Dunlap, 1758.

"Preface." In *Five Sermons.* By George Whitefield. Philadelphia: B. Franklin, 1746.

"Preface." In *Self disclaimed, and Christ exalted: A Sermon Preached at Philadelphia, Before The Reverend Synod of New-York, May 25, 1758.* By David Bostwick. 1748; reprint edition, London, n.p. 1759.

"A Prefatory Discourse to the following Sermons with Relations of some Memoirs of the Author's Conversion and Character." In *The Nature of Regeneration opened, and its absolute Necessity, in order to Salvation, demonstrated, In A Sermon from John iii. 3.* By John Tennent. 2nd edition. London: J. Oswald, 1741.

Remarks Upon A Protestation Presented To The Synod Of Philadelphia, June 1, 1741. Philadelphia: B. Franklin, 1741.

The Righteousness of the Scribes and Pharisees considered. In A Sermon On Matth. V. 20. Preach'd at the Evening Lecture in Boston, January 27, 1740, 1. Boston: J. Draper, 1741.

A Sermon, On 1 Chronicles xxix. 28. Occasioned by the Death of King George the Second, Of happy Memory, who departed this life on the 25th Day of October, in the Year of our Lord, 1760, in the 77th Year of His Age, and the 34th of his Reign; beloved and honored by his Subjects, for his Eminent-Royal-Virtues. Together, With some brief Hints, of the amiable Character of His Majesty King George the Third, Now seated on the British Throne, and the auspicious Omens, that attend his Infant Reign. Preached At Philadelphia, January 25th, 1761, and published at the request of the Audience. Philadelphia: W. Dunlap, 1761.

A Sermon Preach'd at Burlington in New-Jersey, November 23, 1749. Being the Day appointed by his Excellency the Governor, with the advice of His Majesty's Council, For A Provincial Thanksgiving. Before the Governor and others, upon Texts chosen by his Excellency. With a Prefatory Address to Philip Doddridge, D.D. Philadelphia: William Bradford, 1749.

A Sermon Preach'd At Philadelphia, January 7. 1747–8. Being the Day appointed by The Honourable The President and Council, To be observed throughout this Province, As a Day of Fasting and Prayer. With some Enlargement. Philadelphia: William Bradford, 1748.

A Sermon Preach'd at Philadelphia, July 20, 1748. On A Funeral Occasion, Wherein the absolute Certainty, and great Moment, of the Doctrine of the Resurrection Are proved and illustrated; with a Reply to the principal Objections against it. Philadelphia: William Bradford, 1749.

A Sermon Preach'd In Greenwich, September 4, 1746. At The Ordination Of Mr. Andrew Hunter. Philadelphia: William Bradford, [1746].

A Sermon Upon Justification: Preached at New-Brunswick, on the Saturday before the Dispensing of the Holy Sacrament, which was the first Sabbath in August, Anno 1740. Philadelphia: B. Franklin, 1741.

Sermons on Important Subjects: Adapted To the Perilous State of the British Nation, lately preached in Philadelphia. Philadelphia: James Chattin, 1758.

Several Discourses Upon Important Subjects. Wherein I. The Nature, Mode and Seasons of Fasting, are particularly explained; its Necessity and Importance represented, and Objections answered. II. The Nature and Properties of Prayer in general, and the Necessity of Importunity in particular, opened and urged. III. The absolute Certainty and great Moment, of the Doctrine of the Resurrection proved, and illustrated; with a Reply to the principal Objections against it. IV. The Displays of Divine Justice, in the Propitiatory Sacrifice of Christ are represented, the Nature, Necessity and Sufficiency of his Satisfaction, the Imputation of his Righteousness, in Consequence of it. together with an Answer to the most important Objections. V. The General Judgement is briefly represented. Philadelphia: W. Bradford, 1749.

"The Solemn Scene Of The Last Judgment. Open'd in a Sermon, On 2 Thes. i. 6, 7, 8, 9, Preach'd at Maiden-Head in New Jersey, May the 23d, 1737." In *Sermons on Sacramental Occasions By Divers Ministers.* Boston: J. Draper, 1739.

A Solemn Warning To The Secure World, From The God of terrible Majesty. Or, The Presumptuous Sinner Detected, his Pleas Consider'd, and his Doom Display'd. Being an Essay, in which the strong Proneness of Mankind to entertain a false Confidence is proved; The Causes & Foundations of this Delusion open'd and consider'd in a great Variety of Particulars; The Folly, Sinfulness and dangerous Consequences of such a presumptuous Hope expos'd, and Directions propos'd how to obtain that Scriptural and Rational Hope, which maketh not ashamed. In a Discourse from Deut. xxix. 19, 20, 21. Boston: S. Kneeland and T. Green, 1735.

Some Account Of The Principles Of the Moravians: Chiefly collected from several Conversations with Count Zinzendorf; and from some Sermons preached by him at Berlin, and published in London. Being an Appendix To a Treatise on The Necessity of holding fast the truth. London n.p. 1743.

The Substance and Scope of both Testaments, Or, The distinguishing Glory of the Gospel. A Sermon On The Displays of Divine Justice In The Propitiatory Sacrifice of Christ: Representing the Nature, Necessity, and Sufficiency, of his Satisfaction, the Imputation of his Righteousness, in consequence of it, together with an Answer to the most important Objections. Preach'd at Philadelphia, in April, 1749. Philadelphia: William Bradford, 1749.

The Terrors Of The Lord. A Sermon Upon The General Judgment, Preach'd at Maidenhead, in New-Jersey; May the 17th, 1749. Before the Synod of York. Philadelphia: William Bradford, 1749.

Three Letters To The Reverend Mr. George Whitefield. By Benjamin Colman, Gilbert Tennent, and William Tennent. Philadelphia: Andrew Bradford, [1739].

Twenty-Three Sermons Upon The Chief End of Man. The Divine Authority of the sacred Scriptures, The Being and Attributes of God, And the Doctrine of the Trinity, Preach'd at Philadelphia, Anno Dom. 1743. Philadelphia: William Bradford, 1744.

Two Sermons Preach'd at Burlington, in New-Jersey, April 27th, 1749. The Day appointed by His Excellency the Governor, and the Honourable the Council, For A Provincial Fast, Before the Governor and others, upon Texts chosen by his Excellency. Philadelphia: William Bradford, [1749].

Two Sermons Preached at New-Brunswick, In the Year 1741. On The Priestly Office of Christ. And The Virtue of Charity. Boston: S. Kneeland and T. Green, 1742.

"The Unsearchable Riches of Christ Considered, in Two Sermons On Ephes. iii. 8. Preached at New Brunswick in New-Jersey, before the Celebration of the Lord's Supper; which was the first Sabbath in August, 1737." In *Sermons on Sacramental Occasions By Divers Ministers.* Boston: J. Draper, 1739.

RELATED PRIMARY SOURCES

Manuscripts

Bethlehem, Pa., Moravian Archives
  Peter Bohler Papers
  "Journals Box JD: Letters A–Z"
  "Letters: A–Z"
  "Memoirs Box 1: 1744–1760"
  "Pennsylvanica 1740s + Lischy"
  "PhB: Philadelphia: Varia + Letters 1743–1782"
  "Philadelphia I: Diaries: 1743–1751"
  "Philadelphia Lovefeasts 1743–1748"
  Nicholas Zinzendorf Letters
New Brunswick, N.J., Rutgers University Library
  Frelinghuysen Family Papers, 1727–1906
New Haven, Yale University, Beinecke Library
  Jedidiah Andrews Papers
Philadelphia, Pennsylvania Historical Society
  Samuel Blair to Unidentified, 14 March 1742/3
  Simon Gratz Autograph Collection, American Colonial Clergy
  Hazard Papers Miscellaneous
  James Logan Letterbooks
  William Tennent, Sr., Ms. Sermon
Philadelphia, Presbyterian Historical Society
  Abington Presbytery, Minutes 1751–1758
  Donegal Presbytery, "The Records of the Proceedings of the Presbytery of Dunagal." 2 vols.
  First Presbyterian Church, Philadelphia
  New Brunswick Presbytery, Minutes 1738–1798
  New Castle Presbytery, "Records of the Presbytery of New Castle upon Delaware"
  Philadelphia, First Presbytery, Minutes 1706–1716, 1733–1746, 1758–1806
  Second Presbyterian Church, Philadelphia
  William Tennent, Sr., Papers

George Whitefield Letterbook 1745–1746
Princeton, N.J., Princeton University, Firestone Library
Thomas Foxcroft Correspondence
Princeton, N.J., Princeton University, Mudd Library
    "The Minutes of the Proceedings of the Trustees of The College of New
    Jersey, Agreeable to ye Royal Charter obtain'd of his Excellency Governor
    Belcher Esqr," vol. I., 1748–1796

Published Works

Newspapers and Magazines

Boston Weekly News-Letter
Boston Weekly Post-Boy
*The General Magazine and Historical Chronicle, For all the British Plantations
    in America.* 1741; reprint edition, New York: Columbia University
    Press, 1938.
"The Glasgow Weekly History, 1743." In *Massachusetts Historical Society,
    Proceedings* 53 (October 1919–June 1920): 192–217.
Philadelphia American Weekly Mercury
Philadelphia Pennsylvania Gazette
*The Weekly History: or, An Account of the most Remarkable Particular relating
    to the present Progress of the Gospel.* London: J. Lewis, 1741–1742.

Books and Pamphlets

Alison, Francis, and Bostwick, David. *Peace and Union Recommended; And
    Self disclaim'd, and Christ exalted, In Two Sermons, Preached at Phil-
    adelphia, Before The Reverend Synods of New-York and Philadelphia.*
    Philadelphia: W. Dunlap, 1758.
Blair, Samuel. *A Particular Consideration Of A Piece, Entitled, "The Quer-
    ists": Wherein Sundry Passages extracted from The Printed Sermons,
    Letters, and Journals of The Rev. Mr. Whitefield are vindicated from
    the False Glosses and erroneous Senses put upon Them in said "Quer-
    ists"; Mr. Whitefield's Soundness in the true Scheme of Christian Doc-
    trine maintained; and The Author's disingenuous Dealing with him
    exposed.* Philadelphia: B. Franklin, 1741.
————. *The Works Of The Reverend Mr. Samuel Blair, Late Minister of the
    Gospel at Fogs-Mannor, in Chester County, in Pennsylvania.* Phila-
    delphia: William Bradford, 1754.
[Chauncey, Charles.] *A Letter from a Gentleman in Boston, to Mr. George
    Wishart, One of the Ministers in Edinburgh, Concerning The State of*

Religion in New-England. 1742; reprint edition, Edinburgh: Clarendon Historical Society, 1883.

College of New Jersey, Trustees. *A General account of the rise and state of the college lately established in the province of New-Jersey.* New York: James Parker. 1752.

The Conduct of the Presbyterian Ministers, Who sent the Letter to the Archbishop of Canterbury, the Year 1760, considered, and set in a true Light: In Answer to some Remarks thereon. In a Letter to a Friend. By an Elder of the Presbyterian Church. Philadelphia: Andrew Steuart, 1761.

[Cross, Robert.] *A Protestation Presented To the Synod of Philadelphia: June 1. 1741.* Philadelphia: B. Franklin, 1741.

Dickinson, Jonathan. *Danger of Schisms and Contentions With Respect to The Ministry and Ordinances of The Gospel, represented In a Sermon Preached at the Meeting of the Presbytery at Woodbridge, October 10th, 1739: And published at The Desire of some of The Ministers present.* New York: John Peter Zenger, 1739.

————. *A Display of God's special Grace. In A familiar Dialogue Between A Minister and A Gentleman of his Congregation. About The Work of God; in The Conviction and Conversion of Sinners so remarkably of late begun and going on in These American Parts.* Boston: Rogers and Fowle, 1742.

————. *A Display of God's special Grace. In a familiar Dialogue Between A Minister & a Gentleman of his Congregation. About The Work of God, in the Conviction and Conversion of Sinners, so remarkably of late begun and going on in These American Parts.* Philadelphia: William Bradford, 1743.

————. *Familiar Letters To a Gentleman, Upon A Variety of seasonable and important Subjects in Religion,* Boston: Rogers and Fowle; J. Blanchard, 1745.

————. *Remarks Upon A Discourse Intituled An Overture, Presented to The Reverend Synod of Dissenting Ministers sitting in Philadelphia, in the Month of September, 1728.* New York: John Peter Zenger, 1729.

————. *Remarks Upon A Pamphlet, Entitled, A Letter to a Friend in the Country, containing the Substance of a Sermon preached at Philadelphia, in the Congregation of the Rev. Mr. Hemphill.* Philadelphia: Andrew Bradford, [1735].

————. *A Sermon Preached at the opening of the Synod At Philadelphia, September 19, 1722. Wherein is considered the Character of the Man of God, and his Furniture for the Exercise both of Doctrine and Discipline, with the true boundaries of The Churches Power.* Boston: Thomas Fleet, 1723.

————. *The Witness of The Spirit A Sermon Preached at Newark in New-Jersey. May 7th. 1740.* Boston: S. Kneeland and T. Green, 1740.

An Examination and Refutation of Mr. Gilbert Tennent's Remarks Upon the Protestation Presented to the Synod of Philadelphia, June 1, 1741; And The said Protest set in its True Light, and Justified. By Some Members of The Synod. Philadelphia: B. Franklin, 1742.

Finley, Samuel. *Christ Triumphing, And Satan Raging. A Sermon On Math. III. 28. Wherein is proven that the Kingdom Of God Is Come Unto Us at this Day. First Preached at Nottingham in Pensilvania Jan. 20, 1740, 1.* Philadelphia: B. Franklin, 1741.

————. *Satan strip'd of his angelick robe: Being The Substance of Several Sermons Preach'd at Philadelphia, January 1742–3 From 2 Thessalonians 2. 11, 12. Shewing, The Strength, Nature, and Symptoms of Delusion. With an Application to The Moravians.* Philadelphia: William Bradford, [1743].

————. *The successful Minister of Christ Distinguished in Glory. A Sermon, Occasioned by the Death of The late Reverend Mr. Gilbert Tennent, Pastor of The Second Presbyterian Congregation, in Philadelphia. Preached on the 2d Day of September, 1764.* Philadelphia: William Bradford, 1764.

Franklin, Benjamin. *The Autobiography of Benjamin Franklin.* Edited by Leonard W. Labaree et al. New Haven: Yale University Press, 1964.

————. *A Defense Of the Rev. Mr. Hemphill's "Observations: Or, An Answer to The Vindication of The Reverend Commission."* Philadelphia: B. Franklin, 1735.

————. *A Letter to a Friend in the Country, Containing the Substance of a Sermon Preach'd at Philadelphia, in the Congregation of The Rev. Mr. Hemphill, Concerning the Terms of Christian and Ministerial Communion.* Philadelphia: B. Franklin, 1735.

————. *Some Observations on the Proceedings Against The Rev. Mr. Hemphill; With A Vindication of his Sermons.* Philadelphia: B. Franklin, 1735.

Frelinghuysen, Theodorus Jacobus. *Sermons.* Translated by William Demarest. New York: Reformed Protestant Dutch Church, Board of Publications, 1856.

Gillespie, George. *A Letter To The Rev. Brethren of the Presbytery of New-York, or of Elizabeth-Town; In which is shewn The Unjustness of The Synod's Protest, entered last May at Philadelphia, against some of their Rev. Brethren.* Philadelphia: B. Franklin, 1742.

————. *Remarks Upon Mr. George Whitefield, Proving Him a Man under Delusion.* Philadelphia: B. Franklin 1744.

Hamilton, Kenneth G., ed. *The Bethlehem Diary.* Bethlehem, Pa.: Archives of the Moravian Church, 1971.

[Hancock, John.] *The Examiner, Or Gilbert against Tennent. Containing A Confutation of the Reverend Mr. Gilbert Tennent and his Adherents: Extracted chiefly from his Own Writings, and formed upon his Own*

    Plan of comparing the Moravian Principles, with The Standard of Orthodoxy, in distinct Columns. 1743; reprint edition, Philadelphia: B. Franklin, 1743.

Hastings, Hugh, ed. *Ecclesiastical Records [of the] State of New York.* 7 vols. Albany, N.Y.: J. B. Lyons, 1902.

[Husbands, Herman.] *Some Remarks on Religion, With the Author's Experience in Pursuit thereof. For the Consideration of all People; Being the real Truth of what happened.* Philadelphia: William Bradford, 1761.

The Mechanick's Address to the Farmer: Being a short Reply to some of the Layman's Remarks on the Eighteen Presbyterian Ministers Letter to the Archbishop. Philadelphia: Andrew Steuart, 1761.

New Brunswick and New Castle Presbyteries. *A Declaration of the Presbyteries of New-Brunswick and New-Castle Judicially met together at Philadelphia, May 26, 1743.* Philadelphia: William Bradford, [1743].

New Brunswick Presbytery. *The Apology of the Presbytery of New-Brunswick, For Their Dissenting from Two Acts or New Religious Laws, which were made at the last Session of our Synod. Humbly offer'd to the Consideration of the Synod now conven'd at Philadelphia.* Philadelphia: B. Franklin, 1741.

On The Reverend Mr. Gilbert Tennent's powerful and successful Preaching in Boston, and other neighbouring Towns. With a few Words of Advice to awaken'd Souls. And of Warning to The Dispisers of The Gospel Offers of Salvation. [Boston, 1741.]

A Poem Occasion'd by the late powerful and awakening Preaching of the Reverend Mr. Gilbert Tennent. By some young Lads affected therewith. [Boston, 1741?]

Prince, Thomas, ed. *The Christian History Containing Accounts of The Revival and Propagation of Religion in Great-Britain and America for the year 1743.* Boston: S. Kneeland and T. Green, 1743.

————. *The Christian History Containing Accounts of the Revival and Propagation of Religion in Great-Britain and America for the year 1744, 5.* Boston: S. Kneeland and T. Green, 1745.

The Querists, Or An Extract of sundry Passages taken out of Mr. Whitefield's printed Sermons, Journals and Letters: Together With Some Scruples propos'd in proper Queries raised on each Remark. By some Church-Members of the Presbyterian Persuasion. Philadelphia, n.p. 1740.

The Querists, Part III. Or, An Extract of sundry Passages taken out of Mr. G. Tennent's Sermon preached at Nottingham, of The Danger of an Unconverted Ministry. Together With Some Scruples propos'd in proper Queries raised on each Remark. By the same Hands with the former. Philadelphia: B. Franklin, 1741.

A Second Letter To the Congregations of the Eighteen Presbyterian (or New-Light) Ministers, Who wrote the late Contradictory Letter to The Arch-

bishop of Canterbury; With some Remarks on the Two Performances That have appeared in Their Defence. By an old Covenanting and True Presbyterian Layman. Philadelphia: Andrew Steuart, 1761.

Seward, William. *Journal of a Voyage from Savannah to Philadelphia, and from Philadelphia to England, 1740.* London, n.p., 1740.

[Smith, John.] *The Doctrine of Christianity, As held by the People called Quakers, Vindicated: In Answer to Gilbert Tennent's Sermon on the Lawfulness of War.* Philadelphia: B. Franklin and D. Hall, 1748.

Tennent, John. *The Nature of Regeneration opened, and its absolute Necessity, in order to Salvation, demonstrated. In a Sermon From John III. 3. Also The Nature of Adoption, with its Consequent Privileges, explained, in a Sermon on John III. I.* 2nd edition. London: J. Oswald, 1741.

Tennent, William, Sr. "William Tennent's Sacramental Sermon." Edited by Thomas C. Pears, Jr. *Journal of Presbyterian History* 19 (March 1940): 76–84.

Thomson, John. *The Doctrine of Convictions set in a clear Light, Or An Examination and confutation of several Errors relating to Conversion. Being The Substance of a Sermon Preached by the Author to his own and a Neighbouring Congregation, with some Enlargement.* Philadelphia: Andrew Bradford, 1741.

———. *The Government of the Church of Christ, And The Authority of Church Judicatories established on a Scripture Foundation: And the spirit of rash judging arraigned and condemned.* Philadelphia: Andrew Bradford, 1741.

———. *An Overture Presented to the Reverend Synod Of dissenting Ministers, Sitting in Philadelphia, in the Month of September, 1728.* [Philadelphia], n.p. 1729.

A True Copy of a Genuine Letter, Sent to The Archbishop of Canterbury, By Eighteen Presbyterian Ministers, In America: With Some Remarks Thereon; In Another Letter to The Congregations of the Said Minister. By an old Covenanting and true Presbyterian Layman. New York, n.p. 1761.

Whitefield, George. *Five Sermons On The Following Subjects, Viz. I. Christ The Believer's Husband. II. The Gospel Supper. III. Blind Bartimeus. IV. Walking with God. V. The Resurrection of Lazarus.* Philadelphia: B. Franklin, 1746.

———. *George Whitefield's Journals.* Edited by William Wale. Reprint edition, Gainesville, Fla.: Scholar's Facsimiles and Reprints, 1969.

———. *A Letter From the Reverend Mr. Whitefield, To some Church Members of the Presbyterian Perswasion, in Answer to certain Scruples and Queries relating to some Passages in his printed Sermons and other Writings.* Boston: S. Kneeland and T. Green, J. Edwards and S. Eliot, 1740.

———. *Letters of George Whitefield, for the period 1734–1742.* 1771; reprint edition, Carlisle, Pa.: Banner of Truth Trust, 1976.

———. *The Works of the Reverend George Whitefield.* 4 vols. London, n.p. 1771.

Zinzendorf, Nicholas Ludwig von. *Hauptschriften.* 19 vols. Hildescheim: Georg Olms Verlagbuch-handlung, 1962–1978.

Zinzendorf, Nicholas Ludwig von. *Nine Public Lectures on important subjects in religion: Preached in Fetter Lane Chapel in London in the year of 1746.* Translated and edited by George W. Forell. Iowa City: University of Iowa Press, 1973.

SECONDARY SOURCES: SELECTED BIBLIOGRAPHY

Alexander, Archibald. *Biographical Sketches of the Founder and Principal Alumni of the Log College.* Philadelphia: Presbyterian Board of Publication, 1851.

Austin, Richard Cartwright. "The Great Awakening in Philadelphia." B.A. thesis, Swarthmore College, 1956.

Barkley, J. M. "The Presbyterian Church in Ireland: Part I." *Journal of Presbyterian History* 44 (December 1966): 244–265.

Beadle, Elias Root. *The Old and the New, 1743–1876: The Second Presbyterian Church of Philadelphia.* Philadelphia, n.p., 1876.

Berg, J. van den, and Van Dooren, J. P., eds. *Pietismus und Reveil.* Leiden: E. J. Brill, 1978.

Beyreuther, Erich. *Der junge Zinzendorf.* Marburg an der Lahn: Francke, [1957].

———. *Nicholas Ludwig von Zinzendorf in Selbstzeugnissen und Bilddokumenten.* Reinbek bei Hamburg: Rowohlt Monographien, 1965.

———. *Zinzendorf und die Christenheit, 1732–1760.* Marburg an der Lahn: Francke, [1961].

———. *Zinzendorf und die sich allhier beisammen finden.* Marburg an der Lahn: Francke, [1959].

Boudinot, Elias. *Memoirs of the Life of the Reverend William Tennent.* Philadelphia, n.p. 1827.

Brink, Frederick W. "Gilbert Tennent, Dynamic Preacher." *Journal of The Presbyterian Historical Society* 32 (March 1954): 91–107.

Brown, Dale W. *Understanding Pietism.* Grand Rapids, Mich.: Eerdmans Press 1978.

Brown, George, Jr. "Pietism and the Reformed Tradition." *Reformed Review* 23 (1970): 143–152.

Buijtenen, Mari. P. van; Dekker, Cornelius; and Leeuwenberg, Huib, eds.

Unitas Fratrum: *Hernnhuter Studien—Moravian Studies*. Utrecht: Rijksarchief, 1975.

Bushman, Richard L. *From Puritan to Yankee*: *Character and the Social Order in Connecticut, 1690–1765*. Cambridge, Mass.: Harvard University Press, 1967.

Buxbaum, Melvin H. *Benjamin Franklin and the Zealous Presbyterians*. University Park, Pa.: Pennsylvania State University Press, 1975.

Christenson, Merton A. "Franklin on the Hemphill Trial: Deism Versus Presbyterian Orthodoxy." *William and Mary Quarterly*, 3rd series, 10 (July 1953): 422–440.

Christie, John W. "Presbyterians and Episcopalians in 1761." *Ohio Presbyterian Historical Society, Proceedings* 2 (1940): 15–29.

Dallimore, Arnold A. *George Whitefield*: *The Life and Times of the Great Evangelist of the Eighteenth-Century Revival*. 2 vols. Westchester, Ill.: Cornerstone Books, 1970–1979.

Davidson, Robert. *Historical Sketch of First Presbyterian Church of New Brunswick*. New Brunswick. N.J.: Terhune and Son, 1852.

DeJong, Gerald Francis. *The Dutch Reformed Church in the American Colonies*. Grand Rapids, Mich.: Eerdmans, 1978.

Frantz, John B. "The Awakening of Religion Among the German Settlers in the Middle Colonies." *William and Mary Quarterly*, 3rd series, 33 (April 1976): 266–288.

Frelinghuysen, Peter H. B., Jr., *Theodorus Jacobus Frelinghuysen*. Princeton, N.J.: Princeton University Press, 1938.

Gaustad, Edwin Scott. *The Great Awakening in New England*. New York: Harper and Row, 1957.

Gewehr, Wesley M. *The Great Awakening in Virginia, 1740–1790*. Durham, N.C.: Duke University Press, 1930.

Goen, Clarence C. *Revivalism and Separatism in New England*: *Strict Congregationalists and Separate Baptists in the Great Awakening*. New Haven: Yale University Press, 1962.

Goeters, Wilhelm. *Die Vorbereitung des Pietismus in der Reformierten Kirche der Niederlande*. Leipzig: J. C. Inrichs, 1911.

Gollin, Gillian Lindt. *Moravianism in Two Worlds*: *A Study of Changing Communities*. New York: Columbia University Press, 1967.

Goodwin, Gerald J. "The Anglican Reaction to the Great Awakening." *Historical Magazine of the Protestant Episcopal Church* 35 (December 1966): 343–371.

Green, Henry W. "The Trial of the Reverend William Tennent." *Princeton Review* 40 (July 1868): 322–344.

Greschat, Martin, ed. *Zur neueren Pietismusforschung*. Darmstadt: Wissenschaftliche Buchgesellschaft, 1977.

Hall, David D. *The Faithful Shepherd*: *A History of the New England Ministry in the Seventeenth Century*. New York: W. W. Norton, 1972.

————. "Understanding the Puritans." In *Colonial America: Essays in Politics and Social Development*. Edited by Stanley N. Katz, pp. 31–49. Boston: Little, Brown, 1971.

Hamilton, J. T., and Hamilton, K. G. *History of the Moravian Church: The Renewed Unitas Fratrum, 1722–1957*. Bethlehem, Pa.: Interprovincial Board of Christian Education, Moravian Church in America, 1967.

Hardman, Keith J. "Jonathan Dickinson and the Course of American Presbyterianism, 1717–1747." Ph.D. dissertation, University of Pennsylvania, 1971.

Harmelink, Herman. "Another Look at Frelinghuysen and His Awakening." *Church History* 37 (December 1968): 423–438.

Harper, Miles Douglas. "Gilbert Tennent, Theologian of the 'New Light.' " Ph.D. dissertation, Duke University, 1958.

Hatch, Nathan O. "The Origins of Civil Millennialism in America: New England Clergymen, War with France, and the Revolution," *William and Mary Quarterly*, 3rd series, 31 (1974): 407–430.

Heimert, Alan. *Religion and the American Mind: From the Great Awakening to the Revolution*. Cambridge, Mass.: Harvard University Press, 1966.

Heimert, Alan, and Miller, Perry, eds. *The Great Awakening: Documents Illustrating the Crisis and Its Consequences*. Indianapolis: Bobbs-Merrill, 1967.

Henry, Stuart C. *George Whitefield: Wayfaring Witness*. New York: Abingdon Press, 1957.

Heppe, Heinrich. *Geschichte des Pietismus und der Mystik in der Reformierten Kirche*. Leiden: E. J. Brill, 1879.

Hodge, Charles. *The Constitutional History of the Presbyterian Church in the United States of America*. 2 vols. Philadelphia: Wm. S. Martien, 1840.

Ingersoll, Elizabeth A. "Francis Alison: American 'Philosophe,' 1705–1799." Ph.D. dissertation, University of Delaware, 1974.

Ingram, George H. "Biographies of the Alumni of the Log College: 11. William Tennent, Sr., The Founder." *Journal of the Presbyterian Historical Society* 14 (March 1930): 1–27.

————. "Erection of the Presbytery of New Brunswick." *Journal of the Presbyterian Historical Society* 6 (June 1912): 212–233.

————. "History of the Presbytery of New Brunswick: The Trials of Reverend John Rowland and Reverend William Tennent, Jr., 1741–1742." *The Journal of the Presbyterian Historical Society* 8 (September 1915): 114–122.

————. "The Story of the Log College." *Journal of Presbyterian History* 12 (October 1927): 487–511.

Kenney, William Howland. "George Whitefield and the Colonial Revivalism: The Social Sources of Charismatic Authority, 1737–1770." Ph.D. dissertation, University of Pennsylvania, 1966.

————. "George Whitefield, Dissenter Priest of the Great Awakening, 1739–1741." *William and Mary Quarterly*, 3rd series, 26 (January 1969): 75–93.

Klett, Guy S. *Presbyterians in Colonial Pennsylvania*. Philadelphia: University of Pennsylvania Press, 1937.

————. "Some Aspects of the Presbyterian Church on the American Colonial Frontier." *Journal of Presbyterian History* 19 (September 1940): 110–126.

Labaree, Leonard. W. "The Conservative Attitude Toward the Great Awakening." *William and Mary Quarterly*, 3rd series, 1 (October 1944): 331–352.

————. "Franklin and the Presbyterians." *Journal of Presbyterian History* 35 (December 1957): 217–228.

Lang, August. *Puritanismus und Pietismus: Studien zu ihrer Entwicklung von M. Butzer bis zum Methodismus*. Darmstadt: Wissenschaftliche Buchgesellschaft, 1972.

LeBeau, Bryan F. "The Subscription Controversy and Jonathan Dickinson." *Journal of Presbyterian History* 54 (Fall 1976): 317–335.

Lewis, Arthur J. *Zinzendorf, The Ecumenical Pioneer: A Study in the Moravian Contribution to Christian Mission and Unity*. Philadelphia: Westminster Press, 1962.

Lodge, Martin E. "The Crisis of the Churches in the Middle Colonies, 1720–1750." In *Interpreting Colonial America: Selected Readings*. Edited by James Kirby Martin. New York: Dodd and Mead, 1973.

————. "The Great Awakening in the Middle Colonies." Ph.D. dissertation, University of California, Berkeley, 1964.

Loetscher, Frederick W. "The Adopting Act." *Journal of the Presbyterian Historical Society* 13 (December, 1929): 337–355.

————. "Early American Presbyterianism." *Journal of the Presbyterian Historical Society* 13 (March 1928): 23–37.

Luidens, John Pershing. "The Americanization of the Dutch Church." Ph.D. dissertation, University of Oklahoma, 1969.

McLoughlin, William G. *Revivals, Awakenings, and Reform: An Essay on Religion and Social Change in America, 1607–1977*. Chicago: University of Chicago Press, 1978.

Maxson, Charles H. *The Great Awakening in the Middle Colonies*. 1920; reprint ed., Gloucester, Mass.: Peter Smith, 1958.

Mead, Sydney. "The Rise of the Evangelical Conception of the Ministry in America, 1607–1850." In *The Ministry in Historical Perspective*. Edited by H. Richard Niebuhr and Daniel D. Williams. New York: Harper, 1956.

Messler, Abraham. *Forty Years at Raritan*. New York n.p., 1873.

Miller, Howard. *The Revolutionary College: American Presbyterian Higher Education 1707–1837*. New York: New York University Press, 1976.

Minutes of the Presbyterian Church in America 1706–1788. Edited by Guy S. Klett. Philadelphia: Presbyterian Historical Society, 1976.

"Minutes of the Presbytery of New Castle." *Journal of the Presbyterian Historical Society* 15 (June 1932): 73–120, 174–207.

Nichols, James H. "Colonial Presbyterianism Adopts Its Standards." *Journal of Presbyterian History* 34 (March 1956): 53–66.

Nissenbaum, Stephen, ed. *The Great Awakening at Yale College.* Belmont, Calif.: Wadsworth Publishing, 1972.

North Park Theological Seminary, Chicago. *Contemporary Perspectives on Pietism: A Symposium.* Chicago: Covenant Press, 1976.

Ostenhaven, M. Eugene. "The Experimental Theology of Early Dutch Calvinism." *Reformed Review* 27 (Spring 1974): 180–189.

Ott, Philip Wesley. "Christian Experience as Seen in the Writings of Jonathan Dickinson." Th.M. thesis, Princeton Theological Seminary, 1963.

Pears, Thomas Clinton, Jr. "The American Wilderness: A Study of Some of the Main Currents in Colonial American Presbyterianism." Lecture for L. P. Stone Foundation, 1942, at Princeton Theological Seminary.

———. "History by Hearsay or New Light on William Tennent: A Footnote on the 'Documentary History of William Tennent,' &c." *Journal of Presbyterian History* 19 (June 1940): 65–75.

———, ed. *Documentary History of William Tennent and the Log College.* Philadelphia: Department of History of the Office of the General Assembly of the Presbyterian Church in the U.S.A., 1940.

Pettit, Norman. *The Heart Prepared: Grace and Conversion in Puritan Spiritual Life.* New Haven: Yale University Press, 1966.

Pierce, Roderic Hall. "George Whitefield and His Critics." Ph.D. dissertation, Princeton University, 1962.

Pilcher, George W., ed. *The Reverend Samuel Davies Abroad: Diary of a Journey to England and Scotland, 1753–1755.* Urbana, Ill.: University of Illinois Press, 1967.

———. *Samuel Davies: Apostle of Dissent in Colonial Virginia.* Knoxville, Tenn.: University of Tennessee Press, [1971].

Prozesky, Martin H. "The Emergence of Dutch Pietism." *Journal of Ecclesiastical History* 28 (January 1977): 29–37.

Records of the Presbyterian Church in the United States of America. Philadelphia: Presbyterian Board of Publications, 1904.

Reed, Charles Robert. "Image Alteration in a Mass Movement: A Rhetorical Analysis of the Role of the Log College in the Great Awakening." Ph.D. dissertation, Ohio State University, 1972.

Ritter, Abraham. *History of the Moravian Church in Philadelphia, from its foundation in 1742 to the present time.* Philadelphia: Hayes and Zell, 1857.

Rothermund, Dietmar. *The Layman's Progress: Religious and Political Ex-*

perience in Colonial Pennsylvania, 1740–1770. Philadelphia: University of Pennsylvania, 1961.

Schattschneider, David A. "The Missionary Theologies of Zinzendorf and Spangenberg." *Transactions of the Moravian Historical Society* 22 (1975): 213–233.

Schmidt, Martin. "Das pietistische Pfarrerideal und seine altkirchlichen Wurzeln." *In Bleibendes im Wandel der Kirchengeschichte: Kirchenhistorisches Studien*. Edited by Bernd Moeller and Gerhard Ruhbach. Tubingen: J. C. B. Mohr, 1973.

————. "England und der deutsche Pietismus." *Evangelische Theologie* 4/5 (1953): 205–224.

Schrag, F. J. "Theodorus Jacobus Frelinghuysen: The Father of American Pietism." *Church History* 14 (September 1945): 201–216.

Sessler, Jacob John. *Communal Pietism Among Early American Moravians*. New York: Henry Holt, 1933.

Sloan, Douglas. *The Scottish Enlightenment and the American College Ideal*. Teachers College, Columbia University: Teachers College Press, 1971.

Smith, Horace Wemyss. *Life and Correspondence of the Rev. William Smith, D.D.* 2 vols. Philadelphia: Ferguson Bros., 1880.

Stoeffler, F. Ernest. *German Pietism During the Eighteenth Century*. Studies in the History of Religions, vol. 24. Leiden: E. J. Brill, 1973.

————. *The Rise of Evangelical Pietism*. Studies in the History of Religions, vol. 9. Leiden: E. J. Brill, 1965.

————, ed. *Continental Pietism and Early American Christianity*. Grand Rapids, Mich.: Wm. B. Eerdmans Publishing, 1976.

Stout, Harry S. "Religion, Communications, and the Ideological Origins of the American Revolution." *William and Mary Quarterly*, 3rd Series, 34 (October 1977): 519–541.

Tanis, James. *Dutch Calvinistic Pietism in the Middle Colonies: A Study of the Life and Theology of Theodorus Jacobus Frelinghuysen*. The Hague: Martinus Nijhoff, 1967.

————. "The Heidelberg Catechism in the Hands of the Calvinistic Pietists." *Reformed Review* 24 (Spring 1971): 154–161.

Tennent, Mary A. *Light in Darkness: The Story of William Tennent, Sr., and the Log College*. Greensboro, N.C.: Greensboro Printing, 1971.

Thompson, Clark Alva. "Motifs in Eighteenth Century Evangelical Pietism." Ph.D. dissertation, Brown University, 1974.

Towlson, Clifford. *Moravian and Methodist: Relationships and Influences in the Eighteenth Century*. London: Epworth Press, 1957.

Tresch, John W., Jr. "The Reception Accorded George Whitefield in the Southern Colonies." *Methodist History* 6 (January 1968): 17–26.

Trinterud, Leonard J. *The Forming of an American Tradition: A Re-examination of Colonial Presbyterianism*. Philadelphia: Westminster Press, 1949.

Turner, J. D. E. "Reverend Samuel Blair, 1712–1751." *Journal of Presbyterian History* 29 (December 1951): 227–236.

Webster, Richard. *A History of the Presbyterian Church in America, from its Origin until the Year 1760.* Philadelphia: Joseph M. Wilson, 1857.

Weinlick, John R. "Colonial Moravians, Their Status Among the Churches." *Pennsylvania History* 26 (July 1959): 213–225.

———. *Count Zinzendorf.* New York: Abingdon Press, 1956.

Wertenbaker, Thomas Jefferson. *Princeton, 1746–1896.* Princeton, N.J.: Princeton University Press, 1946.

Wettach, Theodor. *Kirche bei Zinzendorf.* Wuppertal: Rolf Brockhaus, 1971.

White, Eugene E. "The Preaching of George Whitefield During the Great Awakening in America." *Speech Monographs* 15 (1948) 33–43.

INDEX

also Conjunct Presbyteries of New
Brunswick and Londonderry
Love, 135–36

McClenachan, William, 159–60
McHenry, Francis, 56
Millennium, 153
Ministry: duty of, 20–21, 42, 69–70,
79–80; education of, 48–54, 69,
144; lay, 93–95, 119–20; uncon-
verted, 44–46, 64–67, 114, 150,
166. *See also* Soul's spiritual con-
dition, judging
Moral reformation, 132, 152–54
Moravians, 96–99, 111–12, 124,
195 n.48. *See also* Zinzendorf,
Count Nicholas Ludwig von
Morgan, Joseph, 16, 180 n.53

New Brunswick Presbytery, 48–49,
50–54, 56–57, 84
New Building, 67, 108–12, 118–19,
121–22, 126–27, 138–39, 193–94
n.22
New Castle Presbytery, 11–12, 32,
36, 50, 72
New York Presbytery, 50, 82, 107,
113, 118–19, 125, 127–28, 155,
187 n.88
Noble, Thomss, 59, 108, 109–10,
138

Ordination, 51–54, 85, 94. *See also*
Examinations of ministerial candidates; Examining Act

Pacific Act, 30
Pastors, choosing, 60–62, 64–67,
79–80
Pemberton, Ebenezer, 63, 125, 143,
146
Perfectionism, 98, 103–4, 151
Philadelphia Presbytery, 28–29, 47,

50, 51, 56, 57, 158, 161, 180
n.54
Pierson, John, 60, 125, 143
Pietism, influence on: Frelinghuysen,
xviii–xx, 12–13, 14, 18–20, 23–
25; Synod of New York, 128;
Tennent, Gilbert, 100–101 (*see
also* Frelinghuysen, Theodorus Jacobus); Zinzendorf, 98–101
Piety, experimental: for Gilbert Tennent, 38, 42, 104–5, 114–15,
120, 123–24, 135–36, 167; for
William Tennent, Sr., 6–9
Preaching. *See* Frelinghuysen, Theodorus Jacobus, homiletics; Tennent, Gilbert, homiletics
*A Protestation Presented to the
Synod of Philadelphia*, 82–83, 85,
115–16, 155–56. *See also* Cross,
Robert

Querists, 72, 76
Querists, Part III, 79–80

Read, James, 108, 110
Roan, John, 128–29
Robinson, William, 128
Rowland, John, 50–54, 56, 57, 68,
91–92, 192 n.56
Rules, ecclesiastical, 29–31, 37–38,
52–54, 57, 64–67, 70–71, 86–88,
114, 166

Salvation, assurance of, 67–68, 79
Second Presbyterian Church, Phila-
delphia, 138–40, 158, 160–62
Self-righteousness, 43–45, 75–76,
166
Seward, William, 108, 110
Smith, William, 150, 159
Soul's spiritual condition, judging,
65, 68, 70–79, 95, 119–20
Spangenberg, August, 111, 192 n.57

War, 131–32, 153–54
Whitefield, George: appeal in colonies, 58–59; criticism of, 58, 67–68, 72, 76–78; first tour in colonies, 55, 58–64; historiographical reputation, xv-xvi; influence on Gilbert Tennent, 55, 59–60, 62–64, 68, 72–73, 108–12, 129–30, 147–48, 195 n.47; and New Building, 108–12, 126 (*See also* New Building); second tour of colonies, 67–68; Unitas Fratrum,

contact with, 96–97, 111–12, 195 n.48 (*see also* New Building). Works: *Letter From the Reverend Mr. Whitefield to Some Church Members of the Presbyterian Persuasion*, 77 (*See also Querists*)

Zanchy, Richard, 181 n.60
Zinzendorf, Count Nicholas Ludwig von, 96, 98–105, 110–12, 113–15, 166, 192 n.57

About the Author

MILTON J COALTER, JR., is Librarian and Assistant Professor
of Bibliography and Research at the Louisville Presbyterian
Theological Seminary and author of a number of articles on the
Awakening movement in America.

Recent Titles in
Contributions to the Study of Religion
Series Editor: Henry W. Bowden

PRESBYTERIAN HISTORICAL SOCIETY PUBLICATIONS

1. *The Presbyterian Enterprise* by M. W. Armstrong, L. A. Loetscher and C. A. Anderson (Westminster Press, 1956; Paperback reprinted for P.H.S., 1963 & 1976)

*2. *Presbyterian Ministry in American Culture* by E. A. Smith (Westminster Press, 1962)

3. *Journals of Charles Beatty, 1762-1769*, edited by Guy S. Klett (Pennsylvania State University Press, 1962)

*4. *Hoosier Zion, The Presbyterian in Early Indiana* by L. C. Rudolph (Yale University Press, 1963)

*5. *Presbyterianism in New York State* by Robert Hastings Nichols, edited and completed by James Hastings Nichols (Westminster Press, 1963)

6. *Scots Breed and Susquehanna* by Hubertis M. Cummings (University of Pittsburgh Press, 1964)

*7. *Presbyterians and the Negro—A History* by Andrew E. Murray (Presbyterian Historical Society, 1966)

8. *A Bibliography of American Presbyterianism During the Colonial Period* by Leonard J. Trinterud (Presbyterian Historical Society, 1968)

9. *George Bourne and "The Book and Slavery Irreconcilable"* by John W. Christie and Dwight L. Dumond (Historical Society of Delaware and Presbyterian Historical Society, 1969)

10. *The Skyline Synod: Presbyterianism in Colorado and Utah* by Andrew E. Murray (Synod of Colorado/Utah, 1977)

*11. *The Life and Writings of Francis Makemie*, edited by Boyd S. Schlenther (Presbyterian Historical Society, 1971)

12. *A Younger Church in Search of Maturity: Presbyterianism in Brazil from 1910 to 1959* by Paul Pierson (Trinity University Press, 1974)

*13. *Presbyterians in the South*, Vols. II and III, by Ernest Trice Thompson (John Knox Press, 1973)

*14. *Ecumenical Testimony* by John McNeill and James H. Nichols (Westminster Press, 1974)

15. *Iglesia Presbiteriana: A History of Presbyterians and Mexican Americans in the Southwest* by R. Douglas Brackenridge and Francisco O. Garcia-Treto (Trinity University Press, 1974)

16. *The Rise and Decline of Education for Black Presbyterians* by Inez M. Parker (Trinity University Press, 1977)

17. *Minutes of the Presbyterian Church in America, 1706-1788* edited by Guy S. Klett (Presbyterian Historical Society, 1977)

*18. *Eugene Carson Blake, Prophet with Portfolio* by R. Douglas Brackenridge (Seabury Press, 1978)

19. *Prisoners of Hope: A Search for Mission 1815-1822* by Marjorie Barnhart (Presbyterian Historical Society, 1980)

20. *From Colonialism to World Community: The Church's Pilgrimage* by John Coventry Smith (Geneva Press, 1982)

21. *Facing the Enlightenment and Pietism: Archibald Alexander and the Founding of Princeton Theological Seminary* by Lefferts A. Loetscher (Greenwood Press, 1983)

22. *Presbyterian Women in America: Two Centuries of a Quest for Status* by Lois A. Boyd and R. Douglas Brackenridge (Greenwood Press, 1983)

23. *Kentucky Presbyterians* by Louis B. Weeks (John Knox Press, 1983)

24. *Gilbert Tennent, Son of Thunder: A Case Study of Continental Pietism's Impact on the First Great Awakening in the Middle Colonies* by Milton J Coalter, Jr. (Greenwood Press, 1986)

*Out of print.